THE ORDEAL OF WOODROW WILSON

Herbert Hoover. Photo by Josh Weiner, courtesy of the Herbert Hoover Presidential Library-Museum

THE ORDEAL OF

WOODROW WILSON

by

HERBERT HOOVER

with a New Introduction by

Mark Hatfield

THE WOODROW WILSON CENTER PRESS
Washington, D.C.

THE JOHNS HOPKINS UNIVERSITY PRESS
Baltimore and London

Editorial Offices
The Woodrow Wilson Center Press
370 L'Enfant Promenade, S.W.
Suite 704
Washington, D.C. 20024-2518 U.S.A.

Order from:
The Johns Hopkins University Press
701 West 40th Street
Baltimore, Maryland 21211-2190
Telephone 1-800-537-5487

First published 1958. Reprinted, with a new introduction by
Mark Hatfield, 1992.
Introduction copyright © 1992
by Mark Hatfield.

Cover photo: Woodrow Wilson in 1914 (left), and 1921.
Courtesy of FPG International

Cover design by Alan Carter.

Printed in the United States of America
∞ Printed on acid-free paper

9   8   7   6   5   4   3   2   1

Library of Congress Cataloging-in Publication Data

Hoover, Herbert, 1874–1964.
  The ordeal of Woodrow Wilson / by Herbert Hoover with a new
introduction by Mark Hatfield.
      p.   cm.
  Originally published: New York : McGraw-Hill, 1958.
  Includes bibliographical references and index.
  ISBN 0-943875-41-2 (pbk.)
  1. Wilson, Woodrow (1856–1924. 2. Hoover, Herbert. 1874–1964.
3. Presidents—United States—Biography. 4. United States—Foreign
relations—1913–1921. 5. World War, 1914–1918—Peace. I. Title.
E767.H78   1992
973.91′3′092—dc20   92-23528
                                                                CIP

WOODROW WILSON INTERNATIONAL CENTER FOR SCHOLARS

The Woodrow Wilson International Center for Scholars is deeply grateful to Senator Mark Hatfield for suggesting the importance of reissuing *The Ordeal of Woodrow Wilson* and for agreeing to write a new introduction for the occasion.

The Center thanks the Herbert Hoover Library in West Branch, Iowa, its director, Richard Norton Smith, its assistant director, Timothy Walch, and its librarian, Mildred Mather, for their enthusiastic support for republishing this book and their assistance with many technical details during the process. The Center is also grateful to the Baker and Hostetler Fund for its generous financial support of this publication.

The Center is the "living memorial" of the United States of America to the nation's twenty-eighth president, Woodrow Wilson. The U.S. Congress established the Woodrow Wilson Center in 1968 as an international institute for advanced study, "symbolizing and strengthening the fruitful relationship between the world of learning and the world of public affairs." The Center opened in 1970 under its own presidentially appointed board of directors.

In all its activities the Woodrow Wilson Center is a nonprofit, nonpartisan organization, supported financially by annual appropriations from the U.S. Congress, and by the contributions of foundations, corporations, and individuals. Conclusions or opinions expressed in Center publications and programs are those of the authors and speakers and do not necessarily reflect the views of the Center staff, fellows, trustees, advisory groups, or any individuals or organizations that provide financial support to the Center.

Woodrow Wilson International Center for Scholars
1000 Jefferson Drive, S.W.
Washington, D.C. 20560
(202) 357-2429

PERMISSIONS

CONTENTS

* * *

INTRODUCTION BY MARK HATFIELD   *ix*

PREFACE   *xxiv*

CHAPTER

1   MY INTRODUCTION TO WOODROW WILSON   1

2   WOODROW WILSON ADMINISTERS THE WAR   10

3   AN UNHAPPY INTERLUDE   14

4   WOODROW WILSON DECLARES AMERICAN IDEALS AS THE BASIS OF PEACE   18

5   WOODROW WILSON LAYS DOWN THE TERMS OF PEACE TO THE GERMANS   28

6   WOODROW WILSON'S BASIS OF PEACE AGREED TO BY THE ALLIES   42

7   THE PRESIDENT DECIDES TO GO TO EUROPE   61

8   WHAT WOODROW WILSON MET IN EUROPE   70

9   WOODROW WILSON'S ADMINISTRATIVE ORDEAL IN PARIS   82

10 THE PRESIDENT'S TROUBLES WITH PEACE IN THE
    BACK BLOCS   115

11 WOODROW WILSON'S ORDEAL OF THE FOOD
    BLOCKADE ON EUROPE   151

12 WOODROW WILSON ESTABLISHES THE LEAGUE OF
    NATIONS   179

13 WOODROW WILSON'S ORDEAL OF SECRET
    NEGOTIATIONS   191

14 THE PRESIDENT'S ORDEAL OF COMPROMISE   207

15 THE DOTTED LINE   233

16 WOODROW WILSON'S ORDEAL OF SMOLDERING ENMITY   253

17 WHAT WOODROW WILSON SAVED AT PARIS   262

18 THE PRESIDENT'S CRUSADE FOR RATIFICATION OF THE
    TREATY   265

19 WOODROW WILSON'S ORDEAL OF STROKE AND
    PARALYSIS   271

20 WOODROW WILSON'S BATTLE FOR RATIFICATION BY
    THE SENATE   279

21 WOODROW WILSON'S STAND FOR RATIFICATION
    IN THE PRESIDENTIAL CAMPAIGN OF 1920   294

    EPILOGUE   300

    APPENDIX   304

    INDEX   309

Note. In the Appendix will be found a list of books and other materials used in the preparation of this volume and reference to where these materials can be located. By doing this, the method of footnoting has been simplified.

Italics in quoted matter in the text are largely the author's.

INTRODUCTION

* * *

Mark Hatfield

"Sometimes people call me an idealist. Well, that is the way I know that I am an American. America is the only idealistic nation in the world."

WOODROW WILSON
September 8, 1919

"He was more than just an idealist: he was the personification of the heritage of idealism of the American people. He brought spiritual concepts to the peace table. He was a born crusader."

HERBERT HOOVER
The Ordeal of Woodrow Wilson

In the summer of 1958 a most unlikely bestseller sent ripples of surprise throughout the literary world. For the first (and thus far only) time in American history, a former President of the United States had chosen to write a book about one of his predecessors. What Herbert Hoover had to say about his World War I colleague and intellectual soulmate, Woodrow Wilson, stirred many readers, not least of all Wilson's aged widow Edith. "You seem to have really understood him," she wrote in gratitude. Wilson's daughter, Nellie, echoed her stepmother's approval, calling *The Ordeal of Woodrow Wilson* a fine and very moving appraisal.

While immensely satisfying to an old man's ego, such praise

should not have come as a surprise, for Wilson and Hoover had much in common—certainly more than Hoover and Harry Truman, another Democratic President with whom Hoover enjoyed a famous friendship, in spite of Truman's 1948 campaign attacks on the Depression-era President. Hoover and Truman, for all the poignancy of their Indian summer rapprochement, would always be seen as a political odd couple. In the wake of World War II, FDR's successor would dispatch his new friend around the world to beg, borrow or cajole enough food to avert global famine. Still later, Truman showed both courage and shrewdness in asking Hoover, the administrative wizard, to reorganize the executive branch of government. But when it came to domestic politics, the two men spoke in different tongues, and it was best to avoid the subject altogether.

Not so with Wilson and Hoover. At first glance there might appear to be little uniting the Princeton educator turned parliamentary-style reformer with the Iowa orphan who made his professional reputation as a "doctor of sick mines." On closer examination, the professor and the engineer prove something of kindred spirits: classical liberals of the nineteenth-century variety struggling to adapt personal freedom to the new age of industrial gigantism, progressives fiercely wedded to economic competition and determined to keep open the sluiceways of individual opportunity. Each was endowed with a powerful intellect; each was deficient in the small gifts with which most public figures acquire popularity. Neither was temperamentally suited to the brutal simplicities of the campaign trail or the rough courtship of those less disinterested than they.

Prior to 1929 Hoover had a natural affinity for Wilson as a leader of lofty instincts and breathtaking vision. After his unhappy White House term, Hoover had still more personal reasons for admiring a tragic hero undone by events beyond his control. Like his Democratic predecessor, Herbert Hoover enjoyed a meteoric rise to the summit of national leadership, only to see his reputation crash along with the American economy. For a long time he and his distinctive brand of "co-operative individualism" were all but ignored, save by his opponents who tarred both with the brush of reaction. Yet there was more to link the two congenital idealists than curdled hopes and public disillusionment. "If you live long enough," Hoover liked to say, "the wheel turns, the pendulum swings." By the mid-1950s, as Americans prepared to mark the centennial of Woodrow Wilson's birth, Hoover himself had at last escaped from the political Coventry where he had passed a generation.

Well advanced into what he called his years of acknowledgment, his former luster largely restored thanks to Harry Truman and a war-ravaged world in desperate need of humanitarian relief, Hoover had at least one critical advantage over Wilson—a robust health denied the World War I President during his brief retirement. For Hoover, longevity indeed proved the best revenge. Not only did he outlive his enemies, but he would help to shape history's view of the turbulent century he had done so much to affect. Mr. Hoover did not dwell in the past, as this writer can attest from numerous encounters between a student pursuing his graduate thesis and the elderly statesman in his Waldorf Towers suite or at the Bohemian Grove. But age has its privileges, among them the right to indulge one's memories. And who among us can lay claim to the historical treasure trove of personal experience and recollection that was Herbert Hoover's?

Hoover's desire to write of the past was still another bond with Wilson, even if readers of both men detect a stylistic gulf separating the professionally trained academic who admitted to disliking the tedium of research, and the amateur for whom there could never be too much documentation to buttress his carefully organized case. In the most curious of all coincidences, each man would write a favorable account of an American President. In 1893, as a promising newcomer to the Princeton faculty, Wilson started a series of articles on George Washington for *Harper's Magazine*. When published in book form three years later, these earned the popular biographer a handsome income, offset by the scorn of less successful (and more rigorous) colleagues. Hoover, by contrast, often wrote as if composing a legal brief. He was after accuracy, not color, with the result that he unintentionally bleached much of the color of daily life and individual character from his laboriously composed pages. *The Ordeal of Woodrow Wilson* is a notable exception. In these pages one revisits a critical time when hope, like sacrifice, was in full flower, only to be dashed by the conventions of power politics.

The book had an interesting genesis. After March, 1921, ensconced in his Washington retirement home on S Street—the Hoovers lived just a few doors up the street—Wilson never got beyond the dedication page of his proposed literary monument, a massive search for the origins of democratic government to be entitled *The*

Philosophy of Politics. Settled into *his* post-Presidential retreat, Suite 31A of New York's Waldorf Towers, Hoover had a literary obsession of his own, crafted over three decades and variously intended to expose Rooseveltian foreign policy leading up to the Second World War, point a finger at Soviet complicity in the suppression of human rights, and indict fuzzy minded diplomats seduced by the siren song of One World internationalism.

Scribbling away for hours each day with the stubby pencils he favored over dictating machines—the latter dismissed as "invitations to verbosity"—Hoover spun off several other works from his magnum opus. These included three volumes of memoirs, and a pair of books written to persuade Hoover's fellow citizens against repeating the errors of Versailles, when cynical Old World statesmen paying lip service to Wilsonian idealism had in fact carved up the continental map for themselves. In the first volume of his memoirs, published in 1943, Hoover wrote at some length about America's wartime leader, whose unceasing purpose it had been from 1914 on to find some ground on which the conflict could be honorably ended. In this, Wilson had been aided by his closest friend and adviser, Colonel Edward M. House, with whom Hoover had established his own intimacy while conducting relief efforts in Belgium and northern France. Unfortunately for Wilson, "both he and the colonel were living in a stratosphere far above the earthly ground on which the war was being fought."

Following the Wilson centennial, in which he played more than an honorary part, Hoover's writing returned to America's wartime crusade and the fascinating, often quixotic personality who broke his lance on the rocks of old-fashioned realpolitik. First, however, the former President turned his attention to *The American Epic*, a profusely documented quartet of volumes written to preserve a record of American generosity following both world wars during times of murderous indifference to the innocent victims of Europe's bloodlust. "Americans don't get much credit abroad these days for what they do," explained Hoover.

As Hoover pored over thousands of yellowing pages, the years fell away. He soon realized that of the dwindling band still alive, he was uniquely qualified to tell the story of those distant events that broke Wilson's heart and denied the world a chance at collective peacemaking. Suddenly he found himself on a historical detour, striding with the great war President through the mirrored halls of Versailles while outside throngs of Parisians chanted "Vive Wilson!" His first draft was dashed off in three weeks. With considerable added detail and interpretation, the manuscript became a truly intimate account of the eighteen critical months when Hoover was part of Wilson's War Cabinet and an informal yet valued adviser at the Peace Conference.

Hoover took pains to assure readers that *The Ordeal of Woodrow Wilson* was neither biography nor history in the conventional sense, but rather a memoir based upon the personal experience of one who had been at Wilson's side through a time of noble purpose and its shabby aftermath. Unfortunately, the author chose to provide little more than a sketch of events leading up to his first encounter with the President, in November, 1915. For us, looking back, it is possible to make out both intriguing parallels and wide divergences in the character and careers of both men. As an adolescent, "Tommy" Wilson hung a portrait of Gladstone over his desk and declared, "I intend to be a statesman too." Yet a life of action seemed foreclosed, in part because of his stiff, somewhat remote personality, but also because Americans grateful to have survived the Civil War were in no mood for heroics.

The materialistic Gilded Age offered an unpromising stage for this high-minded figure. So Wilson the student contented himself with writing constitutions and running debating societies, habitually casting himself as Prime Minister. A desultory year of legal practice in Atlanta was followed by a more congenial life, as Wilson undertook graduate studies at Baltimore's recently established Johns Hopkins University. Longing to do "immortal work," the novice achieved the next best thing in 1885, when his first book, *Congressional Government,* was hailed for its incisive portrayal of the weak executive and strong legislature that characterized late-nineteenth-century Washington.

For all the praise showered upon him, Wilson was unfulfilled. It was not enough to observe government from the sidelines. "I have a strong instinct of leadership," he told his future bride, "an unmistakable oratorical temperament, and the keenest possible delight in affairs. . . . I have a passion for interpreting great thoughts to the world; I should be complete if I could inspire a great movement of opinion."

It is worth noting that the twentieth century's most passionate peacemaker never found peace for himself. All his adult life, Wilson seems to have felt a painful sense of incompleteness, compounded by internal tensions he attributed to his warring Scots and Irish genes. Marriage to Ellen Axson brought a welcome stability, but life as a junior instructor at Bryn Mawr, the Pennsylvania school pioneering in education for women, left Wilson dissatisfied. In the fall of 1888, he left the female academy for Wesleyan College in Middletown, Connecticut, where a year later he published a second work, *The State*, which attracted opinion nearly as favorable as that accorded his first book. Still he was restless. While the Yankee campus was delightful enough, "it is not a sufficiently stimulating place," he lamented.

In 1890, Wilson took up residence at Princeton, his alma mater, where the old pattern reasserted itself. The chronically ambitious instructor and author, thrusting to new heights of academic prestige and student popularity, expressed his frustration to his brother-in-law: "I am so tired of a merely talking profession. I want to do something!" After taking office as Princeton's President in 1902, Wilson did a great deal. His bold reforms in the classroom and his highly publicized battles with campus conservatives over the university's elite dining clubs and a proposed graduate school won him national attention. But they also earned him local derision while destroying some of the most important friendships in his life.

A new pattern took hold, in which the inspired speaker and master administrator played the role of missionary, employing his remarkable oratorical gifts to elevate academic standards while raising the sights of those around him to goals ever higher and less attainable. In 1910, Wilson was swept into office as Governor of New Jersey, where his reforming record and majestic words combined to storm the citadels of conventional politics. In the thoroughly unconventional election year of 1912, Wilson won the presidential nomination at the July Democratic convention on the forty-sixth ballot, defeating Missouri's Champ Clark. Then in the November, 1912, election, Wilson prevailed over three competitors—Theodore Roosevelt, running on the Progressive Party ticket; incumbent President William Howard Taft, the Republican candidate; and Eugene V. Debs, the Socialist candidate—with only a plurality of the popular vote but an overwhelming majority in the electoral college. Wilson's first two years in the White House were marked by a hurricane of legislation, including long overdue tariff reform, establishment of the Federal Reserve System and creation of the Federal Trade Commission.

Yet the fruits of victory can often contain the seeds of later defeat. Just prior to his inauguration, Wilson had remarked that it would be a strange quirk of fate if his Administration were to find itself preoccupied with foreign affairs. After August, 1914, the author of the New Freedom had no alternative. That summer, so full of tragically crossed signals and missed opportunities, marked a turning point for Herbert Hoover as well. Like Wilson, Hoover was frustrated in his nominal profession; not even a considerable fortune amassed in an eighteen-year odyssey through countless exhausted mines and newly discovered fields could quiet his demanding Quaker conscience.

When Wilson wrote, "A boy never gets over his boyhood" he might as easily have described the severe restraints placed upon this orphaned son of a small town farm implements dealer, who learned repression while sitting for hours in an unheated meetinghouse, and stoical self-denial when separated from his siblings and sent to live with a stern uncle and aunt in far-off Newberg, Oregon. In contrast to Wilson, who at college had handed out cards introducing himself as "Senator from Virginia," the uprooted Hoover had a very different boyhood ambition: "to be able to earn my own living, without the help of anybody, anywhere." Thus driven, he went from his uncle's real estate office in Salem, Oregon, to the new Stanford University, where he supported himself typing papers for John Caspar Branner, in whose geology class the young man found his calling. Hoover also made his mark in campus politics, winning election as class treasurer on a slate opposed to fraternity elitists. He soon eliminated a class debt of $2,000. In his spare time he launched the Red Star laundry and organized a campus lecture and concert series.

Graduating in May, 1895, in a very real sense Hoover never left Stanford, for the school had become his emotional as well as intellectual home, a place to belong. He would serve half a century on its board of trustees, and in time establish the Hoover Institution on War, Revolution and Peace, whose tower dominates the Palo Alto landscape just as surely as its ideas have dominated recent Republican presidencies. In 1897, Hoover fibbed about his age to land a mining position in the Australian outback. He impressed his London employers sufficiently to be offered the then fabulous sum of $20,000 a year to manage their growing interests in China. Accompanied by his wife, Lou, Hoover arrived in the Celestial Kingdom in the spring of 1899, and they were soon engulfed in the Boxer Rebellion that threatened Western interests and personnel. After a six-week siege, the Hoovers and their fellow Occidentals in the city of Tientsin were liberated to the strains of a Marine band playing "There'll Be a Hot Time in the Old Town Tonight."

Hoover spent the next decade traveling incessantly. Reputedly the highest-paid engineer of his age, the shy American explored remote frontiers, all the while pining for his native land. To fill long hours on board ship, he and Lou translated from the Latin language the sixteenth-century Georgius Agricola's *De re metallica*, winning a gold medal from the Mining and Metallurgical Society of America for the product of their labors. Yet even as the professional honors came his way, Hoover was as restless as Wilson in his academic cloister. By 1912, "The Great Engineer" was telling friends that he was "rich as any man has much right to be." Nearing his fortieth birthday Hoover confessed a desire to abandon engineering for a career of service back home. Asked specifically what he would do, Hoover replied, "Get into the big game somewhere," before adding, "Just making money isn't enough."

His opportunity came two years later, when the assassination of Austria's Archduke Franz Ferdinand touched off the powderkeg of European alliances and ethnic animosities. What began in the summer of 1914 as a swashbuckling adventure quickly turned into mankind's first total war and history's most prolonged suicide. Asked at the outset to define Germany's military strategy, a blithe Kaiser Wilhelm II replied, "Lunch in Paris, dinner in St. Petersburg." To gratify or deny his appetite, fifty million men put on uniforms; ten million never came home. With them died the last feeble justifications of colonial empire and the automatic belief in machines as agents of human betterment. For the Great War saw the introduction of plastic explosives, poison gas, flame throwers and bombs that could be hurled from airplanes and zeppelins.

Mass propaganda inflamed mass populations. Buried under the weight of so much random death and disillusionment was the benign faith in advancing democracy that Americans called Progressivism. In place of the traditional moral code whereby individuals were held responsible for their actions, there arose Einstein's relativity, Freud's death wish and Lenin's vanguard elite—new formulas spun to explain and justify human insignificance, helplessness and evil.

Seventy-five years later, World War I remains the cradle of modern society, the hinge on which our turbulent century turns. Whole nations disappeared from the map, along with seventeen European thrones. Soviet Communism forced its way on to the world stage, where Wilson's America played a reluctant part. If the Great War produced few conventional heroes, it gave us in Herbert Hoover one who was decidedly unconventional. For most Americans, beginning with President Wilson, the instinctive reaction was to take refuge behind a moat three thousand miles wide. Yet for tens of thousands of Hoover's countrymen trapped on the wrong side of the Atlantic, home seemed impossibly far away—until Hoover and his fellow engineers based in London organized a successful campaign to transport the panicky tourists back to the states.

Hoover's success led United States Ambassador Walter Hines Page to approach him with the much greater assignment of feeding an entire nation trapped between German occupiers and a British blockade. In October, 1914, Hoover agreed to form the Commission for the Relief of Belgium, which over the next four years would provide $1 billion in assistance to the stricken kingdom, including five million tons of food. Hoover taught suspicious Europeans to eat corn. He persuaded German militarists to tolerate the Belgian lace-making industry, so long as patriotic motifs were discontinued. By that autumn, when he picked up rumors that the Wilson Administration might be thinking of "consolidating" Belgian relief at the suggestion of the President's confidential adviser, Colonel House, Hoover and his Commission colleagues were raising and spending $5 million a month, recruiting other volunteers, many of them idealistic young Americans, and sailing an armada of thirty-five ships, each flying the Commission's flag—the sole such banner to be respected by all belligerents.

Wilson, that November, asked his Secretary of the Interior, Franklin Lane, to provide him with information about "the extraordinary American engineer who had stepped forward with such initiative and ability." Ambassador Page responded to the President in January, 1915, "He's a simple, modest, energetic little man who began his career in California and will end it in Heaven; and he doesn't want anybody's thanks."

A month later, Hoover dispatched to Wilson a lengthy report on the Commission's work. The President's response was warm and encouraging. Two months passed. A German U-boat torpedoed the passenger ship *Lusitania*, killing 112 Americans, but Hoover continued his own form of shuttle diplomacy, making at least forty crossings of the North Sea, where the Commission for the Relief of Belgium lost nearly three dozen ships despite promise of safe passage from the Kaiser's Navy.

Hoover never forgot the unsmiling faces of Belgium, where no children played and no scholars gathered in the magnificent library at Louvain, reduced by German shells to a pile of historic rubble. What else did Hoover remember of the Great War and his part in it? His fellow volunteers, to begin with:

> Our American men and women left their professions to perform the dull work of buying millions of tons of food, medical supplies, and clothing; loading and managing great fleets of cargo ships and discharging them; convoying trains and barges from the ports to the place of need; and distributing food to the hungry from tens of thousands of stations and canteens. They operated a telegraph system and bartered food and coal among nations. They settled little wars. They were called upon to advise new and feeble governments at the highest echelons of statesmanship. And they were called upon by the peacemakers in Paris for many political missions.

That is not all that Hoover remembered. "It is impossible to picture the long lines of stumbling refugees trying to carry their children and scant belongings to some desination unknown to them," he wrote long afterward, "the pallid faces; the thin, anemic, and bloated children in the villages and cities; the sweep of contagious disease and the unending procession of funerals—and the heaps of unburied dead." For the rest of his life, he was haunted by nightmares in which dying children beseeched his aid.

All this provided a dramatic backdrop to Hoover's first personal encounter with Wilson. It took place early in November, 1915. According to Colonel House, the best way to win over the President was to discover a common enemy, then enjoy the mutual satisfaction of heaping abuse on the shared foe. It is both amusing and ironic to think that the man who brought Hoover and Wilson together was Henry Cabot Lodge, the self-professed "Scholar in Politics" who thought little of Wilson's intellectual reputation and less of his political vision. This most determined of Wilson's "little group of willful men" was anxious to prosecute Hoover under terms of the Logan Act, which prohibited Americans from transacting diplomatic business with wartime enemies. Not surprisingly, the President lent a sympathetic ear as the Chairman of the Commission for the Relief of Belgium explained his plight.

Wilson's subsequent public commendation of Hoover's work succeeded only in further enraging Lodge. In a chilly Boston encounter with the Senator, the hero of Belgium heard threats, but he also took the occasion to remind Lodge of the Commission's neutral status and high standing with American officials. Lodge's real target became clear when he reproved the Wilson Administration for involving itself morally in any action tending to challenge international rules of blockade and war. Be that as it may, said Hoover, he could not believe that his fellow citizens were averse to saving ten million innocent civilians. A few days later Hoover lunched with Theodore Roosevelt at Oyster Bay, and T.R., no doubt amused by Lodge's belligerence, promised his guest that he would "hold the Senator's hand" if necessary.

Wilson's impression of Hoover as "one of the very ablest men we have sent over there. . . . [S]uch men stir me deeply and make me in love with duty!" is worth remembering seventy-five years later. In the angry, alienated 1990s, idealism, like bipartisanship, seems in short supply. All the more reason, then, for this generation of Americans to rediscover the historic partnership of a Democratic President and a Republican engineer who together set out to save humanity from its own worst instincts.

As his own country drifted closer to war, the President entertained suggestions on how best to utilize Hoover's talents. Walter Hines Page thought him a perfect choice to direct munitions production—an odd recommendation under any circumstances. Colonel House had different ideas, reinforced by a stream of data and advice directed his way by the exceptionally well connected Commission Chairman. While recognizing the likelihood of United States involvement in the war, Hoover cautioned the President against entering the conflict in formal alliance with any power, a stance Wilson had already adopted and would cling to throughout the harsh days of peacemaking at Versailles.

Early in March, 1917, still hoping to win the combatants over to this vision of "peace without victory," Wilson poured out his anxieties to Hoover during a White House visit. At the same time he expressed the hope that if America was dragged into the fighting against her will, she might limit her contribution to the Allied cause to industrial and financial support. He pressed Hoover for his ideas on economic organization in wartime, as if to confirm hints already circulating that the head of the Commission for the Relief of Belgium might soon find himself summoned home in the event of war.

"If we are to have war, with its hatreds, its disturbances, its check to all good causes," Hoover told a reporter, in words that foreshadowed the later American Food Administration, "we should at least have the compensations. So far as we can, we should check extravagances in living, dress, travel and amusement, and set the people to saving. It will be good not only for the conduct of war but for our souls."

When the U.S. at last entered the war in April, 1917, goaded beyond endurance by German attacks on neutral shipping, Hoover provided the administrative spark sought by President Wilson in organizing a domestic food conservation effort of unprecedented scale. With "Food Will Win the War" as his battle cry, the new "food czar" soon had millions of Americans dining on whale steaks and parsnip cutlets, chewing sugarless gum, living in unheated homes and baking "Over the Top" bread to government specifications. Americans were introduced to meatless Mondays and wheatless Wednesdays. Millions of children subscribed to this No Waste Pledge:

> I pledge my allegiance to my flag,
>   in service true I will not lag.
> I'll not despise my crusts of bread,
> Nor make complaint, whatever fed;
> On wheatless days I'll eat no wheat,
>   on other days eat less of sweet;
> I'll waste no pennies, spoil no clothes,
> And so I'll battle 'gainst our foes;
> No slackard, but a soldier keen,
> To do my best in the year eighteen.

A new word entered the language: to "Hooverize" meant to economize on food so that all might eat. Valentine's cards appeared with the romantic message.

> I can Hooverize on dinner,
> And on lights and fuel too.
> But I'll never learn to Hooverize
> When it comes to loving you.

The war ended in 1918, but not Hoover's missionary work among its victims. His postwar American Relief Administration ministered to twenty-one countries from the North Sea to the Urals. The European Children's Fund—forerunner of CARE—fed six million youngsters. In 1922, Hoover even persuaded a Republican Congress to allocate $20 million to feed the new Soviet Union, where millions swept along by Lenin's revolution of the proletariat were threatened by famine, typhus and cholera.

Yet in 1918, the Great Humanitarian, as Hoover was increasingly labeled, stubbed his toe on domestic politics, issuing an appeal supporting Wilson's drive for a Democratic Congress to ratify whatever he might bring back from the Peace Conference.

It is at this point that Hoover begins to tell of Woodrow Wilson's ordeal, and I will not spoil the reader's enjoyment—or diminish the reader's sense of outrage—by stealing a march on the author. Drawing upon thousands of pages of diaries, diplomatic notes, other memoirs and his own prodigious recollections, Hoover traced the sorrowful route from Wilson's initial rapturous European greeting to his subsequent defeat and physical collapse. Hoover, himself often labeled stubborn, took issue with critics of Wilson's alleged obstinacy. Holding to deep convictions of justice and moral right, the President reminded his friend of the original Presbyterians: "what they concluded was right, was thereafter right as against all comers . . . ."

The real problem at Versailles, Hoover insisted, was not Wilsonian idealism but Europe's addiction to prewar hatreds and resentments vastly increased by the horrors of the struggle. Both men tried and failed for months to breach an Allied blockade of food to prostrate Germany, an act of savagery that only sowed the dragon's teeth of future conflict. Having stirred hope among the silent masses of humanity, Wilson suddenly found himself thrown into unfamiliar settings, among men impervious to his eloquence. Conflicts between European imperialism and American democracy arose that were essentially irreconcilable.

"The two worlds were indeed in many ways strangers to each other," wrote Hoover, looking back upon the winter of 1918–19 after also having seen a second global war.

> The American people had been implacably anti-imperial, anti-colonial, and generally anti-the-subjugation-of-one-people-by-another from the day of our Declaration of Independence. . . .
> We had no population pressure or other incentive to colonialism.
> The driving force of Allied statesmen, on the other hand, was not

"self-determination": it was "empire." Its roots in Britain, France, Italy and Japan were centuries deep.

Wilson, the New World archangel with his flaming sword of popular sovereignty and his banner emblazoned with Fourteen Points, was a menacing intruder in the councils of European politicians and an immediate threat to their secret treaties apportioning the continent among the victors. From the start, Wilson made plain that he would not be bound by such agreements. Neither would he consent to wage peace as part of a formal alliance. In this he was seconded by Hoover, who nevertheless wished at times that the President would resort to use of American foodstuffs as a means of compelling attention to his views. Yet Wilson "was too great a man to bargain in that way. American idealism indeed was unfitted to participate in a game played with power as the counters."

Following "the greatest drama of intellectual leadership in all history," Wilson was soon nibbled to death by diplomatic predators. The war had not altered human nature, it turned out, and most of those around the conference table were less interested in preserving future peace than in redressing immediate wrongs and imposing harsh punishments upon those deemed guilty under the terms of a victor's justice. To Hoover, "[r]evenge, reparations and territorial spoils" summed up the clash between Western idealism and Allied greed. The specter of world Communism invaded the gilded halls, and Hoover, while advocating a strict policy of non-recognition of Lenin's outlaw regime, inclined to the view that simple humanity demanded that some neutral of international standing be permitted to minister to starving Russians.

Wilson returned home for a short time early in 1919. Back in Paris, Colonel House agreed to a series of compromises, winning for his efforts repudiation by the President. We now know that Wilson was suffering the visits of the first harbingers of his subsequent breakdown, and historians will forever be gauging the effect of the President's ill health upon his judgment and political skills. As frustrated as Wilson himself, Hoover finally concluded in April, 1919, that if the European Allies were unwilling to accept a peace based on the Fourteen Points, America "should retire from Europe lock, stock and barrel," as no honorable settlement would be possible. He held to this view long after the President retreated, and it became the basis for their eventual disagreement over the final terms of the treaty.

By the start of June, 1919, Hoover was openly critical of the emerging document, and Wilson just as sharp in his replies. A lengthy discussion resolved nothing, but did permit Hoover to warn of the dislocations sure to ensue from huge reparations, disunity in the former Austro-Hungarian state, and the forced transfer of vast ethnic populations to new, so-called liberated states. Worst of all, Germany was the only Great Power to be truly disarmed. Wilson responded by accusing Hoover of making personal attacks. A formal goodbye at the Paris railway platform, and some later unanswered appeals that Wilson accept at least mild senatorial reservations in order to secure his cherished League of Nations, supplied the melancholy climax of the Wilson-Hoover relationship until 1958 and the writing of *The Ordeal of Woodrow Wilson*.

Writing a friend a few months after Wilson's death, Hoover reasserted his earlier admiration. "I believe men should be judged for the good they do," he said. "The whole tendency of modern public criticism is to damn men for their very minor mistakes and to take no proportional vision of their accomplishments. That immortal son of Holland who saved his native land by keeping his fist in a leaky dike no doubt sassed his mother." As for himself, Hoover continued, he had always believed that Wilson's breakdown in the spring of 1919 was a critical factor in the bungled peace. "Therefore, his real history ought to end right there. . . ."

Today's Americans can find many parallels between the postwar scene of 1918–19 and our own world. Once again we are summoned to feed the peoples of the former Soviet Union. Once again we debate the possibility of concerted action to enforce a peaceful "new world order." And once again we are sadly in need of an idealism that transcends partisan politics, one rooted in principles beyond mere party allegiance, one capable of demonstrating the ancient American faith in the ability of one man or woman, fired with a noble purpose, to make a positive difference. Because they shared that faith, Woodrow Wilson and Herbert Hoover were able to bridge whatever surface differences might otherwise have kept them apart. In doing so they drew upon deep reserves of individual character, national patriotism, and global humanitarianism. Long after the passions of their era subsided, their historic partnership still speaks to us of what people of good will and great ideals can achieve in hastening the day when no one wields a sword and no one drags a chain.

JULY, 1992

PREFACE

———————————— * * * ————————————

Herbert Hoover

President Wilson, in the memories of thinking men, is the only enduring leader of those statesmen who conducted the First World War and its aftermath of peacemaking. I served under him in those times. I was a witness to the ordeal and tragedy of Woodrow Wilson. I had some background and a point of vantage from which to evaluate his endeavor to serve mankind.

It may be recalled that for eighteen years before the First World War I had been an administrative engineer, managing large industries in Russia, China, India, Australia, New Zealand, South Africa, Canada, Britain, Belgium, Mexico and the United States. These projects required for their successful conduct some knowledge of their governments, their economics and their history. My relations with their peoples were not as a tourist or a diplomat. I participated in their daily life and work.

With the coming of the First World War, I directed the relief of 10,000,000 people in Belgium and Northern France who were victims of occupation by the German Army and were blockaded by the Allies. To accomplish this purpose I had to obtain agreements with the Germans for protection of our supplies, and with the British and French for permission to pass through their blockade. In these negotiations I had the patronage of the American, Spanish and Dutch Ambassadors or their Ministers in London, Paris, Berlin and Brussels. I was probably the only American civilian allowed to pass freely between these cities. The administration of this huge enterprise required frequent contact with the British, French and German Prime Ministers, their Cabinet members and their military authorities. And in that period I had need for support from President Wilson and members of his Cabinet.

Shortly after we entered the war in April, 1917, I was appointed United States Food Administrator, acting directly under President Wilson. I served upon the President's "American War Council" throughout our participation in the war.

During the peacemaking, and some time after, I administered the Relief and Reconstruction of Europe directly under the President, but on behalf of all the victorious governments. That work required an organization in more than thirty countries with constant dealings with the Prime Ministers and high officials of each of the governments in Europe. Our organization included about 4,000 able Americans and many more thousands of local assistants.[1]

Because this organization was the best equipped to furnish information useful to the peacemakers in Paris and had the only telegraph system connecting those countries, during the Armistice I was called to many sessions of the "Council of Ten," and the later created "Supreme Council," colloquially called the "Big Four." I served on many political missions on their behalf apart from my regular job. And during the Peace Conference I served on President Wilson's "Committee of Economic Advisers."

Why do I recite all this? Because I hope the reader will believe that I am informed and hope he will credit me with objectivity in analysis of President Wilson's high endeavors, his evangelistic idealism, his successes, his difficulties, the purpose of his compromises, and the consequences of the Treaty of Versailles.

With thirty-nine years of contacts with world affairs since that Treaty, and the aid of the mass of subsequent information and disclosures, I can possibly contribute to an understanding of the gigantic tragedy which enveloped Woodrow Wilson and the whole world.

This book is not a life of Woodrow Wilson. It includes no part of his scholastic or political activities prior to the looming of American involvement in the war.

---

[1] I have prepared an extensive memoir of the Belgian Relief, the Food Administration and the Relief and Reconstruction organizations with complete documentation too extensive for elaboration in this text except in their relation to Mr. Wilson.

Writing this memoir some four decades after that war has one advantage. There were many discussions, minutes of meetings, agreements and reasons for decisions and compromises which were only disclosed gradually over years long after. In fact, some important items are now available for the first time. Literally tens of thousands of articles and hundreds of volumes have been published on these events and actions. My own files alone relating to the period when I served with Mr. Wilson exceed a million items. The documentation in other libraries comprise several million more. And the task has been to sort the material from the immaterial.

As I have gone over thousands of these musty papers, memories have sprung vividly to life and often have attested the amount of error and misrepresentation in what has been written about Woodrow Wilson.

My association with him was such that I necessarily formed convictions as to his philosophy of life, his character and his abilities which have deepened during these four decades. My appraisal of him is based solely on my own experiences with him and my knowledge of the forces with which he had to deal.

I have no need to speak of his great scholarly attainments. They were built into a superior mind. He possessed great clarity of thought, with an ability quickly to reduce problems to their bare bones. His public addresses were often clothed with great eloquence. As a Jeffersonian Democrat, he was a "liberal" of the nineteenth-century cast. His training in history and economics rejected every scintilla of socialism, which today connotes a liberal.

His philosophy of American living was based upon free enterprise, both in social and in economic systems. He held that the economic system must be regulated to prevent monopoly and unfair practices. He believed that Federal intervention in the economic or social life of our people was justified only when the task was greater than the states or individuals could perform for themselves.

He yielded with great reluctance to the partial and temporary abandonment of our principles of life during the war, because of the multitude of tasks with which the citizen or the states could not cope. But he often expressed to me the hope that our methods of doing so were such that they could be quickly reversed and free enterprise restored.

Coming from an academic ivory tower with only a brief political career, he at times stumbled badly in the thicket of politics. Some of the appointments to which he was persuaded by politicians were bad. However, of the men whom he selected for the conduct of major war activities few were political appointees and all were men of high ability and integrity.

In evaluating Mr. Wilson's make-up there are a few phenomena to bear in mind. He frequently has been described as "obstinate." In my view this was not true. His mind ran to "moral principles," "justice" and "right." In them he held deep convictions. In some phases of character he partook of the original Presbyterians—what they concluded was right, was thereafter right as against all comers. He often referred with pride to his ancestral inheritance from the Scotch Covenanters of 1638.[2]

The trouble into which he fell with these principles and ideals lay in their conflict with the age-old concepts and aims of nations in Europe. In these conflicts he was at times compelled to choose the lesser of evils. But he was slow to budge. He was not a snob but he had little patience with small minds.

His further difficulty was that at times he became impatient with honest and proper argument against his conclusions, and too often for his own good he construed such argument as personal criticism. He sometimes carried resentment at what he considered personal criticism to the extent of casting loyal and devoted friends into outer darkness. At one time I myself ran into a minor mental barbed-wire entanglement but without serious results. In my work, even when Mr. Wilson did not entirely agree with me, he listened with patience and we were always able to find a path ahead upon which to travel successfully together.

But above all, three qualities of greatness stood out in Woodrow Wilson. He was a man of staunch morals. He was more than just an idealist: he was the personification of the heritage of idealism of the American people. He brought spiritual concepts to the peace table. He was a born crusader.

America is the only nation since the Crusades to fight other peoples' battles at her own gigantic loss. We may be proud of that Crusade even if it did fail to bring peace to mankind. Woodrow

---

[2] For instance, he elaborated upon this inheritance in an address at Manchester, England, December 30, 1918. He spoke of it again at Portland, Oregon, on September 15, 1919.

Wilson, however, did spread lasting ideals over the world.

The story of this period is the story of the leader of this Crusade. It unfolds a tragedy to the world against which he fought—and it becomes the tragedy of Woodrow Wilson.

ACKNOWLEDGMENTS

In the work of sifting out essential from nonessential documents; in comment on the text and in checking quotations and the mechanical work of preparation of this book, I have received most helpful aid from the following persons which I gratefully acknowledge: Felix Morley, Neil MacNeil, H. V. Kaltenborn, Lewis L. Strauss, William I. Nichols, Perrin C. Galpin, Fordyce B. St. John, Walter R. Livingston, Thomas T. Thalken, Bernice Miller, Diana Hirsh, Loretta Camp, Cynthia Fay, and Constance Dibble.

I am also deeply appreciative of the courtesy and cooperation of the many authors or publishers of the books and those responsible for personal material in many libraries for permission to quote and use these important contributions to history. In particular, I should like to thank Mrs. Edith Bolling Wilson and Charles Seymour for their generosity in this regard.

From the unpublished papers of Colonel E. M. House, by permission of Charles Seymour, Curator, Edward M. House Collection, Yale University Library.
From the unpublished papers of Ray Stannard Baker, Princeton University Library, by permission of Mrs. Ray Stannard Baker and Alexander P. Clark, Curator of Manuscripts, Princeton University Library.
From the Papers of Charles L. Swem, Princeton University Library, by permission of the Law Offices of Clarick & Clarick.
From the Diary of Gordon Auchincloss, Yale University Library, by permission of Mrs. Janet Auchincloss.
From the Diary of Vance McCormick, The Hoover Institution, Stanford University, by permission of Vance McCormick.
From the Diary of Hugh Gibson, The Hoover Institution, Stanford University, by permission of Hugh Gibson.

THE ORDEAL OF WOODROW WILSON

1

MY INTRODUCTION TO WOODROW WILSON

My first introduction to President Wilson grew out of a poignant tragedy.

A long-time engineering colleague of mine was in charge of the New York office of the Commission for Relief in Belgium and Northern France. His splendid son, en route to join our staff in Belgium, went down in the German-torpedoed *Lusitania*. The father's grief affected his mind. He became obsessed with the idea that the Relief Commission was responsible for his son's death. As he became more and more disturbed, he sought to embarrass the Commission by laying various charges before Senator Henry Cabot Lodge, with the prospect of having a Senate investigation of the Commission.

The major charge was that I, as its Chairman, had repeatedly violated the century-old Logan Act, which made it a crime for American citizens to negotiate with foreign governments on international matters. It was true enough that I had continuously conducted negotiations with the British, French and Germans to secure immunity for our ships and for the protection of our supplies from the German Army within the occupied territory.

I did not think the matter very serious, but Ambassador Walter Hines Page, in London, warned me that such stuff as the Senator might explode in the columns of the sensational press at home would do the Commission great harm because of the emotional opposition at that time against our becoming involved in the war. Mr. Melville Stone, President of the Associated Press and an old friend, also sent me a warning.

American public confidence in the Commission was the very tenuous thread on which this enterprise hung. Both belligerents were seeking either American support or American neutrality and were cooperative with us because of the great American solicitude for the plight of the Belgians. The answer to Lodge was obvious. So far as I was concerned, I was acting under the patronage of neutral ambassadors and ministers in Europe. This however seemed to irk the Senator even more deeply, because to him it implied that the American Government was getting entangled in the war.

I sailed for the United States on May 7, 1915—it having been arranged by Mr. Stone that I see President Wilson immediately upon my arrival. The President was partly amused and partly confirmed in his long-standing opinion of Senator Lodge. He quickly grasped the situation and his cordiality at once overcame my diffidence. I had prepared a statement that he might possibly issue to the public supporting the Commission. He looked it over, and gave instant directions that it should be given to the press. I also requested that he appoint a nonpartisan committee of seven prominent men to take general charge of our New York office. At once he directed letters to be written to them.

My business with the President was over in less than fifteen minutes. But he detained me for some time, discussing the war and the possibilities of American intervention to make peace. I advised him that the emotional situation among the peoples of the belligerents, if nothing else, made such an effort hopeless at this time.

Mr. Stone arranged a dinner in New York for all the important publishers, editors and heads of the news services, where he explained our predicament. I described our work and difficulties. Frank Cobb, editor of the *New York World*, summed up that they could take care of any outbreaks from the Senator and would so inform him at once. Former President Theodore Roosevelt also promised me "to hold my friend Lodge's hand." Quickly I was able to sail back to my job in Europe.

I had previously had a number of indirect contacts with the President through Colonel Edward M. House. The Colonel was generally regarded as the President's chief adviser on peace and war. He came to Europe on several occasions to explore the possibility of the President's intervention to bring the war to an end. The Colonel visited with me each time, and I was a sort of outpost adviser for him on the political and emotional forces moving in the war as they might bear on the possibilities of bringing about peace.[1]

The Colonel, at the beginning, was entirely ignorant of European politics and the forces behind the statesmen who were in control. Both the President and the Colonel were at that time moving in an idealistic stratosphere far above the earthly ground upon which the war was being fought. It was hard for them to realize that Europe would not recoil from the abyss on the edge of which civilization hung. Leaders on both sides and the peoples behind them had no thought other than victory. The emotions of the German people were whipped into violent hate at every meal of every day when they sat down to face the privations they and their children suffered from the British and French blockade. The people on the Allied side writhed with hate at the aggression of the German militarists. They were still further infuriated at every innocent seaman drowned by submarines and every woman and child killed by bombs from the air. The daily death rolls from the front reached the firesides of every country at war. The masses of people on both sides believed that they were fighting to save their homes from a vicious and brutal enemy.

Certainly the foreign offices wanted to please the Colonel, and they were all men trained in that art. The officials on both sides listened most respectfully to the Colonel's proposals, then gently deferred them.

---

[1] The Colonel told me that he had transmitted this information to the President. As an example, on March 19, 1915, I received a friendly acknowledgment from President Wilson to one of these memoranda:

THE WHITE HOUSE, WASHINGTON

MY DEAR MR. HOOVER:　　　　　　　　　　　　　March 19, 1915

Mr. House has kindly sent me the documents you were kind enough to place in his hands for my inspection.

May I not take this occasion in thanking you for the documents to express my sincere appreciation of the work that you have been doing? It has commanded the admiration and confidence of every one who has had a chance to know of it and I am sure that every American who has had any part in the work of relieving suffering in Belgium will feel, when the whole story is told, that the part you have played is one of distinguished service.

Cordially and sincerely yours,

WOODROW WILSON

My next meeting with President Wilson was on January 31, 1917. Ambassador Page had arranged this appointment. Some explanation of the immediate background is desirable.

In December 1916 the Allied Governments had notified me that they could no longer furnish dollar exchange for the Belgian Relief Commission. I had arranged with New York bankers to place a loan for the Commission of $150,000,000, to be jointly guaranteed by the British, French and exiled Belgian Governments. I arrived in New York on January 21, 1917, to settle the final details of this loan.

At this interview with the President, I told him of the Allies' inability to support the dollar operations of the Belgian Relief much longer and I told him of the successful completion of the loan to the Belgian Relief Commission. He expressed great satisfaction at this outcome.

The conversation then again drifted to the European situation and I gave him an appraisal as I saw it.

By this time, the President was under great pressures that the United States should join in the war.[2] I was convinced from his remarks that he had no intention at this time of having the United States drawn into the European conflict, a position which I heartily approved.

However, the next morning we had a terrible shock. On Feb-

---

[2] These pressures arose from pro-Allied committees in the United States. Both of the President's advisers, Colonel House and Ambassador Page, joined in these pressures. They were further augmented by vigorous organized propaganda of the French and British Governments.

Colonel House's Diary indicates the President's attitude at this time. An entry on January 4, 1917, says:

Lansing desires the President to press the submarine issue and to send Bernstorff home.... The President told him the other day that he did not believe the people of the United States were willing to go to war because a few Americans had been killed.

On January 11, 1917, House made the following entry:

... He [Wilson] thought Lansing was not in sympathy with his purpose to keep out of war.

The President's determination to keep out of the war, even with this provocation, was indicated by Colonel House, who states in his Diary on February 1:

The President was insistent that he would not allow it to lead to war if it could possibly be avoided. He reiterated his belief that it would be a crime for this Government to involve itself in the war to such an extent as to make it impossible to save Europe afterward. He spoke of Germany as "a madman that should be curbed." I asked if he thought it fair to the Allies to ask them to do the curbing without doing our share. He noticeably winced at this, but still held to his determination not to become involved if it were humanly possible to do otherwise.

ruary 1, the Germans declared their unlimited submarine war. They torpedoed three of our Belgian Relief food ships within the next three days, despite the guaranteed immunity from attack and the plain marking and flags on these ships, exactly as the Germans had stipulated. Only one of our ships en route reached Rotterdam. Sixteen others were ordered into English ports by the British Navy or the shipowners. We were compelled to stop loading and the Relief was paralyzed.

On February 3, President Wilson recalled our American Ambassador from Germany in protest against the conduct of the Germans.

I urgently needed to return to Europe to negotiate renewed protection for our Relief ships. But as all passenger traffic in the North Atlantic had been suspended, I was forced to remain in New York and negotiate by cable.

On February 13, Colonel House discussed with me the question of what part the United States should take in case we did become involved. At his request I gave him a memorandum, which I understood he wished to send to the President. The pertinent paragraphs are:

13th February 1917

DEAR COLONEL HOUSE:

Apropos of my conversation with you this morning, my own views as to immediate steps to be taken in case we go to war with Germany are as follows:

1. I trust that the United States will enter into no political alliance with the Allied Governments, but will confine itself to naval and military *cooperation*.

2. The first step for such cooperation would be to bring to bear the whole weight of our naval, shipping, and other resources to supply England, France, and Italy with food-stuffs and munitions.

3. It will probably be necessary for us to open to them all the facilities of which we are capable, to enable finance of such purchases in the United States.

4. Although, as you know, I have had no sympathy with the food blockade of Germany, this measure has proceeded to such a length that from a military point of view it is necessary that it should be now continued to the end and we would therefore need address ourselves to the reinforcement of it at every point. You are also aware that the Allied Governments have found themselves embarrassed by the necessity of bending to the demands of this country in connection with trade with the northern neutral governments. As a

consequence, a considerable leakage of their native food supplies filters into Germany from these quarters, but by cooperation with the Allied Governments in the restriction of permits for the shipment of food-stuffs from this country to these neutral Powers, we could no doubt further restrict the native supplies now going into Germany.

5. It would probably be necessary for this government to direct as much American shipping to the assistance of the Allies as possible, but we can go one further if we join with the Allies by pressure upon neutral shipping to serve the Allies. For instance, if we cooperate with the Allies in refusing bunker coal to shipping except on terms that they serve the Allies beyond their regulated self-needs, we can force a great deal of neutral shipping into the service of the Allied Governments. There are other means by which pressure can be directed to this end as well. . . .

In paragraph 6, I explored the possibility of allowing the French Army to recruit more American men for their army and the need of mosquito vessels to protect shipping.

7. It appears to me that the political situation which will eventuate out of this war makes it absolutely necessary that this country should not only be protected by a large defensive force, but that we should have a force in being when peace approaches. As our terms of peace will probably run counter to most of the European proposals, our weight in the accomplishment of our ideals will be greatly in proportion to the strength which we can throw into the scale.

8. It appears that the world will be faced with a food shortage before the next harvest and that some measures will be necessary for the control of food consumption in this country if we are adequately to supply the Western Allies. Such measures do not need to take the form of rationing the people, or any drastic measures of that character, but there are many indirect methods of repressing food consumption, such as the suppression of the consumption of grain and sugar for brewing and distilling purposes and a long list of other measures with which we are well familiar.

HERBERT HOOVER[3]

---

[3] In sending this letter to the President on February 13, Colonel House attached the following:

Here is a copy of a letter from Hoover in which he outlines his idea and the best way to serve in the event of war with Germany. I think you will agree with most of his suggestions.

On February 16 the President wrote to Ray Stannard Baker:

Here is a letter so pertinent to the inquiries now being made by the Council of National Defense that I am taking the liberty of sending it to you for consideration. It comes from a very experienced man.

I was in Washington on February 14 and 15, to consult Secretary of State Lansing because Ambassador Page, on February 12, had sent a cable to the Secretary of State urging that the Belgian Relief Commission should end its activities. To this I did not agree, believing from my cable negotiations that I could restore our ship immunities. I was already making progress toward this goal both with the Germans and the British.

I had no intention of troubling the President but while in Washington, Secretary of the Interior Franklin K. Lane, an old friend, sent me to see him. This was my third meeting with him. Our discussion naturally dwelt on the plight of the Belgian people and of the Relief Commission. I told him of my hopes of restoring the German guarantees of safety for our ships but added that our financial outlook was desperate as our projected loan had necessarily failed. On a sudden thought, I suggested that possibly Congress could grant an appropriation for expenditures in the United States and that I believed the Allies would meet our European currency outlays. The President at once responded that he believed this should be done and that at a favorable moment he would recommend it.

Our discussion then turned to the war situation and the dangers of our becoming involved. I told him that I did not believe the Germans wanted us in the war but in their madness anything could happen.

As I was leaving, the President commented upon my letter to Colonel House of a few days before and said that when I returned to Europe it might prove helpful if I could study the Allied economic organizations in the conduct of the war. I came away convinced that the President earnestly, and even emotionally, intended to avail himself of every device to keep out, short of sacrifice of national honor.

On February 24, having, as I thought, restored the German guarantees, we began again to load food ships for Belgium. On March 12, I obtained passage on a Spanish jalopy—half sail, half steam—for Cadiz. En route the wireless reported that the Germans had torpedoed seven American and five Belgian Relief ships without a chance for the crews. It also brought news of the revolution ousting the Czar in Russia.

I stopped at Madrid and settled with the Spanish Minister of Foreign Affairs the possibility that his nationals would need to represent the Belgian Relief Commission inside Belgium and Northern France in case the United States became involved in the war.[4]

At once on my arrival in Paris and later in London I began the studies that the President had suggested. On April 6, 1917, the United States declared war. While in Washington, Secretary Lane had told me that if we became involved in the war I would be wanted in Washington for food organization. From this and the President's conversations noted above, I was not surprised when Ambassador Page notified me that Mr. Wilson wanted me to return to Washington to organize the American food activities. I accepted on condition that I conduct the Belgian Relief at the same time. I also

---

[4] As I have had occasion several times to mention the Belgian and Northern France Relief Commission in this book, I give the following short sketch for those unfamiliar with that operation.

I organized the Commission for Relief in Belgium in October 1914 at the urgent request of the representatives of the people in Belgium, the exiled government at Le Havre, and American Ambassador Walter Hines Page. At that time, the 10,000,000 people in Belgium and Northern France, normally dependent on imports for 70 per cent of their food, were being crushed between the millstones of the Allied blockade of Germany and the German armies which had invaded them.

With the approval of our State Department I secured as "patrons" of the Commission Ambassador Walter Hines Page in London, Ambassador James W. Gerard in Berlin, and American Minister Brand Whitlock in Brussels. We also secured as "patrons" the Spanish Ambassador in London, Merry del Val; the Spanish Ambassador in Berlin, Luis Polo de Bernabé; the Spanish Minister in Brussels, the Marquis de Villalobar; the Netherlands Minister in Brussels, and the cooperation of the Netherlands Minister of Foreign Affairs, J. Loudon. Although these officials could not themselves, as representatives of their governments, negotiate matters concerning the relief, they could pave the way for myself and my colleagues. The Commission was operated wholly by Americans until the United States entered the war and thereafter we operated up to the Belgian frontier with Dutch and Spanish representatives in the German occupied areas. We had created a system of distribution committees of leading Belgians in Belgium and leading French men and women in Northern France.

The Commission started with only charitable funds from over the world but in February 1915, I got subsidies from the British and French Governments at the rate of $90,000,000 annually, increasing the rate to $300,000,000 annually by January 1917.

The United States joined in the support of the Commission after we came into the war. The requirements rose to a rate of $360,000,000 annually.

Our imports of food under the most vigorous rationing started at the rate of 720,000 tons annually and rose to a rate of 1,260,000 tons by January 1917, and to a rate of 1,600,000 tons at the time of the Armistice. During the unlimited German submarine war in 1917, the Belgians suffered terribly before we were able to restore the protection agreements for our ships.

The Belgian Relief was the pioneer of the World War Food Administration. It involved not only the importation of food, but the eventual control of food processing; the stimulation of agricultural production; and the requisition of agricultural products, which we combined with the imports to ration their people. The work required the development of special care of 2,500,000 children and the provision for millions of the destitute with not only food but clothing, medical supplies, fuel and housing.

asked to delay my return for a few weeks to solve certain urgent problems in the Relief and to examine the Allied civilian war organization, including their food needs. I arrived in Washington on May 6, 1917. I saw Mr. Wilson on May 8 and 10, and on May 19 I was appointed United States Food Administrator, directly responsible to the President.

2

WOODROW WILSON ADMINISTERS THE WAR

The purpose of this book is solely to unfold the President's plans, his obstacles, his methods, his successes and the causes of the tragedy which came to him in his efforts to bring lasting peace to the world. It is appropriate, however, to touch briefly upon his organization of the American Government and people for the conduct of the war. On the military side, the Secretary of War, Newton D. Baker, fortunately, was a good administrator. There could have been no better selections than General Peyton C. March as Chief of Staff, and General John J. Pershing to command our overseas army. In the Navy Department, the President had the advantage that its normal organization was almost on a war footing. The Secretary of the Navy, Josephus Daniels, was assured a good administration by the long-experienced admirals under him, including Admiral William S. Benson, Admiral Mark Bristol and Admiral William S. Sims in command of our naval forces in Europe.

On the civilian side, new agencies had to be created to meet the demands both for supplies for our military forces, and for the civilian and military necessities of the Allies. These new agencies, in order to control raw materials, food, coal, imports, exports and shipping, had many problems in common. Among them was the need, with the huge drain on our supplies, to stimulate production and reduce domestic consumption. With the law of supply and demand upset by the forced drain for the Allies it was also necessary to control domestic prices, distribution, exports and imports in order to protect supplies for our own people and prevent speculation and profiteering.

These governmental activities were strange in American life and Congress was tardy, fearful and often inadequate in conferring the powers upon the President which were vital to enable the civilian agencies to contribute their part in winning the war.

To meet the cry that these were dictatorial powers, the President at the beginning developed the idea that they should be administered by boards, commissions, councils or committees. I had reported to him mistakes the Allies had made by this sort of organization at the start, and their ultimate but slow recognition that administration must be conducted by a single head. As a matter of fact, a single executive had been the basic concept of organization of our Government and our business world ever since the foundation of the Republic. I was fortunate in persuading the President that a new term, "Administrator," would not connote dictatorship and I, therefore, did not have to go through the unhappy experiences of some of my colleagues.

However, after a few months of stumbling and bitter experience, the President returned to our traditional methods of organization with a single executive in authority, and the boards, commissions, committees and councils relegated to purely advisory functions.

The President made appointments irrespective of political faiths. No more splendid men could have been found than Bernard M. Baruch, who directed the War Industries Board; Secretary of the Treasury W. G. McAdoo, who was also Railway Administrator; Harry A. Garfield, who directed the Fuel Administration; Charles M. Schwab, who directed ship construction; Edward N. Hurley, who managed the overseas shipping; and Vance M. McCormick, who directed the controls over imports, exports and blockade matters. Mr. Wilson was fortunate in having David F. Houston as Secretary of Agriculture and Franklin K. Lane as Secretary of the Interior. Thousands of competent men of all professions answered the President's call as volunteers to staff these new organizations.[1]

---

[1] I should like to mention the thousands of men and women who volunteered to aid in the War Administration but space forbids. I may, however, mention a few leading men in these agencies. On the War Industries Board were heads of important

In my job I was confronted with a crop failure immediately following the declaration of war which plagued us from the harvest of 1917 to the harvest of 1918. But despite the difficulties and frustrations, with the loyal support of the housewives, the processors, and the middlemen, we so reduced consumption as to make possible huge exports from what was statistically a vacuum.[2]

Early in my relations with the President, I learned that he preferred a letter or a memorandum to personal interviews whenever it was possible. Further, where it was necessary to secure his written authority by personal interviews, he liked to have a possible draft document ready to sign. This accounts for the large number of such documents in this text and in my other memoirs — few of which have ever been published.

The following letter is of interest in indicating the President's attitude toward the Allies:

THE WHITE HOUSE, December 10, 1917

MY DEAR MR. HOOVER:

I have noticed on one or two of the posters of the Food Administration the words, "Our Allies." I would be very much obliged if you would issue instructions that "Our Associates in the War" is to be substituted. I have been very careful about this myself, because we have no allies and I think I am right in believing that the people

---

divisions, Arch W. Shaw, Alexander Legge, Judge Robert S. Lovett, and Robert S. Brookings. In the Coal Administration were heads of divisions, Mark L. Requa, Walter Hope and Henry Taylor, Sr. On the War Trade Board were John Beaver White, Alonzo E. Taylor and Clarence M. Woolley. In the Food Administration there were heads of divisions, Joseph P. Cotton, Julius H. Barnes, Judge Curtis H. Lindley, Edgar Rickard, Gertrude B. Lane, Ray Lyman Wilbur, George Rolph and Robert A. Taft.

I may add that after having served in the organizations which I directed, four became United States Senators, four governors, one an ambassador, one a minister, one a Federal judge, and two Assistant Secretaries of State, and many became leaders in the professions and industry.

[2] I had a momentary diversion from the treadmill of the Food Administration. Colonel House, knowing of my prewar experience in Russia, often discussed the current situation there with me. The Communists had overthrown the Kerensky Government in 1917. In June 1918, the Colonel developed the idea that I should head a Food Relief expedition to Communist Russia as a method of calming that tempest. While I had no confidence in their accepting the conditions that would be necessary for success, I stated that I would serve in any capacity that the President requested. The President, however, brought the Colonel's project to an end by a letter to Mr. Baruch on July 15, 1918, stating that he wanted me in Washington.

I had a further diversion in a visit to Europe in July and August 1918 to coordinate all Allied food activities under the "Food Council of the Allied and Associated Powers" and to bring about better distribution of shipping.

of the country are very jealous of any intimation that there are formal alliances.

You will understand, of course, that I am implying no criticism. I am only thinking it important that we should all use the same language.

WOODROW WILSON

With our Food Administration's guaranteed prices for farm products and Secretary Houston's leadership of our devoted farmers, we produced in the crop of 1918 the greatest surplus of food in all our history, enabling us to export over three times as much as our prewar average.

Our War Department under the President's leadership organized armies of over 3,000,000 men. The Navy expanded its already great strength.

Our war agencies met every requirement of our armed forces and of the Allies, even though great shipping difficulties arose due to the slowness of our shipbuilding program.

The President's religious and moral upbringing expressed itself in a zeal for financial integrity which characterized the conduct of a war practically without corruption.

With his ability to delegate work, his loyalties to subordinates, and his speed in evaluating problems, he proved a great administrator. A comparative study of the administration of any war in our history since Lincoln's time down to the present would easily confirm this.[3]

---

[3] I emphasize this point because various persons, including Colonel House in his Diary, were constantly criticizing the President's administrative abilities.

For instance, there is an entry in the Colonel's Diary under date of July 4, 1917 (House Papers, Yale University Library):

. . . I urged him [the President] to let me organize a war machine for him. It is the kind of thing I know how to do . . . I assured him that it could be done in a few weeks and in a way to give him entire freedom from details . . . if he would let me select it regardless of party, the result would inure to his credit. . . .

Among other things I told him that he did not have the kind of ability necessary to organize the country for war. I softened this by saying that the ability to organize was not rare and could be found in plenty, but the ability to frame and force policies of government was rare, and he should confine his time to that. I shook him, but did not entirely convince him that I was right. . . .

For further substantiation of the President's administrative abilities see Chapters 9 and 10.

3

AN UNHAPPY INTERLUDE

In the last stages of the war came an unhappy incident to which I refer here only because it detracted from the President's strength in negotiating the peace and later in securing ratification of the Peace Treaty by the Senate.

The end of the war was evidently approaching in October 1918, and the Congressional elections were to take place on November 5.

On October 24, Mr. Wilson made an appeal for the election of a Democratic Congress, accompanied by an attack upon Republicans and their party members of Congress. The more controversial paragraphs read:

MY FELLOW COUNTRYMEN:

The Congressional elections are at hand. They occur in the most critical period our country has ever faced or is likely to face in our time. If you have approved of my leadership and wish me to continue to be your unembarrassed spokesman in affairs at home and abroad, I earnestly beg that you will express yourselves unmistakably to that effect by returning a Democratic majority to both the Senate and the House of Representatives. . . .

The leaders of the minority in the present Congress have unquestionably been pro-war, but they have been anti-administration. At almost every turn since we entered the war they have sought to take the choice of policy and the conduct of the war out of my hands and put it under the control of instrumentalities of their own choosing. . . .

The return of a Republican majority to either House of the Congress would, moreover, certainly be interpreted on the other side of the water as a repudiation of my leadership. Spokesmen of the Republican Party are urging you to elect a Republican Congress in order to back up and support the President, but even if they should in this way impose upon some credulous voters on this side of the water, they would impose on no one on the other side. It is well understood there as well as here that the Republican leaders desire not so much to support the President as to control him.

The peoples of the allied countries with whom we are associated against Germany are quite familiar with the significance of elections. They would find it very difficult to believe that the voters of the United States had chosen not to support their President by electing to the Congress a majority controlled by those who are not in fact in sympathy with the attitude and action of the Administration.

I need not tell you, my fellow-countrymen, that I am asking your support not for my own sake or for the sake of a political party, but for the sake of the nation itself in order that its inward unity of purpose may be evident to all the world.

If in these critical days it is your wish to sustain me with undivided minds, I beg that you will say so in a way which it will not be possible to misunderstand, either here at home or among our associates on the other side of the sea. I submit my difficulties and my hopes to you.

Woodrow Wilson

This statement was not only a shock to me but also a mystery. The President had shown no partisanship in his appointments to the war agencies. In fact, he had appealed to many Republicans to undertake large responsibilities at great personal sacrifice.[1] It came

---

[1] The Republicans in important positions in Mr. Wilson's administration included General Pershing, General Robert E. Wood, Admiral Mark Bristol, Admiral W. S. Sims, and such men as President Harry Garfield of Williams College, Julius Rosenwald, Alexander Legge, Judge Robert S. Lovett, Benedict Crowell, Robert S. Brookings, William H. Taft, Daniel Willard, Edward Stettinius, Charles Schwab, myself, and scores of others. I had all my adult life been a registered Republican and taken part in Republican organizations. However, from 1914, when I first assumed war responsibilities in the Belgian Relief Commission, until after the Senate defeat of the Treaty in 1920, with this one exception of supporting the President's appeal, I engaged in no political party activities. After that time I resumed my party affiliations and directed them to support the ratification of the Treaty of Versailles.

as a great shock to these Republican officials and to the majority of Republican members of the Congress. Most of them had supported his call for the declaration of war and some of the President's recommendations of war powers, particularly the coal and food control, had been bogged down by antagonistic Democratic Senators but had finally been enacted by the efforts of Republicans. Above all, this letter was construed by his opponents to be an attack on the patriotism of Republicans in general. Up to this time they had no great fighting material for their campaign, but this gave them a powerful issue, both in its implications and its cry of partisanship in the midst of the nation's greatest crisis. It is idle talk to speculate about what might otherwise have been the outcome of the election.

The mystery lies in the identity of the politicians who pushed Mr. Wilson into an action so entirely foreign to his nature and his previous nonpartisan conduct of war affairs. There can be no doubt of the great pressures exerted upon him by some Democratic members of Congress and certain outside groups apparently stimulated by his Secretary, Joseph P. Tumulty, and Postmaster General Albert S. Burleson. On the other hand, according to their memoirs, the essence of the statement was opposed by four Cabinet members, Secretary of State Lansing, Secretary of Agriculture Houston, Secretary of the Interior Lane and Attorney General Gregory.[2]

---

[2] A memorandum of Attorney General Thomas W. Gregory on this incident, among the House Papers at Yale University Library, is illuminating:

... The letter was not merely the worst political mistake that he could make, but it was utterly un-Wilsonian. For more than a year there has been in Washington thousands of loyal Republicans, working under Wilson's leadership for the country, at $1.00 a year, and sacrificing their private interests and forgetting their political affiliations. There were scores of Republicans in the Senate and House who had voted consistently for Wilson's policies and held up his hands during the struggle, at a time when many of his own party were hamstringing him. The letter seemed to stigmatize everyone who was not a member of the Democratic party, and it immediately raised an electoral issue and gave an opportunity to the Republicans which up to then had been lacking. Previously they had no fight in them. Now they had good reason to complain of a document which had injected a partisan issue at a moment when they might claim they had forgotten everything in order to win the war. Without this issue the Democrats would have carried the elections easily, on the basis of Wilson's prestige and the fact that the war had been won. None of us knew anything of the letter until it appeared. I myself read it with horror in the morning paper. It seems probable to me that Wilson decided to write the letter in a moment of extreme weariness, for these were harrowing days, at the end of a long session when his nerves were taut and his intellectual sentinels ·vere not on the lookout for danger. Otherwise I cannot conceive of his writing the letter, which, as I have said, is so thoroughly un-Wilsonian.

Deeply as I believed that this appeal was a mistake and a wholly unwarranted reflection on many good men, on November 2, I addressed a letter to Frederic Coudert, a Republican friend, in which I supported the President's appeal for a Congress favorable to him. I did so because I believed that the President's hand in the Treaty negotiations would be greatly weakened if the election went against him. The publication of this letter created a storm around my head. The Chairman of the Republican National Committee denounced me violently.

The Republicans won both the Senate and the House of Representatives. Subsequent events show that the President's influence at Paris[3] and his influence with the Senate to obtain ratification of the peace were definitely damaged.

I received the following note from the President:

THE WHITE HOUSE, 4 November, 1918

MY DEAR HOOVER:

Your letter to Mr. Coudert has touched me very deeply, and I want you to know not only how proud I am to have your endorsement and your backing given in such generous fashion, but also what serious importance I attach to it, for I have learned to value your judgment and have the greatest trust in all your moral reactions. I thank you from the bottom of my heart.

Cordially and sincerely yours,
WOODROW WILSON

---

[3] For its adverse effect on the President's influence in Paris see Chapter 16.

4

WOODROW WILSON DECLARES AMERICAN IDEALS
AS THE BASIS OF PEACE

While the war was still being fought, Mr. Wilson began the enumeration of the principles which should form the basis of the peace which must follow the inevitable victory over Germany and her allies. These were defined in four major addresses from January to December 1918. The President subsequently, for negotiation purposes, unified them as the "Fourteen Points and subsequent addresses." They were Woodrow Wilson's proclamation to all mankind of the New World ideals of peace.

But even prior to these four addresses the President, in urging the declaration of war on April 2, 1917, indicated some of his determinations as to the peace. In this eloquent address he first reviewed the submarine war against the United States, the conspiracies, spies, and sabotage within our borders. He described the ruthless character of the militarists in control of Germany, denounced them for making war against all mankind, and stated that this menace must be destroyed. Then he went on to say:

> We have no quarrel with the German people. We have no feeling towards them but one of sympathy and friendship. It was not upon their impulse that their government acted in entering this war. . . .
>
> A steadfast concert for peace can never be maintained except by a partnership of democratic nations. No autocratic government could be trusted to keep faith within it or observe its covenants.

It must be a league of honour. . . . Only free peoples can hold their purpose and their honour steady to a common end and prefer the interests of mankind to any narrow interest of their own.

Mr. Wilson concluded:

... The world must be made safe for democracy. Its peace must be planted upon the tested foundations of political liberty. We have no selfish ends to serve. We desire no conquest, no dominion. We seek no indemnities for ourselves, no material compensation for the sacrifices we shall freely make. We are but one of the champions of the rights of mankind. We shall be satisfied when those rights have been made as secure as the faith and the freedom of nations can make them . . .

The right is more precious than peace, and we shall fight for the things which we have always carried nearest our hearts, for democracy, for the right of those who submit to authority to have a voice in their own governments, for the rights and liberties of small nations, for a universal dominion of right by such a concert of free peoples as shall bring peace and safety to all nations and make the world itself at last free. . . . America . . . God helping her . . . can do no other.

However, the principles laid down in this address were not a part of the precise "basis of peace" which he later stated.

In the first of the four addresses of 1918, he laid down "Fourteen Points," which, when added to those in his subsequent addresses, made a total of thirty-eight "points," "principles," "ends," "particulars" and "declarations." Some of them were enlargements and explanations and part repetitions of those previously given.[1]

---

[1] Mr. Wilson had no ghost writer. He composed the first draft of his addresses on his own typewriter. He sometimes submitted them to his colleagues for their opinions but he seldom adopted changes in his fundamental ideas.

It is desirable to point out that in some of the unpublished sections of Colonel House's Diary he has a tendency to assume the credit for inspiring Wilson's major speeches and originating the "points." I have not accepted this claim. Some of the "points" were expressions of American ideals as old as the Revolution of 1776, about which Mr. Wilson as a historian had often written and spoken. Many of the "points" as to specific countries were based on cries for freedom poured into American ears for decades, such as those relating to Poland, the southern Slavs, Czechoslovakia, the Baltic States and the restoration of Alsace-Lorraine and Belgium. Some of these ideas could be found in Professor Wilson's teachings. The Colonel, in volumes of his own writings in the House Papers, shows no such powers of expression or historical background.

The Colonel was a useful adviser and a most capable negotiator for the President. But Woodrow Wilson was no Charlie McCarthy.

In order to make clear the later events, I present each of the thirty-eight points in the President's exact words. To simplify my references to them in ensuing chapters, they are numbered in brackets at the end of each paragraph.

The first of these epochal addresses was to the Congress, on January 8, 1918. He began with a discussion of the effect of the recent German treaties with the Communists and continued:

> No statesman who has the least conception of his responsibility ought for a moment to permit himself to continue this tragical and appalling outpouring of blood and treasure unless he is sure beyond a peradventure that the objects of the vital sacrifice are part and parcel of the very life of society and that the people for whom he speaks think them right and imperative as he does. . . .
>
> We entered this war because violations of right had occurred which touched us to the quick and made the life of our own people impossible unless they were corrected and the world secured once for all against their recurrence. What we demand in this war, therefore, is nothing peculiar to ourselves. It is that the world be made fit and safe to live in; and particularly that it be made safe for every peace-loving nation which, like our own, wishes to live its own life, determine its own institutions, be assured of justice and fair dealings by the other peoples of the world, as against force and selfish aggression. All the peoples of the world are in effect partners in this interest, and for our own part we see very clearly that unless justice be done to others it will not be done to us.
>
> The program of the world's peace, therefore, is our program, and that program, the only possible program, as we see it, is this:
>
> I. — Open covenants of peace, openly arrived at, after which there shall be no private international understandings of any kind but diplomacy shall proceed always frankly and in the public view. [1]
>
> II. — Absolute freedom of navigation upon the seas, outside territorial waters, alike in peace and in war, except as the seas may be closed in whole or in part by international action for the enforcement of international covenants. [2]
>
> III. — The removal, so far as possible, of all economic barriers and the establishment of an equality of trade conditions among all

the nations consenting to the peace and associating themselves for its maintenance. [3][2]

IV. — Adequate guarantees given and taken that national armaments will be reduced to the lowest point consistent with domestic safety. [4]

V. — Free, open-minded, and absolutely impartial adjustment of all colonial claims, based upon a strict observance of the principle that in determining all such questions of sovereignty the interests of the populations concerned must have equal weight with the equitable claims of the Government whose title is to be determined. [5]

VI. — The evacuation of all Russian territory and such a settlement of all questions affecting Russia as will secure the best and freest cooperation of the other nations of the world in obtaining for her an unhampered and unembarrassed opportunity for the independent determination of her own political development and national policy and assure her of a sincere welcome into the society of free nations under institutions of her own choosing; and, more than a welcome, assistance also of every kind that she may need and may herself desire. The treatment accorded Russia by her sister nations in the months to come will be the acid test of their good will, of their comprehension of her needs as distinguished from their own interests, and of their intelligent and unselfish sympathy. [6]

VII. — Belgium, the whole world will agree, must be evacuated and restored, without any attempt to limit the sovereignty which she enjoys in common with all other free nations. No other single

---

2 In a letter to Senator F. M. Simmons ten months later (October 28, 1918), the President defined this point:

I of course meant to suggest no restriction upon the free determination by any nation of its own economic policy, but only that whatever tariff any nation might deem necessary for its own economic service, be that tariff high or low, it should apply equally to all foreign nations. . . . This leaves every nation free to determine for itself its own internal policies, and limits only its right to compound those policies of hostile discriminations between one nation and another. . . . The experiences of the past among nations have taught us that the attempt by one nation to punish another by exclusive and discriminatory trade agreements has been a prolific breeder of that kind of antagonism which oftentimes results in war and that if a permanent peace is to be established among nations every obstacle that has stood in the way of international friendship should be cast aside. It was with this fundamental purpose in mind that I announced this principle in my address of Jan. 28 . . . to inject the bogey of free trade which is not involved at all, is to attempt to divert the mind of the nation from the broad and humane principle of durable peace. . . .

act will serve as this will serve to restore confidence among the nations in the laws which they have themselves set and determined for the government of their relations with one another. Without this healing act the whole structure and validity of international law is forever impaired. [7]

VIII. — All French territory should be freed and the invaded portions restored, and the wrong done to France by Prussia in 1871 in the matter of Alsace-Lorraine, which has unsettled the peace of the world for nearly fifty years, should be righted, in order that peace may once more be made secure in the interest of all. [8]

IX. — A readjustment of the frontiers of Italy should be effected along clearly recognizable lines of nationality. [9]

X. — The peoples of Austria-Hungary, whose place among the nations we wish to see safeguarded and assured, should be accorded the freest opportunity of autonomous development. [10]

XI. — Rumania, Serbia, and Montenegro should be evacuated; occupied territories restored; Serbia accorded free and secure access to the sea; and the relations of the several Balkan States to one another determined by friendly counsel along historically established lines of allegiance and nationality; and international guarantees of the political and economic independence and territorial integrity of the several Balkan States should be entered into. [11]

XII. — The Turkish portions of the present Ottoman Empire should be assured a secure sovereignty, but the other nationalities which are now under Turkish rule should be assured an undoubted security of life and an absolutely unmolested opportunity of autonomous development, and the Dardanelles should be permanently opened as a free passage to the ships and commerce of all nations under international guarantees. [12]

XIII. — An independent Polish State should be erected which should include the territories inhabited by indisputably Polish populations, which should be assured a free and secure access to the sea, and whose political and economic independence and territorial integrity should be guaranteed by international covenant. [13]

XIV. — A general association of nations must be formed under specific covenants for the purpose of affording mutual guarantees of political independence and territorial integrity to great and small states alike. [14]

The President concluded this address:

We have spoken, now, surely, in terms too concrete to admit of any further doubt or question. An evident principle runs through the whole program I have outlined. It is the principle of justice to all peoples and nationalities, and their right to live on equal terms of liberty and safety with one another, whether they be strong or weak. Unless this principle be made its foundation, no part of the structure of international justice can stand. The people of the United States could act upon no other principle, and on the vindication of this principle they are ready to devote their lives, their honor, and everything that they possess. The moral climax of this, the culminating and final war for human liberty, has come, and they are ready to put their own strength, their own highest purpose, their own integrity and devotion to the test.

On February 11, 1918, the President again addressed the Congress. After explaining the reasons for rejection of a peace plan proposed by Count von Hertling, Chancellor of Germany, he enunciated "four principles" to be applied. But before stating these principles he made the following important demands or declarations:

There shall be no annexations. [15]
No contributions, no punitive damages. [16]
Peoples are not to be handed about from one sovereignty to another by an international conference or an understanding between rivals and antagonists. [17]
National aspirations must be respected; peoples may now be dominated and governed only by their own consent. "Self-determination" is not a mere phase. It is an imperative principle of action, which statesmen will henceforth ignore at their peril. [18]
We cannot have general peace for the asking, or by the mere arrangements of a peace conference. It cannot be pieced together out of individual understandings between powerful states. All the parties to this war must join in the settlement of every issue anywhere involved in it. [19]

In presenting his "four principles" he said:

This war had its roots in the disregard of the rights of small nations and of nationalities which lacked the union and the force to make good their claim to determine their own allegiances and their own forms of political life. Covenants must now be entered into which will render such things impossible for the future; and those covenants must be backed by the united force of all the nations that love justice and are willing to maintain it at any cost.

After all, the test of whether it is possible for either government to go any further in this comparison of views is simple and obvious. The principles to be applied are these:

First, that each part of the final settlement must be based upon the essential justice of that particular case and upon such adjustments as are most likely to bring a peace that will be permanent; [20]

Second, that peoples and provinces are not to be bartered about from sovereignty to sovereignty as if they were mere chattels and pawns in a game, [21]

even the great game, now forever discredited, of the balance of power; [22]

Third, every territorial settlement involved in this war must be made in the interest and for the benefit of the populations concerned, and not as a part of any mere adjustment or compromise of claims amongst rival states; [23] and

Fourth, that all well defined national aspirations shall be accorded the utmost satisfaction that can be accorded them without introducing new or perpetuating old elements of discord and antagonism that would be likely in time to break the peace of Europe and consequently of the world. [24]

The President added this affirmation:

. . . We believe . . . in a new international order under which reason and justice and the common interests of mankind shall prevail . . . [25] Without that new order the world will be without peace and human life will lack tolerable conditions of existence and development. Having set our hand to the task of achieving it, we shall not turn back.

The President delivered the third of these major addresses on the basis of peace at Mount Vernon on July 4, 1918. After paying tribute to George Washington and his ideals he enunciated four "ends" which he said "must be conceded before there can be peace":

The Past and the Present are in deadly grapple and the peoples of the world are being done to death between them.

There can be but one issue. The settlement must be final. There can be no compromise. No halfway decision would be tolerable. No halfway decision is conceivable. These are the ends for which the associated peoples of the world are fighting and which must be conceded them before there can be peace:

I. — The destruction of every arbitrary power anywhere that can separately, secretly, and of its single choice disturb the peace of the world; or, if it cannot be presently destroyed, at the least its reduction to virtual impotence. [26]

II. — The settlement of every question, whether of territory, of sovereignty, of economic arrangement, or of political relationship, upon the basis of the free acceptance of that settlement by the people immediately concerned, and not upon the basis of the material interest or advantage of any other nation or people which may desire a different settlement for the sake of its own exterior influence or mastery. [27]

III. — The consent of all nations to be governed in their conduct towards each other by the same principles of honor and of respect for the common law of civilized society that govern the individual citizens of all modern states in their relations with one another; to the end that all promises and covenants may be sacredly observed; no private plots or conspiracies hatched, no selfish injuries wrought with impunity, and a mutual trust established upon the handsome foundation of a mutual respect for right. [28]

IV. — The establishment of an organization of peace which shall make it certain that the combined power of free nations will check every invasion of right and serve to make peace and justice the more secure by affording a definite tribunal of opinion to which all must submit and by which every international readjustment that cannot be amicably agreed upon by the peoples directly concerned shall be sanctioned. [29]

These great objects can be put into a single sentence. What we seek is the reign of law, based upon the consent of the governed and sustained by the organized opinion of mankind. [30]

On September 27, 1918, in New York, Mr. Wilson spoke again about the basis for peace, citing five "particulars" and prefacing these with three other "points":

If it be in deed and in truth the common object of the governments associated against Germany and of the nations whom they govern, as I believe it to be, to achieve by the coming settlements a secure and lasting peace, it will be necessary that all who sit down at the peace table shall come ready and willing to pay the price, the only price, that will procure it; and ready and willing, also, to create in some virile fashion the only instrumentality by which it can be made certain that the agreements of the peace will be honored and fulfilled. . . . [31]

That indispensable instrumentality is a League of Nations formed under covenants that will be efficacious. Without such an instrumentality, by which the peace of the world can be guaranteed, peace will rest in part upon the word of outlaws, and only upon that word. . . . [32]

And, as I see it, the constitution of that League of Nations and the clear definition of its objects must be a part, is in a sense the most essential part, of the peace settlement. . . . [33]

These, then, are some of the particulars, and I state them with the greater confidence because I can state them authoritatively as representing this Government's interpretation of its own duty with regard to peace:

First, the impartial justice meted out must involve no discrimination between those to whom we wish to be just and those to whom we do not wish to be just. It must be a justice that plays no favorites and knows no standard but the equal rights of the several peoples concerned; [34]

Second, no special or separate interest of any single nation or any group of nations can be made the basis of any part of the settlement which is not consistent with the common interest of all; [35]

Third, there can be no leagues or alliances or special covenants and understandings within the general and common family of the League of Nations. [36]

Fourth, and more specifically, there can be no special, selfish economic combinations within the League and no employment of any form of economic boycott or exclusion except as the power of economic penalty by exclusion from the markets of the world may be vested in the League of Nations itself as a means of discipline and control; [37]

Fifth, all international agreements and treaties of every kind must be made known in their entirety to the rest of the world. [38]

. . . In the same sentence in which I say that the United States will enter into no special arrangements or understandings with particular nations let me say also that the United States is prepared to assume its full share of responsibility for the maintenance of the common covenants and understandings upon which peace must henceforth rest. We still read Washington's immortal warning against "entangling alliances" with full comprehension and an answering purpose. But only special and limited alliances entangle; and we recognize and accept the duty of a new day in which we are permitted to hope for a general alliance which will avoid entanglements and clear the air of the world for common understandings and the maintenance of common rights.

The reader will observe that the twenty-three supplementary "points" to the original fourteen at times repeat them in other terms or amplify them. But they all became important in the formal documents of the peace negotiations as the "Fourteen Points and the subsequent addresses."

In two post-armistice addresses abroad, the President further developed his ideas. In an address at Manchester, England, on December 30, 1918, he emphasized his point [22] referring to abolition of the balance of power:

> ... I want to say very frankly to you that she [the United States] is not now interested in European politics, but she is interested in the partnership of right between America and Europe. If the future had nothing for us but a new attempt to keep the world at a right poise by a balance of power the United States would take no interest, because she will join no combination of power which is not the combination of all of us. She is not interested merely in the peace of Europe, but in the peace of the world. ...

He returned to this point again in an address at Rome, on January 3, 1919:

> We know that there can not be another balance of power. That has been tried and found wanting, for the best of all reasons that it does not stay balanced inside itself, and a weight which does not hold together cannot constitute a makeweight in the affairs of men. ...

I was present at three of the President's major speeches. I was profoundly moved by these expressions of the idealism of the American people and the New World. But I was haunted by my knowledge that they were doctrines strange to the Old World. Nevertheless, the proposition that lasting peace could be had only by organized unity of the world and the rights of nations to self-determination and independence came as a brilliant light and an inspiring hope to peoples who had suffered from domination and war over the centuries.

WOODROW WILSON LAYS DOWN THE TERMS
OF PEACE TO THE GERMANS

When at last the enemy states sought an Armistice, they directed their request to President Wilson rather than to any Allied leader, and proposed that the basis of negotiations be the "Fourteen Points and the subsequent addresses."

The President at once took personal control of the negotiation. His purpose in doing so was threefold:

First, to assure before peace negotiations the withdrawal of enemy troops from occupied territory and the reduction of the strength of the enemy armies to impotence.

Second, to establish securely the "Fourteen Points and the subsequent addresses" as a basis for peace for Germany and the other enemy states.

Third, and of equal or greater importance as we shall see in the next chapter, to secure agreement from the Allies that they, too, would adhere to the "Fourteen Points and the subsequent addresses" as the basis of peace.

To make clear the unfolding of what in my opinion is the greatest drama of intellectual leadership in all history, I present the events as they occurred day by day. That the reader may more quickly grasp the magnitude of this intellectual drama, I have introduced summary headings, the reading of which illuminates the great scenes of action. However, inasmuch as the documentation of these vital agreements by the Central Powers is fundamental to the consideration of subsequent events, the texts of the pertinent dispatches[1] are reproduced almost in their entirety. I have added the major breaks in the enemy front at the dates on which they occurred. The italics throughout are mine.

September 16, 1918

Austria Requests a Conference

The Chancellor of the Austro-Hungarian Government, on September 16, 1918, requested a conference to consider an armistice. The President rejected the idea of a conference.

September 26

The Surrender of Bulgaria

The Bulgarian front began to crumble in the midst of attack by the Allied armies commanded by General Franchet d'Esperey. On September 26 the Bulgarian Army asked for a truce for forty-eight hours. This being refused, they made an unconditional surrender on September 30. The same day Chancellor von Hertling of Germany and his Cabinet resigned.

October 4

The Reichstag Revolution

On October 4, by action of the Reichstag, Prince Max of Baden succeeded to the Chancellorship of Germany, with a Cabinet which included Philip Scheidemann, representing the Social Democratic party, and Matthias Erzberger, the leader of the Catholic Centrist party.

October 6–7

Germany and Austria
Request an Armistice

Through the Swiss Legation in Washington, the United States Government, on October 6, received the following note:

> The German Government requests the President of the United States of America to take steps for the restoration of peace, to notify

---

[1] All these dispatches are quoted from the United States Department of State, *Papers Relating to the Foreign Relations of the United States* [The World War, supplement 1], vol. I, United States Government Printing Office, Washington: 1933, pp. 338–405 *passim*, and I have not considered it necessary to footnote each one.

all belligerents of this request, and to invite them to delegate plenipotentiaries for the purpose of taking up negotiations. *The German
Government accepts, as a basis for the peace negotiations, the
program laid down by the President of the United States in his
message to Congress of January 8, 1918, and in his subsequent
pronouncements, particularly in his address of September 27....*
In order to avoid further bloodshed, the German Government requests to bring about the immediate conclusion of a general armistice on land, on water, and in the air.

MAX, PRINCE OF BADEN

The next day our Government received the following note from
the Austro-Hungarian Government through the Swedish Legation
in Washington:

The Austro-Hungarian Monarchy, which has waged war always
and solely as a defensive war and repeatedly given documentary
evidence of its readiness to stop the shedding of blood and arrive
at a just and honorable peace, hereby addresses itself to (Monsei-
gneur) the President of the United States of America and offers to
conclude with him and his allies an armistice on every front,
on land, at sea, and in the air, and to enter immediately upon
negotiations *for a peace for which the fourteen points in the Message of President Wilson to Congress of January 8, 1918, and the
four points contained in President Wilson's address of February
12 [11], 1918, should serve as a foundation, and in which the view-
points declared by President Wilson in his address of September
27, 1918, will also be taken into account.*

OCTOBER 8
THE PRESIDENT DEMANDS EVACUATION OF INVADED TERRITORY

As these statements accepting the "Fourteen Points and the
subsequent addresses" were only as *a basis for negotiations* they
could be a trap to "negotiation," with the German armies standing
intact. Therefore, on October 8, the President, through the Swiss
Legation in Washington, demanded the evacuation of Allied territory, saying:

Before making reply to the request of the Imperial German
Government, and in order that that reply shall be as candid and
straightforward as the momentous interests involved require, the
President of the United States deems it necessary to assure himself
of the exact meaning of the note of the Imperial Chancellor. Does

the Imperial Chancellor mean that the Imperial German Government accepts the terms laid down by the President in his *address to the Congress of the United States on the 8th of January last and in subsequent addresses, and that its object in entering into discussions would be only to agree upon the practical details of their application?*

The President feels bound to say with regard to the suggestion of an armistice that he would not feel at liberty to propose a cessation of arms to the Governments with which the Government of the United States is associated against the Central Powers so long as the armies of these Powers are upon their soil. The good faith of any discussion would manifestly depend upon the consent of the Central Powers immediately to withdraw their forces everywhere from invaded territory.

The President also feels that he is justified in asking whether the Imperial Chancellor is speaking merely for the constituted authorities of the Empire who have so far conducted the war. He deems the answers to these questions vital from every point of view.

OCTOBER 10

THE ALLIES DEMUR

The three Allied Prime Ministers, meeting in Paris, naturally wanted not only the evacuation of occupied territory but also disarmament. On October 9 they sent the following telegram to the President:

PARIS, October 9, 1918, 8 P.M.
[Received October 10, 10:55 A.M.]

The Allied Governments have taken cognizance of the reply addressed by President Wilson to the Chancellor of the German Empire, with the greatest interest.

They recognize the elevated sentiments which have inspired this reply. Limiting themselves to most urgent question, that of the armistice, they agree with the President of the United States that the preliminary condition of all discussion of this question is the evacuation of all invaded territory. But they think for the conclusion of an armistice itself this condition, while necessary, would not be sufficient. It would not prevent the enemy from profiting by a suspension of hostilities to install himself, after the expiration of an armistice not followed by peace, in a better military position than at the moment of the expiration of hostilities. He would be left the facility of retiring from a critical situation to save his war material, reconstitute his units, shorten his front and retire without loss of men to new positions which he would have the time to choose and fortify.

The conditions of an armistice cannot be fixed until after consultation with military experts and in accordance with the military situation at the moment of engaging in negotiations. These considerations have been forcibly exposed by the military experts of the Allied Powers and especially by Marshal Foch. They are of equal interest to the armies of the Governments associated in the battle against the Central Empires.

To these considerations the Allied Governments draw the entire attention of President Wilson.

The President, however, was not to be rushed, for he had other vital questions to settle which needed step-by-step development.

OCTOBER 12

THE GERMANS AND AUSTRIANS AGREE TO EVACUATE OCCUPIED TERRITORY

The German Chancellor's reply to the President's questions of October 8 was dated October 12 and was received through the Swiss Legation in Washington on October 14:

In reply to the question of the President of the United States of America the German Government hereby declares:

The German Government has accepted the terms laid down by President Wilson in his address of January 8 and in his subsequent addresses as the foundations of a permanent peace of justice. Consequently its object in entering into discussions would be only to agree upon practical details of the applications of these terms.

The German Government believes that the Governments of the powers associated with the United States also accept the position taken by President Wilson in his addresses.

The German Government, in accordance with the Austro-Hungarian Government, for the purpose of bringing about an armistice declares itself ready to comply with the propositions of the President in regard to evacuation.

The German Government suggests that the President may occasion the meeting of a mixed commission for making the necessary arrangements concerning the evacuation.

The present German Government which has undertaken the responsibility for this step towards peace has been formed by conferences and in agreement with the great majority of the Reichstag. The chancellor, supported in all of his actions by the will of this majority, speaks in the name of the German Government and of the German people.

October 14
The President Demands Reduction in Enemy Arms

While evacuation of occupied territories was an important step, Mr. Wilson now pressed for the reduction of the German armies. He sent the following note to the Germans through the Swiss Legation:

The unqualified acceptance by the present German Government and by a large majority of the German Reichstag of the terms laid down by the President of the United States of America in *his address to the Congress of the United States on the 8th of January, 1918, and in his subsequent addresses* justifies the President in making a frank and direct statement of his decision with regard to the communications of the German Government of the . . . 12th of October, 1918.

It must be clearly understood that the process of evacuation and the conditions of an armistice are matters which must be left to the judgment and advice of the military advisers of the Government of the United States and the Allied Governments, and the President feels it his duty to say that no arrangement can be accepted by the Government of the United States which does not provide absolutely satisfactory safeguards and guarantees of the maintenance of the present military supremacy of the armies of the United States and of the Allies in the field. He feels confident that he can safely assume that this will also be the judgment and decision of the Allied Governments.

The President feels that it is also his duty to add that neither the Government of the United States nor, he is quite sure, the Governments with which the Government of the United States is associated as a belligerent will consent to consider an armistice so long as the armed forces of Germany continue the illegal and inhumane practices which they still persist in. At the very time that the German Government approaches the Government of the United States with proposals of peace its submarines are engaged in sinking passenger ships at sea, and not the ships alone but the very boats in which their passengers and crews seek to make their way to safety; and in their present enforced withdrawal from Flanders and France the German armies are pursuing a course of wanton destruction which has always been regarded as in direct violation of the rules and practices of civilized warfare. Cities and villages, if not destroyed, are being stripped of all they contain . . . often of their very inhabitants. The nations associated against Germany can not be expected to agree to a cessation of arms while acts of inhumanity, spoliation, and desolation are being continued which they justly look upon with horror and with burning hearts.

It is necessary, also, in order that there may be no possibility of misunderstanding, that the President should very solemnly call the attention of the Government of Germany to the language and plain intent of one of the terms of peace which the German Government has now accepted. It is contained in the address of the President delivered at Mount Vernon on the Fourth of July last. It is as follows: "*The destruction of every arbitrary power anywhere that can separately, secretly, and of its single choice disturb the peace of the world; or, if it cannot be presently destroyed, at least its reduction to virtual impotency.*" *The power which has hitherto controlled the German Nation is of the sort here described. It is within the choice of the German Nation to alter it. The President's words just quoted naturally constitute a condition precedent to peace, if peace is to come by the action of the German people themselves. The President feels bound to say that the whole process of peace will, in his judgment, depend upon the definiteness and the satisfactory character of the guarantees which can be given in this fundamental matter.* It is indispensable that the Governments associated against Germany should know beyond a peradventure with whom they are dealing. . . .

OCTOBER 19

THE PRESIDENT PROPOSES TO THE AUSTRIANS

A CHANGE IN POINT 10

On October 19, the President replied through the Swiss Legation to the Austro-Hungarian Government note of October 6:

The President deems it his duty to say to the Austro-Hungarian Government that he cannot entertain the present suggestions of that Government because of certain events of utmost importance which, occurring since the delivery of his address of the 8th of

January last, have necessarily altered the attitude and responsibility of the Government of the United States. Among the fourteen terms of peace which the President formulated at that time occurred the following:

> X. The people of Austro-Hungary, whose place among the nations we wish to see safeguarded and assured, should be accorded the freest opportunity of autonomous development.

Since that sentence was written and uttered to the Congress of the United States, the Government of the United States has recognized that a state of belligerency exists between the Czecho-Slovaks and the German and Austro-Hungarian Empires and that the Czecho-Slovak National Council is a *de facto* belligerent Government clothed with proper authority to direct the military and political affairs of the Czecho-Slovaks. It has also recognized in the fullest manner the justice of the nationalistic aspirations of the Jugo-Slavs for freedom.

The President is, therefore, no longer at liberty to accept the mere "autonomy" of these peoples as a basis of peace, but is obliged to insist that they, and not he, shall be the judges of what action on the part of the Austro-Hungarian Government will satisfy their aspirations and their conception of their rights and destiny as members of the family of nations.

October 20
German Evasion of Army Reduction

On October 20 the German Government, through the Swiss Legation, pretended to answer but in truth sought to evade answering the points raised in the President's statement of October 14, when he insisted upon reduction of the German armies. The reply stated:

> In accepting the proposal for an evacuation of the occupied territories, the German Government has started from the assumption that the procedure of this evacuation and *of the conditions of an armistice should be left to the judgment of the military advisers, and that the actual standard of power on both sides in the field has to form the basis for arrangements safeguarding and guaranteeing the standard.* The German Government suggests to the President to bring about an opportunity for fixing the details. It trusts that the President of the United States will approve of no demand which would be irreconcilable with the honor of the German people, and with opening a way to a peace of justice.

The Germans then protested the President's charges of destruction and inhumanity, and continued:

As the fundamental conditions for peace, the President characterizes the destruction of every arbitrary power that can separately, secretly and of its own single choice disturb the peace of the world. To this the German Government replies: Hitherto the representation of the people in the German Empire has not been endowed with an influence on the formation of the Government. The Constitution did not provide for a concurrence of the representation of the people in decisions on peace and war. These conditions have just now undergone a fundamental change. The new Government has been formed in complete accord with the wishes of the representation of the people, based on the equal, universal, secret, direct franchise. The leaders of the great parties of the Reichstag are members of this Government.

In the future no government can take or continue in office without possessing the confidence of the majority of the Reichstag. The responsibility of the Chancellor of the empire to the representation of the people is being legally developed and safeguarded.

The first act of the new Government has been to lay before the Reichstag a bill to alter the Constitution of the Empire so that the consent of the representation of the people is required for decisions on war and peace. The permanence of the new system is, however, guaranteed not only by constitutional safeguards, but also by the unshakable determination of the German people, whose vast majority stands behind these reforms and demands their energetic continuance.

The question of the President, with whom he and the Governments associated against Germany are dealing, is therefore answered in a clear and unequivocal manner by the statement that the offer of peace and an armistice has come from a Government which, free from arbitrary and irresponsible influence, is supported by the approval of the overwhelming majority of the German people.

October 23

Unequivocal Acceptance Demanded

On October 23, at a meeting of the "President's War Council" at the White House there were present Baruch, Hurley, Williams, McCormick and myself. We had before us the German note of October 20, which was evasive as to reduction of German armies. The

President read his proposed reply. We all approved it. In the conversation McCormick remarked that he would like to see a complete surrender and an occupation of Berlin. I remarked that I wanted to see a quick end to the war and that I took no stock in a triumphal march down the Unter den Linden.

The President's reply sent by Secretary Lansing through the Swiss Chargé in Washington stipulated that the German armies be reduced, that military terms of the Armistice should be formulated by the Allies and that any militarist control of Germany be removed. The note read:

WASHINGTON, *October 23, 1918*

SIR:

I have the honor to acknowledge the receipt of your note of the 22d transmitting a communication under date of the 20th from the German Government and to advise you that the President has instructed me to reply thereto as follows:

Having received the solemn and explicit assurance of the German Government that it unreservedly accepts the terms of peace laid down in his address to the Congress of the United States on the 8th of January, 1918, and the principles of settlement enunciated in his subsequent addresses, particularly the address of the 27th of September, and that it desires to discuss the details of their application, and that this wish and purpose emanate, not from those who have hitherto dictated German policy and conducted the present war on Germany's behalf, but from Ministers who speak for the Majority of the Reichstag and for an overwhelming majority of the German people; and having received also the explicit promise of the present German Government that the humane rules of civilized warfare will be observed both on land and sea by the German armed forces, the President of the United States feels that he can not decline to take up with the Governments with which the Government of the United States is associated the question of an armistice.

He deems it his duty to say again, however, that the only armistice he would feel justified in submitting for consideration would be one which should leave the United States and the powers associated with her in a position to enforce any arrangements that may be entered into and to make a renewal of hostilities on the part of Germany impossible. The President has, therefore, transmitted his correspondence with the present German authorities to the Governments with which the Government of the United States is associated as a belligerent, with the suggestion that, if those Governments are disposed to effect peace upon the terms and principles indicated, their military advisers and the military advisers of the United States be asked to submit to the Governments associated against Germany *the necessary terms of such an armistice as will fully protect the interests of the peoples involved and ensure to the Associated Governments the unrestricted power to safeguard and enforce the details of the peace to which the German Government has agreed,* provided they deem such an armistice possible from the military point of view. Should such terms of armistice be suggested, their acceptance by Germany will afford the best concrete evidence of her unequivocal acceptance of the terms and principles of peace from which the whole action proceeds.

THE PRESIDENT DEMANDS REMOVAL
OF THE MONARCHISTS

The President would deem himself lacking in candor did he not point out in the frankest possible terms the reason why extraordinary safeguards must be demanded. Significant and important as the constitutional changes seem to be which are spoken of by the German Foreign Secretary in his note of the 20th of October, *it does not appear that the principle of a Government responsible to the German people has yet been fully worked out or that any guarantees either exist or are in contemplation that the alterations of principle and of practice now partially agreed upon will be permanent.* Moreover, it does not appear that the heart of the present difficulty has been reached. It may be that future wars have been brought under the control of the German people, but the present war has not been; and it is with the present war that we are dealing. *It is evident that the German people have no means of commanding the acquiescence of the military authorities of the Empire in the popular will; that the power of the King of Prussia to control the policy of the Empire is unimpaired; that the determining initiative still remains with those who have hitherto been the masters of Germany.*

Feeling that the whole peace of the world depends now on plain speaking and straightforward action, *the President deems it his duty to say, without any attempt to soften what may seem harsh words, that the nations of the world do not and can not trust the word of those who have hitherto been the masters of German policy;* and to point out once more that in concluding peace and attempting to undo the infinite injuries and injustices of this war the Government of the United States can not deal with any but veritable representatives of the German people who have been assured of a genuine constitutional standing as the real rulers of Germany. *If it must deal with the military masters and the monarchical autocrats of Germany now, or if it is likely to have to deal with them later in regard to the international obligations of the German Empire, it must demand, not peace negotiations, but surrender.* Nothing can be gained by leaving this essential thing unsaid.[2]

October 27

The Germans Give Assurances Demanded
by the President

On October 27, the German Government, through the Swiss Legation, gave the assurances the President had demanded, that their new government was in actual control, saying:

> The German Government has taken cognizance of the reply of the President of the United States. The President knows the far-reaching changes which have taken place and are being carried out in the German constitutional structure. The peace negotiations are being conducted by a government of the people in whose hands rests, both actually and constitutionally, the authority to make decisions. The military powers are also subject to this authority. The German Government now awaits the proposals for an armistice, which is the first step toward a peace of justice, as described by the President in his pronouncements.

---

[2]Colonel House with a staff sailed for Europe on October 17, arriving in Paris on October 26.

Two days before the Colonel left for Paris, Lansing, Baker and Daniels discussed with the President his proposed note to the Germans of October 23. House's Diary does not give their opinions but apparently the President made no substantial changes. However, under date of October 24, House says:

> I am still disturbed over the President's reply to the German Note of October 22nd. . . .
> . . . He had gone into a long and offensive discussion which may have the effect of stiffening German resistance and welding the people together back of their military leaders. . . .
> . . . The Germans may accept the President's terms without question, but if they do not and the war is prolonged, he has taken the entire responsibility upon himself.

The chief importance of this footnote is its indication that Mr. Wilson was the master of the situation and not dominated by Colonel House.

OCTOBER 29

THE AUSTRIANS ACCEPT THE CHANGE IN POINT 10
AND AGREE TO PEACE TERMS

On October 29, the Austro-Hungarian Government sent the following communication through the Swedish Legation:

> In reply to the note of President Wilson to the Austro-Hungarian Government dated October 18 [19] of this year, with regard to the decision of the President to take up with Austria-Hungary separately the question of armistice and peace, the Austro-Hungarian Government has the honor to declare that *it adheres both to the previous declarations of the President and his opinion of the rights of the peoples of Austria-Hungary, notably those of the Czecho-Slovaks and the Jugo-Slavs, contained in his last note. Austria-Hungary having thereby accepted all the conditions which the President had put upon entering into negotiations on the subject of the armistice and peace,* nothing, in the opinion of the Austro-Hungarian Government, longer stands in the way of beginning those negotiations. The Austro-Hungarian Government therefore declares itself ready to enter, without waiting for the outcome of other negotiations, into negotiations for a peace between Austria-Hungary and the Entente states and for an immediate armistice on all the Austro-Hungarian fronts and begs President Wilson to take the necessary measures to that effect.

OCTOBER 29

THE PRESIDENT INSISTS ON DECISIVE YET MODERATE
ARMISTICE TERMS

The President sent a dispatch to Colonel House on October 29, officially paraphrased as follows:

> My deliberate judgment is that our whole weight should be thrown for an armistice which will not permit a renewal of hostilities by Germany, but which will be as moderate and reasonable as possible within that condition, because lately I am certain that too much severity on the part of the Allies will make a genuine peace settlement exceedingly difficult if not impossible.... Foresight is better than immediate advantage.[3]

---

[3]What was going on among the German militarists during these negotiations is made clear in General Ludendorff's book, in which he recounts a meeting on August 14 of the German and Austrian leaders in Berlin:

There can be no doubt that Mr. Wilson, by his courage and skill, had turned the German request for an armistice during which to negotiate the peace with their armies still standing into a complete surrender, and more, he had fully established his "basis of peace" with them. His problem now was to secure the Allied adherence to the principles of the "Fourteen Points and the subsequent addresses."

> I reviewed the military situation, the condition of the army, and the position of our allies, and explained that it was no longer possible by an offensive to force the enemy to sue for peace. Defense alone could hardly achieve this object, and so the termination of the war would have to be brought about by diplomacy.... The Emperor was very calm...and instructed him (the Foreign Secretary) to open up peace negotiations, if possible, through the medium of the Queen of the Netherlands.

Apparently they made no headway on this line, and Ludendorff continues as of October 1:

> Today the troops are now their own; what may happen to-morrow cannot be foreseen.... The line might be broken at any moment and then our proposal would come at the most unfavorable time.... Our proposal must be forwarded immediately from Berne to Washington. The army could not wait forty-eight hours longer.

However, the German generals apparently believed that the armies would be retained intact while negotiations were in progress. Therefore, the President's note of October 23 came as a great shock to Ludendorff:

> On October 23rd or 24th Wilson's answer arrived. It was a strong answer to our cowardly note. This time he had made it quite clear that the armistice conditions must be such as to make it impossible for Germany to resume hostilities, and to give the powers allied against her unlimited power to settle themselves the details of the peace accepted by Germany. In my view, there' could no longer be doubt in any mind that we must continue the fight. I felt quite confident that the people were still to be won over to this course.

On the evening of October 24, General von Hindenburg issued an order to the troops to resume hostilities, saying:

> Wilson's answer is a demand for unconditional surrender. It is thus unacceptable to us soldiers. It proves that our enemies' desire for our destruction, which let loose the war in 1914, still exists undiminished. It proves, further, that our enemies use the phrase "peace of justice" merely to deceive us and break our resistance. Wilson's answer can thus be nothing for us soldiers but a challenge to continue our resistance with all our strength.

Prince Max was apparently strong enough as Chancellor by this time to demand that the Emperor relieve both Ludendorff and von Hindenburg of their commands.

6

WOODROW WILSON'S BASIS OF PEACE
AGREED TO BY THE ALLIES

The President, having now established the "Fourteen Points and the subsequent addresses" as the basis of peace with the enemy governments and also having established the military basis of the Armistice, including the withdrawal of enemy troops from occupied countries and the demobilization of their armies, now had the task of winning the Allied acceptance of these terms as the basis of peace.

Again I believe that this phase of his efforts can best be presented by the actual text of dispatches[1] in their proper sequence along with a summary of the events, day by day.

OCTOBER 23

THE PRESIDENT SUBMITS HIS BASIS OF PEACE
TO THE ALLIES

The President presented to the Allies the terms of the basis of peace on October 23. The presentation took the form of identical dispatches from the Secretary of State to the diplomatic representatives in Washington of Belgium, Brazil, China, Cuba, France, Great Britain, Greece, Guatemala, Haiti, Honduras, Italy, Japan, Mon-

---

[1]The texts are quoted from United States Department of State, *Papers Relating to the Foreign Relations of the United States* [The World War, supplement I], vol. I, United States Government Printing Office, Washington: 1933, pp. 383-469. Since the original dispatches follow the sequence given in this text, as in the preceding chapter I do not cumber the pages with specific references.

tenegro, Nicaragua, Panama, Portugal, Russia, Serbia, and Siam, as follows:

WASHINGTON, *October 23, 1918*

EXCELLENCY:

I have the honor to enclose herewith certain communications which have passed between the Government of the United States and the Government of Germany, relative to an armistice and the terms of a treaty of peace between the belligerents in the present war, with the request that you transmit the same to your Government.

The President instructs me to make request that your Government take this correspondence under careful consideration and communicate, at its convenience, its views and conclusions concerning it.

The President desires especially an expression of the decision of Your Excellency's Government as to its willingness and readiness to acquiesce and take part in the course of action with regard to an armistice which is suggested in my note of October 23, 1918, to the Chargé d'Affaires of Switzerland, in which is set forth the decision of the President with regard to the submission of the question of an armistice to the Governments with which the Government of the United States is associated in the prosecution of the war against Germany, and with regard to the manner in which the terms of an armistice are to be determined provided an armistice at this time is deemed possible from the military point of view.

I wish to point out to your Government that the President has endeavored to safeguard with the utmost care the interests of the peoples at war with Germany in every statement made in the enclosed correspondence, and that it is his sincere hope that your Government will think that he has succeeded and will be willing to cooperate in the steps which he has suggested.

ROBERT LANSING

OCTOBER 28

Czechoslovakia and Estonia each declared itself an independent republic. And on October 29 the Serbians, Croatians, Slovenes, Montenegrins and the Banat proclaimed the unification of the Southern Slavs and their independence under a constitutional monarchy.

October 30

Lloyd George and Clemenceau
Question the President's Basis of Peace

Prime Ministers Lloyd George and Clemenceau asked for a detailed explanation of many of the "Fourteen Points." On October 29, House cabled the President that he had engaged Walter Lippmann, the journalist, and Frank Cobb, the editor of the New York *World,* to draw up an explanation. However, the President's response was not an entire acceptance of their interpretation.

Washington, *October 30, 1918*

Analysis of fourteen points satisfactory interpretation of principles involved but details of application mentioned should be regarded as merely illustrative suggestions and reserved for peace conference. Admission of inchoate nationalities to peace conference most undesirable.

Woodrow Wilson

The same day House cabled the President an account of a meeting with the Allied leaders on the "Fourteen Points":

For the President:

Lloyd George, Balfour, and Reading lunched with me today and George stated that it was his opinion that if the Allies submitted to Germany's terms of armistice without more [discussion?], Germany would assume that the Allies had accepted President Wilson's fourteen points and other speeches without qualification. So far as Great Britain was concerned, George stated, point 2 of speech of January 8, 1918, respecting freedom of the seas, could not be accepted with [out] qualification. He admitted that if point 2 was made a part of point 14 concerning League of Nations, and assuming League of Nations was such a one as Great Britain could subscribe to, it might be possible for Great Britain to accept point 2. He said that he did not wish to discuss freedom of the seas with Germany and [if] freedom of the seas was a condition of peace Great Britain could not agree to it. Before our discussion ended it seemed as though we were near an agreement concerning this matter along the lines of interpretation of point 2 heretofore cabled you in cable No. 5 to the Department.

We then went to conference at Quai d'Orsay attended by Clemenceau, Pichon, George, Balfour, Sonnino and myself. Conference opened with discussion of fourteen points enumerated in President's address of January 8 last. Clemenceau and others balked at number [*Point*] 1 until I read them interpretation thereof as cabled to you in telegram No. 5[2]. They then all accepted number [*Point*] 1. After number [*Point*] 2 had been read, George made a short speech worded so as to excite Clemenceau. He reversed his position taken a short time before with me privately *and said respecting point 2: "We cannot accept this under any circumstances; it takes away from us the power of blockade. My view is this, I want to see character of League of Nations first before I accept this proposition. I do not wish to discuss it with Germany. I will not make it a condition of peace with Germany." I stated that if these views were persisted in the logical consequences would be for the President to say to Germany: "The Allies do not agree to the conditions of peace proposed by me and accordingly the present negotiations are at an end."* I pointed out that this would leave the President free to consider the question afresh and to determine whether the United States should continue to fight for the principles laid down by the Allies. My statement had a very exciting effect upon those present. *Balfour then made a forceful speech to the effect that it was clear that the Germans were trying to drive a wedge between the President and the Allies and that their attempts in this direction must be foiled.*

It was then suggested that France, England and Italy confer together and submit tomorrow drafts of the proposed answers to the President's communication asking whether they agree to his terms of peace, stating where they can agree with the President and where they disagree. I then offered to withdraw from the conference so that they would feel at liberty to discuss the matter between themselves. They all stated that they had no secret from America and that they wished me to remain. Accordingly it was agreed after further discussion and after the reading of the terms agreed upon by the inter-Allied naval conference now in session in Paris for the naval armistice that we should meet Wednesday afternoon to consider draft answers by the Allies to the President's communication transmitting correspondence between the President and Germany.

French Prime Minister and Italian Prime Minister are not at all in sympathy with the idea of League of Nations. Italian Prime Minister will probably submit many objections to fourteen points.

---

[2]This refers to the Colonel's October 29 telegram embodying the Lippmann-Cobb "interpretations" of the "Fourteen Points."

French Prime Minister, George and I agreed to meet Wednesday morning without Italian Prime Minister for the purpose of further discussion.

It is my view that privately George and Balfour believe that the proposed terms of the naval armistice and those of the military armistice are too severe. They wish to get just as much as they can but they wish to be able to continue negotiations in the event that Germany refuses to accept the terms proposed.

An exceedingly strict censorship by the French War Office makes it impossible for American correspondents to send any communications to the United States respecting the progress of the present conference. I am examining into this matter and it may be advisable to take drastic steps in order that the United States can arrange for herself what news of political character shall be communicated to her people.

                                                    EDWARD HOUSE

Late the same day House again telegraphed the President, proposing strong action.

                                        PARIS, *October 30, 1918, 4 p.m.*

FOR THE PRESIDENT:

It is my intention to tell Prime Ministers today that if their conditions of peace are essentially different from the points you have laid down and for which the American people have been fighting, that you will probably feel obliged to go before Congress and state the new conditions and ask their advice as to whether the United States shall continue to fight for the aims of Great Britain, France and Italy.

The last thing they want is publicity and they do not wish it to appear that there is any cause for difference between the Allies. Unless we deal with these people with a firm hand everything we have been fighting for will be lost.

I told the British privately you anticipate that their policy would lead to the establishment of the greatest naval program by the United States that the world had ever seen. I did not believe that the United States would consent for any [power] to interpret for them the rules under which American commerce could traverse the sea. I would suggest that you quietly diminish the transport of troops giving as an excuse the prevalence of influenza or any other reason but the real one. I would also suggest a little later that you begin to gently shut down upon money, food and raw material. I feel confident that we should play a strong hand and if it meets with your approval I will do it in the gentle and friendly [way] almost certain [to prevail?].

HOUSE

The President Bars Any Variation from the "Fourteen Points and the Subsequent Addresses"

A few hours after receiving House's advice the President replied, refusing any concessions as to the freedom of the seas or the League of Nations:

WASHINGTON, *October 30, 1918*

I feel it my solemn duty to authorize you to say that I cannot consent to take part in the negotiation of a peace which does not include freedom of the seas because we are pledged to fight not only to do away with Prussian militarism but with militarism everywhere. Neither could I participate in a settlement which did not include league of nations because peace would be without any guarantee except universal armament which would be intolerable. I hope I shall not be obliged to make this decision public.

WOODROW WILSON

October 31

The Allies Accept With One Reservation

A few hours later Colonel House advised the President that the Allies had accepted the "Fourteen Points and the subsequent addresses" as the basis of peace, but with a reservation on freedom of the seas, saying:

PARIS, *October 30*

FOR THE PRESIDENT:

Lloyd George, Clemenceau and I met for 45 minutes this morning alone at the office of the Minister of War. Just before we entered Clemenceau's office George handed me a proposed answer to the President which the British authorities had drafted. I quote the draft in full.

"The Allied Governments have given careful consideration to the correspondence which has passed between the President of the United States and the German Government. Subject to the qualifications which follow, they declare their willingness to make peace with the Government of Germany on the terms of peace laid down in the President's address to Congress of January 8, 1918, and the principles of settlement enunciated in his subse-

quent addresses. They point out, however, that clause 2, relating to what is usually described as the freedom of the seas, is open to various interpretations, some of which they could not accept. They must therefore reserve to themselves complete freedom on this subject when they enter the peace conference.

"Further, in the conditions of peace laid down in his address to Congress of January 8, 1918, the President declared that invaded territories must be restored as well as evacuated and freed. The Allied Governments feel that no doubt ought to be allowed to exist as to what this provision implies. By it they understand that compensation will be made by Germany for all damage done to the civilian population of the Allies and their property by land, by sea and from the air."

I told George that I was afraid his attitude at yesterday's meeting had opened the flood gates; Clemenceau, Sonnino would have elaborate memoranda to submit containing their objections to the President's fourteen points, and that I doubted whether Clemenceau would accept ... [*the answer*] drafted by British which was in marked contrast to the position taken by George yesterday.

It developed at the conference that Clemenceau was having prepared an elaborate brief setting forth France's objections to the President's fourteen points. *I promptly pointed out to Clemenceau that undoubtedly Sonnino was preparing a similar memorandum and that if the Allied Governments felt constrained to submit an elaborate answer to the President containing many objections to his program it would doubtless be necessary for the President to go to Congress and to place before that body exactly what Italy, France and Great Britain were fighting for and to place the responsibility upon Congress for the further continuation of the war by the United States in behalf of the aims of the Allies. As soon as I had said this George and Clemenceau looked at each other significantly.*

Clemenceau at once abandoned his idea of submitting an elaborate memorandum concerning the President's fourteen points and apparently accepted the proposed answer drafted by the British. I suggested that the word "illegal" be placed before the words "damage done to the civilian population of the Allies," in the last sentence of draft of proposed answer. George accepted this suggestion but Clemenceau stated [that he] preferred that the draft should be left as it was. I believe that the suggestion would be accepted by all if the President sees fit to insist upon it. I am not entirely clear yet that this is necessary.

I ascertained that George and Clemenceau believed that the terms of the armistice, both naval and military, were too severe and that they should be modified. George stated that he thought it might be unwise to insist on the occupation of the east bank of the Rhine; Clemenceau stated that he could not maintain himself in the Chamber of Deputies unless this was made a part of the armistice to be submitted to the German forces and that the French Army would also insist on this as their due after the long occupation of French soil by the Germans, but he gave us his word of honor that France would withdraw after the peace conditions had been fulfilled. I am inclined to sympathize with position taken by Clemenceau.

I pointed out the danger of bringing about a state of Bolshevism in Germany if terms of armistice were made too stiff, and the consequent danger to England, France and Italy. Clemenceau refused to recognize that there was any danger of Bolshevism in France. George admitted it was possible to create such a state of affairs in England and both agreed that anything might happen in Italy.

I asked Clemenceau where he thought it would be wise to hold the peace conference. He answered, "Versailles," but however, did not argue with us when George stated that he and I had agreed on Geneva. I stated that I thought this matter should be discussed later. Upon leaving the conference, George and I again agreed that the conference had better be held in neutral territory than in a belligerent country and I still have in mind to urge Lausanne.

It was agreed that this afternoon we would discuss, first, results [terms?] of an armistice with Austria; second, the terms of the armistice with Turkey (with this I explained we have nothing to do); third, the terms of the armistice with Germany. It was agreed that there should be a meeting at my headquarters tomorrow morning of Clemenceau, George, Orlando, Marshal Foch, and myself, with Geddes at hand to advise concerning naval questions. Uninterruptedly, I am in constant consultation with our military and naval authorities.

In the event that answer drafted by British and quoted above is adopted by Allies as their answer to your communication I would strongly advise your accepting it without alteration.

House

OCTOBER 31

THE PRESIDENT HOLDS TO FREEDOM OF THE SEAS

On October 31 the President telegraphed to Colonel House about the freedom of the seas issue, saying:

> WASHINGTON, October 31, 1918
>
> I fully and sympathetically recognize the exceptional position and necessities of Great Britain with regard to the use of the seas for defence both at home and throughout the Empire and also realize that freedom of the seas needs careful definition and is full of questions upon which there is need of the freest discussion and the most liberal interchange of views, but I am not clear that the reply of the Allies quoted in your 12 definitely accepts the principle of freedom of the seas and means to reserve only the free discussion of definitions and limitations.... Terms one, two, three, and fourteen are the essentially American terms in the programme and I cannot change what our troops are fighting for or consent to end with only European arrangements of peace. Freedom of the seas will not have to be discussed with Germany if we agree among ourselves beforehand but will be if we do not. Blockade is one of the many things which will require immediate redefinition in view of the many new circumstances of warfare developed by this war. There is no danger of its being abolished.
>
> WOODROW WILSON

TURKEY ASKS FOR AN ARMISTICE

In the meantime Secretary of State Lansing was occupied with armistice proposals from Turkey. On October 31, he dispatched the following note to the Turkish Government:

> I did not fail to lay before the President the note which you addressed to him on the 14th instant, and handed to me on that date.
>
> Acting under the instructions of your Government, you enclosed with that note the text of a communication received by the Minister for Foreign Affairs of Spain, from the Chargé d'Affaires of Turkey at Madrid, on October 12, in which the good offices of the Government of Spain were sought to bring to the attention of the President the request of the Imperial Ottoman Government that he take upon himself the task of the reëstablishment of peace, and that he notify all belligerent states of the request and invite them

to delegate plenipotentiaries to initiate negotiations; the Imperial Ottoman Government accepting as a basis for the negotiations the programme laid down by the President in his message to Congress of January 8, 1918, and in his subsequent declarations, especially his speech of September 27. It is further requested by the Imperial Ottoman Government that steps be taken for the immediate conclusion of a general armistice on land, on sea, and in the air.

By direction of the President, I have the honor to inform your Excellency that the Government of the United States will bring the communication of the Turkish Chargé d'Affaires to the knowledge of the Governments at war with Turkey.

The Turks ultimately surrendered under the President's terms.

NOVEMBER 1

The Hungarians and the Austrians declared their separation from each other and proclaimed themselves independent republics.

NOVEMBER 3
BELGIANS AND ITALIANS OBJECT TO
THE PRESIDENT'S BASIS OF PEACE

On November 3 House informed the President that the Belgian and Italian representatives objected to some of the "points," reporting:

PARIS, *November 3*

FOR THE PRESIDENT:
Yesterday afternoon we had a meeting of the Supreme Council at Versailles in which we made further progress on the military terms of armistice for Germany. We did not reach the naval terms because both Lloyd George and Clemenceau wanted to wait for Austria's reply which [must?] come in by Sunday midnight. I disagreed with this procedure believing it a waste of time.

The Belgians are protesting articles 3 and 5 of the fourteen points. The Italians are protesting article 9.

The three Prime Ministers meet this afternoon at 3 o'clock at my headquarters to discuss the fourteen points. As a matter of fact Clemenceau and Orlando will accept anything that the English will agree to concerning article 2. I have spent almost every minute outside my conference discussing this article with the British. I am insisting that they must recognize the principle, that it is a strong case for discussion at the peace conference or before and

I am having the greatest difficulty in getting them to admit even that much.

I have contended that they might notwithstanding [*as well*] refuse to accept the principle that laws governing war upon land [*formed*] a subject for discussion. I believe if I could get the matter postponed until you come that some satisfactory solution might be arrived at.

EDWARD HOUSE

NOVEMBER 3

THE PRESIDENT AGREES THAT FREEDOM OF THE SEAS
SHOULD BE SUBJECT TO NEGOTIATION

Within a few hours, House sent another telegram to the President on the freedom of the seas issue as follows:

PARIS, *November 3, 1918, 9 p.m.*

My entire time outside of the scheduled conferences of Prime Ministers has been spent in working for a solution of the difficulties mentioned in my No. 38. It had become very clear that the conference to be held at my headquarters at 3 o'clock this afternoon was to be a critical one and I was fully prepared to exert strong pressure in order to secure from the Allies an acceptance of the President's fourteen points set forth in his speech of January 8, 1918, and of his subsequent addresses.

At 3 o'clock this afternoon, Lloyd George, Clemenceau, Orlando and Hymans (representing the Belgian Government) met with me at my headquarters for a talk over the fourteen points. George opened the discussion by stating that he was prepared to stand by the proposal answer cabled in my No. 12. I pointed out that the following phrase of this answer was not satisfactory to the President inasmuch as it was not clear that the Allies accepted the principle of the freedom of the seas: "They must therefore reserve to themselves complete freedom on this subject when they enter the peace conference." I then read to the conference a paraphrase of the President's telegram to me dated October 31, in answer to my No. 12. Clemenceau then stated, "We accepted the principle of the freedom of the seas," and turning to George he said, "You do, also, do you not?" George answered: "No, it is impossible for any British Prime Minister to do this." He then stated: "We are quite willing to discuss the freedom of the seas in the light of the new conditions which have arisen by reason of the war." I stated: "Why do you not say so?" He said: "I am perfectly willing to say that to the President and I will instruct the British Ambassador in Washington to so inform the President." I said: "I would prefer to have you so inform me and I will inform the President."

I am now in receipt of the following letter:

British Embassy
Paris, November 3d, 1918

My Dear Colonel House:

I write to confirm the statement I made in the course of our talk this afternoon at your house when I told you that "We are quite willing to discuss the freedom of the sea in the light of the new conditions which have arisen in the course of the present war." In our judgment this most important subject can only be dealt with satisfactorily through the freest debate and the most liberal exchange of views.

I send you this letter after having had an opportunity of talking the matter over with the Foreign Secretary, who quite agrees.

Ever sincerely,

D. Lloyd George

Also on the same day Colonel House telegraphed the President:

The Belgian representative proposed a number of modifications of point number 3. None of these received approval. One change, however, was requested by the Allied representatives to point 3. They wish it to be understood that the words ["so far as possible"] qualify the entire point. This they suggest could be accomplished by transposing them to the beginning of the point, so that point 3 would read: "So far as possible the removal, etc., etc." I assented to this suggestion and stated that I thought it would probably be unnecessary for the President to point out this change to Germany. All other points were agreed upon without reservation.

Situation now is therefore as follows. The proposed answer cabled you in my No. 12 will be sent to the President along with the terms of the military and naval armistice to be offered to Germany. The President will then send the answer received from the Allies to the German Government with the statement that the military authorities of the Allies and the United States are prepared to receive the German military authorities and to communicate to them the terms upon which an armistice will be granted to Germany. The letter quoted above that I received from George must not be published unless it becomes necessary. If I do not hear from you to the contrary, I shall assume that you accept the situation as it now is. This I strongly advise. Any other decision would cause serious friction and delay.

A conference will be held at my headquarters Monday morning.

Edward House

NOVEMBER 4

METHOD OF PRESENTING THE ARMISTICE

Colonel House, on November 4, advised the President as to further military preparations, if necessary, and the method proposed for handling the military armistice:

Paris, *November 4, 1918, 4 p.m.*

For the President:

A meeting was held at my headquarters this morning at 11 o'clock attended by Lloyd George, Clemenceau, Orlando, Doctor Benes (representing the Czecho-Slovaks) and myself. Marshal Foch and the Allied military and naval authorities were in attendance also.

The conference agreed to the following resolutions:

1. To approve the plan of operations against Germany through Austria proposed by Marshal Foch, General Bliss, General Wilson and General de Robilant.

2. That Marshal Foch shall have the supreme strategical direction of operations against Germany on all fronts including the southern and eastern.

3. That the military advisers of the British, French and Italian and the United States Governments shall immediately examine the following:

(*a*) The possibility of taking immediate steps to send a force which shall include the Czecho-Slovak forces on the French and Italian fronts to Bohemia and Galicia with the following [objects]: to organize these countries against invasion by Germany; to prevent the export to Germany of oil, coal or any other material, and to render these available to the Allied forces; to establish airdromes for the purpose of bombing Germany.

(*b*) The immediate cooperation of General Franchet d'Espérey in these objects.

The procedure to be adopted by the Supreme War Council this afternoon was agreed upon as follows:

(a) To approve the attached terms for an armistice with Germany.

(b) To communicate the terms of armistice to President Wilson, inviting him to notify the German Government that the next step for them to take is to send a *parlementaire* to Marshal Foch who will receive instructions to act on behalf of the Associated Governments.

(c) To communicate to President Wilson the attached memorandum [of] observations by the Allied Governments on the correspondence which has passed between the President and the German Government, in order that they may be forwarded to Germany together with the communication in regard to an armistice.

(d) To invite Colonel House to make the above communications on their behalf to President Wilson.

(e) To authorize Marshal Foch to communicate the terms as finally approved to envoys properly accredited by the German Government.

(f) To associate a British admiral with Marshal Foch on [the] naval aspects of the armistice.

(g) To leave [discretion to] Marshal Foch and the British admiral in regard to minor technical points in the armistice.

NOVEMBER 4

THE PRESIDENT'S BASIS OF PEACE AGREED TO BY THE ALLIES

House continued the above cable:

The memorandum of observations by the Allied Governments on the correspondence which has passed between the President and the German Government now reads as follows:

The Allied Governments have given careful consideration to correspondence which has passed between the President of the United States and the German Government. *Subject to the qualifications which follow they declare their willingness to make peace with the Government of Germany on the terms of peace laid down in the President's address to Congress of January 1918, and the principles of settlement enunciated in his subsequent addresses.* They must point out, however, that clause 2, relating to what is usually described as the freedom of the seas, is open to various interpretations, some of which they could not accept. They must therefore reserve to themselves complete freedom on this subject when they enter the peace conference.

Further, in the conditions of peace laid down in his address to Congress of January 8, 1918, the President declared that invaded territories must be restored as well as evacuated and freed; the Allied Governments feel that no doubt ought to be allowed to exist as to what this provision implies. By it they understand that compensation will be made by Germany for all damage done to the civilian population of the Allies and their property (by the forces of Germany) [sic] by the aggression of Germany by land, by sea and from the air.

Main change in this from draft cabled you in my No. 12 is the insertion of the words "by the aggression of Germany" in the last sentence. This, with Lloyd George's letter quoted in my No. 38 [41], makes the situation quite satisfactory for the moment. The terms of the military and naval armistice will be finally adopted this afternoon at Versailles and will be cabled you in full as soon as they have been adopted. Lloyd George leaves today at 2 o'clock for England, accordingly he will not be present at the conference this afternoon.

EDWARD HOUSE

The Allies had now accepted the President's terms in full with the exception of the point on the freedom of the seas and some minor changes in wording.

NOVEMBER 5

THE PRESIDENT TRANSMITS TO THE GERMANS THE
TWO ALLIED CHANGES IN THE BASIS OF PEACE

The following dispatch was sent to the Germans through the Swiss Embassy on November 5 by Secretary Lansing, stating the two changes in the President's basis of peace agreed upon with the Allies:

In my note of October 23, 1918, I advised you that the President had transmitted his correspondence with the German authorities to the Governments with which the Government of the United States is associated as a belligerent with the suggestion that, if those Governments were disposed to accept peace upon the terms and principles indicated, their military advisers and the military advisers to the United States be asked to submit to the Governments associated against Germany the necessary terms of such an armistice as would fully protect the interests of the peoples involved and insure the associated Governments the unrestricted power to safeguard and enforce the details of the peace to which the German Government agreed, provided they deem such an armistice possible from the military point of view.

The President is now in receipt of a memorandum of observations by the Allied Governments on this correspondence, which is as follows:

The Allied Governments have given careful consideration to the correspondence which has passed between the President of the United States and the German Government. Subject to the qualifications which follow, they declare their willingness to make peace with the Government of Germany on the terms of peace laid down in the President's address to Congress of January 8, 1918, and the principles of settlement enunciated in his subsequent addresses.

They must point out, however, that clause 2, relating to what is usually described as the freedom of the seas, is open to various interpretations, some of which they could not accept. They must, therefore, reserve to themselves complete freedom on this subject when they enter the peace conference.

Further, in the conditions of peace, laid down in his address to Congress of January 8, 1918, the President declared that invaded territories must be restored as well as evacuated and freed, the Allied Governments feel that no doubt ought to be allowed to exist as to what this provision implies. By it they understand that compensation will be made by Germany for all damage done to the civilian population of the Allies and their property by the aggression of Germany by land, by sea and from the air.

I am instructed by the President to say that he is in agreement with the interpretation set forth in the last paragraph of the memorandum above quoted. I am further instructed by the President to request you to notify the German Government that Marshal Foch has been authorized by the Government of the United States and the Allied Governments to receive properly accredited representatives of the German Government and to communicate to them terms of an armistice.

Robert Lansing

NOVEMBER 5

THE BIRTH OF FREE POLAND

On November 5 Poland announced itself an independent republic.

NOVEMBER 9

GERMANY PROCLAIMS ITSELF A REPUBLIC

On November 9 the Republic of Germany was proclaimed from the steps of the Reichstag and Friedrich Ebert succeeded Prince Max as Chancellor. The Kaiser fled to Holland.

NOVEMBER 11

THE ARMISTICE AGREEMENT IS SIGNED BY THE GERMANS, AND THE PRESIDENT TRANSMITS ITS TERMS TO CONGRESS

The German representatives met with the Allied Military Commission at General Foch's headquarters on November 7, 1918, and while making many protests signed the Armistice Agreement on November 11.

The same day the President addressed the Congress. His essential paragraphs were:

> In these anxious times of rapid and stupendous change it will in some degree lighten my sense of responsibility to perform in person the duty of communicating to you some of the larger circumstances of the situation with which it is necessary to deal.
>
> The German authorities who have, at the invitation of the Supreme War Council, been in communication with Marshal Foch have accepted and signed the terms of armistice which he was authorized and instructed to communicate to them.

The President then read the terms of the Armistice Agreement. I do not give the entire text, as it mostly concerned the evacuation of occupied territory, the surrender of arms, naval vessels, railway equipment, the repatriation of prisoners of war and impressed labor and other military matters, together with the surrender of seized property. Some minor changes had been made, but too late to be included in the President's text.

Some of the provisions in the Armistice Agreement, however, had a relationship to subsequent political settlements, and I present a summary of these articles here:

Article Twelve provided for withdrawal of German troops in occupied areas, but stated in respect to Russian territories that the German troops now there should withdraw within the frontiers of Germany "as soon as the Allies, taking into account the internal situation of these territories, shall decide that the time for this has come."

Article Fifteen provided "renunciation of the treaties of Bucharest and Brest-Litovsk and of the supplementary treaties."

Article Sixteen provided that the Allies should have free access to the territories evacuated by the Germans on their eastern frontier either through Danzig, or by the Vistula, in order to convey supplies to the populations of those territories and for the purpose of maintaining order.

Article Nineteen provided that, with the reservation that any future claims and demands of the Allies and the United States of America remained unaffected, the following financial conditions were required:

Reparation for damage done.

While the Armistice lasted, no public securities were to be removed by the enemy, which was to serve as a pledge to the Allies for the recovery or reparation for war losses.

Immediate restitution of the cash deposit in the National Bank of Belgium and, in general, immediate return of all documents, specie, stock, shares, paper money together with plant for the issue thereof, touching public or private interests in the invaded countries.

Restitution of the Russian and Rumanian gold yielded to Germany or taken by that power.

This gold to be delivered in trust to the Allies until the signature of peace.

Article Twenty-six provided that the existing blockade conditions set up by the Allied and Associated Powers were to remain unchanged and all German merchant ships found at sea were to remain liable to capture. The Allies and the United States would give consideration to the provisioning of Germany during the Armistice to the extent recognized as necessary.

Article Thirty-three declared that no transfers of German merchant shipping of any description to any neutral flag were to take place after signature of the Armistice.

With respect to the Communist revolution, then in progress in Russia, the President told the Congress in his November 11 speech:

> The peoples who have but just come out from under the yoke of arbitrary government and who are now coming at last into their freedom will never find the treasures of liberty they are in search of if they look for them by the light of the torch. They will find that every pathway that is stained with the blood of their own brothers leads to the wilderness, not to the seat of their hope.

THE PRESIDENT INFORMS CONGRESS OF HIS IDEAS UPON PEACE WITH COMMUNIST RUSSIA

In his address of November 4 informing Congress of the terms of the Armistice, the President said:

> They [*the Russians*] are now face to face with their initial test. We must hold the light steady until they find themselves. And in the meantime, if it be possible, we must establish a peace that will justly define their place among the nations, remove all fear of their neighbors and of their former masters, and enable them to live in security and contentment when they have set their own affairs in order. I, for one, do not doubt their purpose or their capacity. There are some happy signs that they know and will choose the way of self-control and peaceful accommodation. If they do, we shall put our aid at their disposal in every way that we can. If they do not, we must await with patience and sympathy the awakening and recovery that will assuredly come at last.

Woodrow Wilson had accomplished one of the most monumental feats of international action of any statesman of history. Singlehanded he had maneuvered the Germans from their island of safety where they might have negotiated with their armies still standing, into almost complete surrender.

And, equally vital, he had won Allied agreement to the basis of peace laid down in his "Fourteen Points and the subsequent addresses" with the exception only of one point—the freedom of the seas.

It was a vast triumph for Woodrow Wilson and a war-weary mankind.

7

THE PRESIDENT DECIDES TO GO TO EUROPE

The President had done much to bring about the effective defeat of the enemy and its disarmament. He had established the terms of peace with both the Allies and the enemy.

He now decided to go to Europe—his friends advised both for and against—to personally head the American Delegation at the Peace Conference. The President's decision was his own, and it became one of the pivotal acts of the titanic world drama.

From my own experience, I was convinced that Mr. Wilson's New World idealism would clash seriously with the Old World concepts of the Allied statesmen, and I feared that the President's dominant voice in creating world opinion would be stilled if he became involved in the inevitable restraints of personal negotiation.

There were others who, for the same reasons, opposed the President's going. They included Secretary of State Robert Lansing, Vance McCormick, Chairman of the War Trade Board, Dr. Harry Garfield, Fuel Administrator, Bernard Baruch, Chairman of the War Industries Board, Frank I. Cobb, editor of the New York *World* and a close friend of the President. Secretary of Agriculture David F. Houston thought he should pay no more than a short visit and not participate in the conference.[1]

The best formulation of the reasons against the President's going was that of Mr. Cobb. At this time he was one of Colonel

---

[1]Lansing's and Houston's reasons can be found in their books. McCormick and Doctor Garfield are quoted in an interview with Stephen Bonsal given later and Bernard Baruch told me personally.

House's assistants in Paris. On November 4 he gave a memorandum to the Colonel which was transmitted to the President. It read as follows:

Paris, November 4, 1918

The moment President Wilson sits at the council table with these Prime Ministers and Foreign Secretaries he has lost all the power that comes from distance and detachment. Instead of remaining the great arbiter of human freedom he becomes merely a negotiator dealing with other negotiators. He is simply one vote in a Peace Conference bound either to abide by the will of the majority or disrupt its proceedings under circumstances which having come to a climax in secret, can never be clearly explained to the public. Any public protest to which the President gave utterance would thus be only the complaint of a thwarted and disappointed negotiator.

The President's extraordinary facility of statement would be lost in a conference. Anything he said to his associates would be made mediocre and commonplace by the translators, and could carry none of the weight of his formal utterances.

Furthermore, personal contact between the President and these Prime Ministers and Foreign Secretaries, who are already jealous of his power and resentful of his leadership in Europe, must inevitably develop new friction and endless controversy. They would miss no opportunity to harass him and wear him down. They would seek to play him off one against the other, a game in which they are marvelously adroit, since it has been the game of European diplomacy since the days of Metternich and Talleyrand. The President cannot afford to play it.

In Washington, President Wilson has the ear of the whole world. It is a commanding position, the position of a court of last resort, of world democracy. He cannot afford to be maneuvered into the position of an advocate engaged in personal dispute and altercation with other advocates around a council table. In Washington, he is a dispassionate judge whose mind is unclouded by all these petty personal circumstances of a conference. If his representatives are balked by the representatives of the other Powers in matters which he regards as vital to the lasting peace of the world, he can go before Congress and appeal to the conscience and hope of mankind. He can do this over the head of any Peace Conference. This is a mighty weapon, but if the President were to participate personally in the proceedings, it would be a broken stick.

The President, if he is to win this great battle for human freedom, must fight on his own ground and his own ground is Washington. Diplomatic Europe is all enemy soil for him. He cannot make a successful appeal to the people of the world here. The official surroundings are all unfavorable. The means of minimizing its effect are all under the control of those who are opposed to him. One of his strongest weapons in his conflict is the very mystery and uncertainty that attach to him while he remains in Washington.

When we left New York, I believed that it was not only desirable but necessary for President Wilson to come to Europe. Since our arrival here, my opinion is changed completely, and I am wholly convinced now that the success of the Peace Conference from the American point of view depends on the President's directing the proceedings from Washington where he can be free from immediate personal contact with European negotiators and European diplomacy.

FRANK I. COBB

Stephen Bonsal, from an interview with Doctor Garfield, gave this account of the doctor's conversation with Mr. Wilson. It has value in that it indicates the President's reasons for going. Doctor Garfield had remained to talk with Mr. Wilson after a meeting of the War Council three or four days after the Armistice. Bonsal reported:

...the President said, "What is on your mind, Harry?"...
"I want to ask you not to go to Europe," said Garfield. "Not to take an active part in the Peace Conference. I and many of your other friends for whom I am speaking fear that if you do go you will have to descend from your present position of world arbiter. You will necessarily become a combatant in the hurly-burly. You will become a contestant in the struggle, in the struggle of which you are the only possible referee."

The President... [replied], "...I am indeed confronted with a difficult decision. But now listen to me and weigh my thought. Here in America I understand what is going on throughout the country. I know even before the public what is likely to happen at the Capitol. But Europe is far away, and the voices that come to me from there are so confusing. Half my time, and more, is occupied with decoding dispatches that come from Europe—and must come to me personally. So you see—at least I see—that by going abroad I would save time and would be helped by more direct contacts." . . .

Downstairs Garfield found that McCormick was waiting for him. "What did you talk about so long with the President?" he asked.

"I begged him not to go to Europe—to remain here on top of the uneasy world," said Garfield.

"That is exactly what I talked to him about," answered McCormick. . . .

The President's private secretary, Charles L. Swem, gave perhaps the best summation of the President's attitude. He said:

> It was inevitable that he should himself go to the Peace Conference. Every habit of thought bound him, every dictate of principle to which he responded, every circumstance of the time, made it impossible for him to be absent when the Conference of settlement met. He had striven to win the war that he might have a part in the settlement that followed. . . .
>
> . . . here was a duty, as he saw it. His articles of peace had been accepted as the basis of the Armistice and he was determined to see them written into the Treaty. He had little faith in the conversion of the Allied leaders, whom he had brought to his way of thinking and speaking with obvious reluctance. They had submitted, because they were desperate. They were converted under political duress. They would be in control again, without the compulsion of fear or circumstance to follow the principles of the Armistice. It would require an authoritative voice from America if the American programme was to be fulfilled.
>
> To one of Mr. Wilson's mind, this situation left him no alternative had he sought one. His inability . . . to clothe others with presidential authority, led inevitably to the decision to go himself. He had supreme confidence in himself and only in himself to secure what he fought for. What he himself lacked, the prestige of his office would do more toward supplying than all the "best minds" the spacious quarters of the *George Washington* would hold. Whether he acted wisely or not in going in person . . . is beside the question; it was constitutionally impossible for him to do otherwise than he did. He could not work at long distance, nor through others, in a matter of such import. It is not likely that he gave more than a passing thought to the question; the decision

was made for him when the Conference was set for Paris. . . .

It was a tragic moment when, three days before sailing, he stood before a Congress hostile to his intention and, speaking to an organized silence on the part of friend and foe alike, officially announced his decision. No patter of applause interrupted his usually moving sentences; there was scarcely a stir in the chamber as if the whole performance were a concerted effort to stare down by silence a presumptuous actor; but, grimly, modestly, in his usual apologetic delivery of all his written utterances, he concluded with his reasons for breaking precedent:

I am the servant of the nation. I can have no private thought or purpose of my own in performing such an errand. . . . The gallant men of our armed forces on land and sea have consciously fought for the ideals which they knew to be the ideals of their country; I have sought to express those ideals; they have accepted my statement of them as the substance of their own thought and purpose as the associated governments have accepted them; I owe it to them to see to it, so far as in me lies, that no false or mistaken interpretation is put upon them, and no possible effort omitted to realize them. It is now my duty to play my full part in making good what they offered their life's blood to obtain. I can think of no call to service which could transcend this.

Colonel House, in an entry in his Diary on July 24, 1919, states that he had advised the President to go to Europe, but that he was to discover that the Prime Ministers were not enthusiastic over Mr. Wilson's decision. Gordon Auchincloss states that on November 14 House sent the following telegram to the President:

Americans here whose opinions are of value are practically unanimous in the belief that it would be unwise for you to sit in the Peace Conference. They fear that it would involve a loss of dignity and your commanding position.

Clemenceau has just told me that he hopes you will not sit in the Congress because no head of a state should sit there. The same feeling prevails in England. Cobb cables that Reading and Wiseman voice the same view. Everyone wants you to come over to take part in the preliminary conferences. It is at these meetings that peace terms will be worked out and determined just as the informal conferences determined the German and Austrian armistices. It is of vital importance I think for you to come as soon as possible for everything is being held in abeyance.

... Clemenceau believes that the preliminary discussions need not take more than three weeks. The peace conference he believes may take as long as four months.

...I believe it would be well to have seven delegates with two Republicans and one of those Root and the other McCall. This may avoid criticism and opposition....

In announcing your departure I think it important that you should not state that you will sit in at the Peace Conference. That can be determined after you get here. There is reason enough for your coming because of the impossibility of keeping in touch and exercising a guiding hand at such a distance.

The French, English and Italian Prime Ministers will head their delegations.

The President replied to House on November 16:

EDWARD HOUSE:

Your 107 [November 14 telegram] upsets every plan we had made. I infer that the French and English leaders desire to exclude me from the Conference for fear I might there lead the weaker nations against them. If I should come to the Conference and stay outside I would be merely the center of a sort of sublimated convenient lobby and all weak parties would resort to me, and there would be exactly the same jealousy that was excited by the Germans addressing themselves exclusively to me.

I play the same part in our Government as the Prime Ministers play in theirs. The fact that I am head of the State is of no practical importance. I object very strongly to the fact that dignity must prevent our obtaining the results we have set our heart on. It is universally expected and generally desired here that I should attend the Conference, but I believe that no one would wish me to sit by and try to steer from the outside.

I am thrown into complete confusion by the change of program. The program proposed for me in telegram of the French Prime Minister excludes [the wording here is not clear] and the rest seems to me a way of pocketing me.

I hope you will be very shy of their advice and give me your own independent judgment after reconsideration.

WILSON

So the President was determined to go. Coincident with the problem of the President's participation in the Conference was a second question concerning the composition of the American delegation.

Attorney General Gregory, in a memorandum to Charles Seymour in August 1924, stated that he had proposed some members from the Senate but that the President had refused to accept them.

In his memorandum found among the House Papers, he continued:

> I then said to him, "Mr. President, I have four names to suggest for the Peace Commission: three Republicans and an Independent. The choice of any two of these men will absolutely assure the approval of the Senate to whatever Treaty you bring back and will make impossible any organized opposition. These men agree in sum with your policies, they would be of valuable assistance and would not obstruct. The effect upon the country and the Republican Party would be of the utmost value. They are, Root, Taft, Governor McCall of Massachusetts, and Mr. Eliot."

Joseph Tumulty states in his book that both he and Secretary Lansing had urged the appointment of Root.

Three of the final four selections were of the first stature — Colonel House, General Tasker Bliss and Secretary Lansing — but none of these had political influence in the all-important Senate. The fourth member, Henry White, was a career ambassador of distinction and was no doubt useful in procedure and protocol. He was a Republican, but without influence in the Senate, and owing to his years he was not often consulted in important matters.

Mr. Wilson would have been far better off to include one or two of the following former Secretary of State Elihu Root, former President William Howard Taft, and Charles Evans Hughes, all of whom had earnestly supported the League.

I had been delegated by the President to go to Europe and negotiate the setting up of the organization for postwar relief and reconstruction. When I arrived in Paris on November 26, I found Colonel House still worrying about what part the President should take in the Conference. As often before, he tried out one of his ideas on me: that Mr. Wilson should be made the head of a committee on the League of Nations, but that he should not engage in the negotiations for the settlement of Europe.

House believed that there was general understanding about the creation of a League, and that this would not take long. He thought that the Conference should set up a number of committees to deal with the enemy treaties: one on the questions of boundaries, one covering future economic controls and reparations and one on military controls. These committees were to be given a few months to make their recommendations to the Conference. The Colonel's view was that, after setting up the League, the President could be more influential working through the American members of these committees from Washington and would be free for public comment on subjects before the Conference.

The President arrived in Paris on December 14 and I heard no more about the Colonel's plans. Certainly they were not adopted.

In a conversation with the President on December 16, after having settled several problems of my organization, he made some expression of his satisfaction that the Allied leaders so strongly supported his ideas. I commented that he must not ignore the shapes of evil inherent in the Old World system. He brushed this aside with a remark that Europe had a changed spirit as the result of the blood bath through which it had passed. But one day, three months later, Mr. Wilson remarked wearily that I had been right.

Between his arrival and the opening of the Peace Conference, the President delivered seven addresses in France, England and Italy. Most of his themes were comradeship, friendship, freedom, right and justice and the League of Nations for lasting peace. He complimented his listeners on their patriotism, courage and sacrifices and stressed their mutual satisfaction in victory. Only on one point did he stir up immediate criticism by European statesmen when he elaborated on his opposition to "military alliances" and "balances of power."

He was received everywhere with almost religious fervor by immense outpourings of people. The ovations were greater than had ever come before to a mortal man.

His eloquent development of his basis of peace, with its "independence of peoples," "self-determination," "no annexations," "justice," "right," a "new order," "freedom of mankind" and a "lasting peace," had stirred hope among the masses everywhere in the world. To them, no such man of moral and political power and no such an evangel of peace had appeared since Christ preached the

Sermon on the Mount. Everywhere men believed that a new era had come to all mankind. It was the star of Bethlehem rising again.

For the moment, Woodrow Wilson had reached the zenith of intellectual and spiritual leadership of the whole world, never hitherto known in history.

8

WHAT WOODROW WILSON MET IN EUROPE

To understand the immense tragedy which befell Woodrow Wilson and the whole world, it is necessary to understand the forces which dominated the new stage upon which he now appeared.

The guns of the first total war of history had been silenced. But the tumult had not quieted among the 95 per cent of the human race who had taken part in the war. This had been no war fought as of old by soldiers on battlefields, with little civilian involvement. In those days civilians were rarely assaulted. Now for the first time civilians had been attacked from the air and on the seas. Even women and children had to be organized to supply services or to work the farms and factories. Millions of homes mourned their injured and dead.

By the time the President arrived in Paris, revolutions creating seventeen constitutional republics had swept over Europe. Ten new nations had declared their independence and had set up constitutional governments, or soon were to do so. The peoples of the old enemy states had discarded their dictators or rulers. All of Europe, outside of Russia, was now to be under constitutional government and enjoy personal freedoms.

When the President arrived, the delegations of twenty-seven nations of the Allied and Associated Powers had been approved to sit at the peace table. The delegations of seven nations who had declared themselves self-governing peoples, not yet "recognized,"

and seven little nations neutral in the war came there to peer into
the windows, anxious for their future. The representatives of the five
enemy countries were later allowed to sit on a hard bench outside
in the halls while their fate was discussed. And the Communists,
from their stronghold in Moscow, were lurking in the shadows,
creating trouble for all the new nations and their elders.

To add to the turmoil, each of the forty-one delegations of
these nations had, from extensive headquarters, organized propaganda agencies and employed press agents. The military and some
departments of the Allied Governments also had press agents and
issued propaganda. To these were added a host of representatives
from social, scientific and economic organizations from over the
earth, each with propagandist weapons with which to instill the
higher thought.

Also the sixty-odd inter-Allied agencies, which I shall mention
later, found that their life expression required periodic press statements and reports for circulation to all those who had desires or
hopes and sufficient wastepaper baskets. And there were present
300 reporters from all over the world.[1]

Many of the forces confronting Mr. Wilson were no help to him
in finally establishing the "Fourteen Points and the subsequent addresses" to which the Allies and enemy states had agreed.

The American people, at the time of the Armistice, presented
the President with no problem concerning the Allies. With victory
our people forgot, at least temporarily, their prejudices against some
of the Allied nations. We thrilled with admiration for our comrades
in war, for their courage and steadfastness, and our emotions over-
flowed in sympathy for their trials and suffering. Everywhere our
people acknowledged our debt to them for the ancient foundations
of freedom, for their development of law and for their contributions
to literature, art, science and invention—all of which underlay our
civilization. American oratory blossomed with references to their
glorious victories on the battlefields where in centuries past their
men had fought for the establishment of liberty and government by
law. Our people admired their noble cathedrals, which marked the
rule of religious faith, and their monuments to men and women

---

[1] To aid historians a systematic collection of this propaganda can be consulted
in the Hoover Institution at Stanford University.

who had fought and died in the advancement of great causes.

Mr. Wilson, as a student and teacher, had lived almost all his life steeped in these inheritances.

But the issue at Versailles was not that of America making peace with European culture. It was the rough job of making peace among 400,000,000 people in Europe living cheek by jowl amid economic desperation, ancient and rival traditions of power and violent forces of hate and revenge. And in the Middle East and Asia another 11,000,000 people involved were there with their own demands. Mr. Wilson's magnificent ideals were to be tried by fire, stoked by political veterans.

From the start the President was met with settings unfamiliar to him and obstacles he had never imagined. Fundamentally he was confronted with the irreconcilable conflicts between Old and New World concepts of government and of social and economic life. The two worlds were indeed in many ways strangers to each other. Our ancestors had fled from Europe because they were already in conflict with its ideas of class stratification, religion and freedom, and we had drifted farther and farther apart over the course of three centuries.

ALLIED IMPERIALISM AND COLONIALISM

The American people had been implacably anti-imperial, anti-colonial, and generally anti-the-subjugation-of-one-people-by-another from the day of our Declaration of Independence. Through the Monroe Doctrine, we had stopped the expansion of European empires in the Western Hemisphere. By the Spanish-American War, we had freed Cuba, Puerto Rico and the Philippines from the Spanish Empire. We had established the independence of Cuba and were now building self-government in Puerto Rico and the Philippines.

The freedom of the New World and its lack of any spirit of empire were the more complete because of our abundant resources and our relative paucity of population. We had no population pressure or other incentive to colonialism. The driving force of Allied statesmen, on the other hand, was not "self-determination": it was "empire." Its roots in Britain, France, Italy and Japan were centuries-deep. Both national glory and the standards of living of the people in the "mother country" in each empire had been built upon, and their economy had been geared to, returns from imperial possessions.

Rivalries and conflicts between the various empires and their world-wide holdings had relied, and would inevitably have to continue to rely, upon military strength, military alliances, power politics and balances of power.[2]

SELF-DETERMINATION

With our Declaration of Independence came the American concept that nations have the right to determine their own independence and form of government. We had expressed public sympathy with the efforts of many nations toward these ends, beginning with the Greek declaration of freedom from the Turks a hundred years earlier. Conflict was inevitable between our ideas of free men and the very base of any peace settlement in Europe.

With his flaming banner of the "Fourteen Points and the subsequent addresses," his eloquence about self-determination, his denunciations of annexations and "bandying peoples about," Mr. Wilson was a menacing intruder in the concepts of British, French and Italian statesmen and a threat to their secret treaties dividing all Europe, which I review later on.

Allied leaders did no doubt welcome the President's stimulation of independence among the subject peoples of the disintegrating empires of Germany, Austria, Turkey and Russia. From their former imperial rivals the Allies were soon to pick up some valuable pieces, especially from Germany and Turkey. Far from uprooting the theory and practice of empire, as Mr. Wilson idealistically hoped, the Allies were greatly to expand their holdings.

MILITARY ALLIANCES AND THE BALANCE OF POWER

One of the first signs of resistance to the President's "Fourteen Points and the subsequent addresses" resulted from the speech he made at Manchester, England, on December 30, 1918, in which he assailed the balance of power and military alliances as roots

---

[2]On November 26, 1918, a month after Britain had agreed to the "Fourteen Points and the subsequent addresses," according to Ray Stannard Baker, Winston Churchill, then British Minister of Munitions, speaking at Dundee, said that "he was a friend of the League of Nations, but it was no substitute for the supremacy of the British fleet; and he declared that none of the German colonies would ever be restored to Germany, and none of the conquered parts of Turkey would ever be returned to Turkey."

of evil in the Old World. No echo resounded from the hearts of the Allied statesmen. On the contrary, Prime Minister Clemenceau thought it necessary to make an immediate reply—the same day. In a speech before the Chamber of Deputies, he said:[3]

> There is an old system of alliances called the "balance of power." It seems to be condemned nowadays, but if such a balance had preceded the war, if England, the United States, France, and Italy had agreed, say, that whoever attacked one of them attacked the whole world, the war would not have occurred. This system of alliances, which I do not renounce, will be my guiding thought at the Peace Conference if your confidence sends me there.

He received a three-to-one vote of confidence.

THE PESTILENCE OF EMOTIONS

Still more difficulties confronted Mr. Wilson from the emotions which surged through all twenty-seven nations admitted to the peace table.

In the blood of many of the delegations at Versailles were the genes of a thousand years of hate and distrust, bred of religious and racial persecution and domination by other races. The impelling passion for vengeance of past wrongs rose with every hour of the day. Nor was it the delegates alone who were thus infused. Back home their people were at fever heat, demanding retribution from their enemies. England had just reelected Lloyd George on a platform of "Hang the Kaiser" and of wringing from the foe fantastic sums in indemnities. Clemenceau had received a vote of confidence from the French Assembly with a program to render Germany innocuous for all time and to collect every centime of every Frenchman's losses.

All the warring nations of Europe were economically exhausted, desperate, and most of them were hungry. Those twenty-seven nations were less interested in preserving peace for some distant future than in immediately righting their wrongs and ensuring their economic recovery. Their representatives in Paris well knew that they would have to go home to their people, still torn by these emotions, to seek approval of the agreements at the Peace Conference. They had to bring back to their people annexations and reparations. Their continuation in power depended upon that.

---

[3] *The New York Times,* December 31, 1918.

Such were the destructive forces which sat at the peace table. As a historian, Mr. Wilson was no doubt familiar with their age-old background, but he did not seem to realize their dynamism. He believed that the horrors of war and the prospects of freedom and peace had instilled a new spirit of righteousness and idealism in the leaders of men. And his popular reception seemed to have confirmed it.

American Emotions

In this discussion of the emotional obstacles to peace, it must not be overlooked that the American people also had violent dislikes of the enemy countries. We resented the original aggression of the Germans that precipitated the war and all their subsequent activities. Many chairs at our firesides were also empty.

While the United States was more remote from the scene than our Allies, and had suffered less, we were not free from hate and the desire for vengeance. For example, a few days after the Armistice I stated that we must lift the blockade on food to the enemy states or we would have anarchy in Europe. The applause was hardly overwhelming, and there was comment that a bit of anarchy would be good for them.

But like President Wilson and his principal advisers, a substantial part of the American people even at the height of their emotions believed that civilization had to live with these 60,000,000 Germans and that our purpose must be to disarm them, ban their militarists; require them to pay such reparations as were practicable to obtain; and support the efforts of the good men in Germany to build up their new government of, and by, the people.

Because of this attitude the President and many of us in Paris had to meet the charge of being soft or pro-German. I particularly resented this, as I had ample reasons for disliking the German militarists and Junker class generally. I was an eyewitness to the savagery of the German Army in their invasion of Belgium. I had, for two years, to pass by the wantonly destroyed university and cathedral of Louvain and the gaunt skeletons of destroyed villages. Even in my dreams forty years after I was haunted by the monument at Dinant, which pathetically records the names of over two hundred men, women and children who had been seized as hostages and mowed down with machine guns because someone had fired a shot

from a roof. I was an eyewitness to the brutal deportation of work-
men to German work camps. And my only purpose for enduring these
sights was to take part in saving 10,000,000 human beings from starvation because of the Germans.

But whatever the disagreeable emotions of Americans were,
they did not impede the course of Woodrow Wilson.

SUSPICIONS ENTERTAINED OF THE PRESIDENT

The Allies regarded the President's latent power to press the
adoption of his ideas upon them with vast suspicion. A leader more
versed in the European school of diplomacy might have dictated
the peace. He could have demanded his share of territorial spoils
and enemy reparations, and could have traded them for concessions
to his views. He could have stopped the huge American loans upon
which many of these nations depended for their continued existence. He even could have threatened to cut off the daily bread
which America alone could supply.

The Allies in their dealings with us concerning the Relief and
Reconstruction organization very clearly revealed their fears and
suspicions that the President might use these powers and proposed
that all resources of the Allied and Associated nations be pooled
in a fashion that would prevent such action. The use of such power
would not have been in accord with American ideals. The President's disavowal of its application, in advance, no doubt weakened
him in his negotiations. He was too great a man to bargain in that
way. American idealism indeed was unfitted to participate in a game
played with power as the counters.

EXTREME NATIONALISM IN THE NEW STATES

Another of Mr. Wilson's problems in Paris developed as a
result of his policies of "self-determination," "independence" and
related ideas announced in many of his "points." These were to
kindle a fire of extreme nationalism in the newly created states of
Eastern Europe, fully evident at the Peace Conference by exaggerated demands for territory based not only on racial justifications
but on economic or defense motives, and sometimes also on purely
historical boundaries of the dim past.

The President's Inability to Bind the American Government

Still another of Mr. Wilson's obstacles stemmed from the difference between the American and Allied forms of government. Ours is a government of separate powers. Under the parliamentary governments of the Allies, the executive and legislative leadership is combined. A prime minister spoke for the majority of his parliament and could assure the ratification of treaties into which he entered. Moreover on the floor of the lower house he could look his opponents in the eye and deliver them instant answers. Under our separation of powers, the President could give no such assurances. Furthermore, the Congressional election of 1918 had damaged the confidence of the Allied statesmen in the President's ability to speak for the American people and the Congress.

The Americans were Amateurs in the Ancient Art of Diplomacy

A crucial American weakness at the peace table was our lack of diplomats skilled and experienced in the ancient art of diplomacy. Under our way of government, much of our personnel in foreign fields changed with elections, in contrast with the continuity of the career diplomatic service of European nations. Those countries were thus represented in Paris by staffs of old hands fully experienced in this art, whereas our representatives were mostly amateurs and college professors.

Moreover, because Americans are derived from the many races in Europe, they often retain a subcurrent of sympathy with their origins which sometimes clouds their objectives and influences their representatives in the Congress. These influences would also affect our various positions in international affairs.

To match the Europeans in power politics, and to enjoy the same continuity of skilled diplomatic staffs, we would need to be something other than a free people as we conceive it.

Confirmation of all this may be had from an analysis of our inexperienced group of peacemakers at Paris, who worked in a sort of daze with the skilled men they encountered.

The Secret Treaties

The President was to meet many other obstacles in peacemaking aside from the inherent conflict of New and Old World concepts of national life and the forces of emotion or extreme nationalism.

A maze of secret agreements had been entered into by the Allies, before America entered the war, by which they had already allotted the spoils of victory among their four Allied empires. These treaties were themselves proof of the implacable forces of imperial expansion which dominated the Allies. If the treaties were to be respected, the results would be far removed from Mr. Wilson's gospel of peace for mankind. They would nullify many of the "Fourteen Points and the subsequent addresses," which the Allies had reluctantly adopted as the basis for peace.

For a full understanding of the potency of these treaties at the peace table, I enumerate the major agreements:

1. In March 1915, by an exchange of diplomatic notes among Russia, Britain, France, and later Italy, it was agreed that Russia was to have Constantinople and free passage through the Dardanelles. She was also to annex a part of Northern Persia and to have a sphere of influence over other Persian territory, with a neutral zone between her spheres and that of the British, which was to extend over all South Persia. The Russians further agreed to support British and French spheres of influence in Mesopotamia, which covered Iraq, Jordan and Syria.

2. On April 26, 1915, the Pact of London was signed by Britain, France and Italy. It assured to Italy, if she entered the war, the Trentino, Brenner Pass, Istria, Trieste, parts of Dalmatia, some Adriatic islands, and a share in Anatolia. She was specifically not to have the port of Fiume, that being reserved for Serbia. These territories were defined with the precision of the metes and bounds of a New England farm.

3. In May 1916, the Sykes-Picot Treaty between Britain and France provided that France was to have the coast of Syria as far south as Acre, and a hinterland stretching to the Tigris River. Great Britain was to have the Mediterranean ports of Acre and Haifa, and a portion of Mesopotamia between Bagdad and the Persian Gulf. It was agreed that certain Arab states were to be divided into spheres of influence, in which the sphere holders were to have "prior rights over local resources and loans" and to "furnish

foreign advisers and officials." The treaty excluded any other power from any rights in the old Turkish Empire except those already ceded to Russia. The Italians, hearing of this, decided to be included, and in August 1917, they obtained Smyrna and a large zone of influence to the north.

4. In August 1916, France, Britain and Russia made a treaty with Rumania by which she was to come into the war, and for this was to receive Transylvania from the old Austrian Empire and Dobruja from Bulgaria.

5. On February 16, 1917, Japan and Britain signed a treaty by which Japan was to get the German titles to the Chinese province of Shantung and all German islands in the Pacific north of the equator. Britain was to have all German islands south of the equator.

6. In February and March 1917, the Russians and French entered into several agreements. The gist of them was that Alsace-Lorraine should be restored to France; that France be given the Saar; and that a neutral state should be created from the German territory west of the Rhine (the "left bank"). The Russians were confirmed in their annexation of Constantinople and free passage of the Dardanelles. They were also to have a free hand in the eastern possessions of the Austrian and German Empires, including the disposition of Poland. When the treaty was disclosed by the Communists in November 1917, Mr. Balfour, the British Foreign Secretary, declared Britain had not approved it and would not do so.

7. In March 1917, by a further exchange of notes between Russia and France, the Russians were to have 60,000 square miles of territory between the Persian frontier and the Black Sea. France was to have a slice of Turkey on the Mediterranean coast, the extent to be settled with the British.

This carving up of Europe and the Middle East and Far East seemed fairly complete.

In view of subsequent events it is desirable to examine how much the President knew of these treaties and how much weight he gave to them. On that score it can be said at once that if he knew of them, his agreement with the Allies, by which they accepted the "Fourteen Points and the subsequent addresses," had canceled all of them, for they were in utter conflict with a dozen of the "points."

In any event, only part of these treaties could possibly have been known to him.

Some of these treaties, in which Russia was involved as a party, were published by the Communist Government in Moscow on November 22, 1917, to embarrass the Allies. Parts of these disclosures were repeated at that time in the *New York Evening Post*. One of the treaties, the Sykes-Picot Agreement, was published in the *Manchester Guardian* on January 19, 1918. On May 11, 1918, the London *Daily Herald* published the Communist disclosures with maps. These publications did not excite much interest at the time.

Mr. Balfour, the British Foreign Minister, visited the United States in April and May 1917, a few weeks after we entered the war. Colonel House records in his Diary on April 28, 1917, a conversation with Mr. Balfour in which, at one point, the Colonel asked:

> ... what treaties were out between the Allies as to the division of spoils after the war. He [Balfour] said they had treaties with one another, and that when Italy came in they made one with her in which they had promised pretty much what she demanded.
>
> Balfour spoke with regret at the spectacle of great nations sitting down and dividing the spoils of war, or as he termed it, "dividing up the bearskin before the bear was killed." I asked him if he did not think it proper for the Allies to give copies of these treaties to the President for his confidential information. He thought such a request entirely reasonable and said he would have copies made for that purpose. ...

Ray Stannard Baker states as of May 18, 1917:

> Balfour sent the President, as he had promised, texts of "the various Agreements" [secret treaties]. ...

But the treaties sent embraced only four of the above list, there being important omissions. Baker adds:

> The President did not answer this letter in writing, nor refer to it in writing at any time, so far as the author has been able to discover, nor did he [Wilson], apparently, give the treaties themselves any study.

Three of these secret treaties gave rights to Russia, which the remaining Allies immediately repudiated as invalid because of the

Communist revolution. However, the Allies subsequently claimed any rights these treaties provided for themselves. A fourth treaty, giving Japan rights in China, was not disclosed to the President until two months after his arrival in Paris. A fifth treaty was effectively resolved by the system of mandates. A sixth treaty, giving annexations to Rumania, was a *fait accompli* by force of arms before the President arrived in Paris.

In Chapter 13 I review what happened to these secret treaties at Paris. But my conviction is that the President attached no great importance to any of those which had been disclosed prior to Paris. It is entirely possible that the partial disclosures by Balfour were the cause of the President's subsequent strong enunciation of certain of the thirty-eight "points." When the Allies, on November 4, 1918, accepted the "Fourteen Points and the subsequent addresses" as the basis of peace, these treaties were so much in conflict with this agreement that the President would naturally conclude they no longer had any force.[4]

But in the larger sense, the forces which weakened the President's influence at Paris were far deeper than the intrigues or the secret agreements between Allied statesmen. Here was the collision of civilizations that had grown centuries apart. Here the idealism of the Western World was in clash with the racial mores and the grim determination of many nations at the peace table to have revenge, reparations and territorial spoils.

At the Peace Conference the ordeal of Woodrow Wilson began and the forces inherent in the Old World took over the control of human fate.

---

[4]A great storm over the secret treaties was raised by the Senate enemies of ratification of the Treaty with Germany in 1919. Hearings were held by the Senate Foreign Relations Committee in August. Their purpose was not to learn what had been done by the Conference in respect to the treaties but to illustrate the undesirability of joining with them in the League of Nations.

9

WOODROW WILSON'S ADMINISTRATIVE ORDEAL
IN PARIS

This and the two following chapters of this memoir are included to demonstrate the huge administrative burdens which Woodrow Wilson carried in Paris at the same time he was negotiating world peace. They will indicate his administrative abilities and, above all, his humane spirit. They will also show how the overwork required may have contributed to his final stroke.

To understand the scene in Paris, it is necessary to know something of the organizing of the Peace Conference itself. This was achieved by a process of evolution, and the result was never wholly ideal. Aside from plenary sessions, the negotiations started with the "Council of Ten," which theoretically included only the President, the Secretary of State and the Prime Ministers of Britain, France and Italy, their Foreign Ministers and two Japanese representatives. However, these principals brought so many assistants with them that at times the Council of Ten seemed a sort of town meeting. Also, there was a constant leakage of information.

After Mr. Wilson's return to Paris on March 15, 1919, from his visit home, he proposed that the three Prime Ministers and himself comprise exclusively what became known as the "Supreme Council" or, colloquially, the "Big Four."

The Council of Ten continued under the four Foreign Ministers and Japanese delegates. While Secretary of State Lansing represented the United States on this body, Colonel House also sat in.

The Colonel's relationships to the Peace Conference were never very clear, but he can best be described as the President's handy man. The Council of Ten became a kind of "Court of the First Instance," sifting certain matters for the Big Four.

The detailed work of the Peace Conference staff was divided into committees. The first concerned the League of Nations, and was under the chairmanship of the President. Other committees were set up to deal with reparations; international labor legislation; international control of ports, waterways and railways; financial and economic problems; territorial boundaries; military and disarmament questions. All these committees prepared draft articles for the Treaty along lines designated by the Council of Ten or Big Four.

A multitude of inter-Allied councils, committees or boards for administrative coordination had grown up during the war. Most of these continued during the peacemaking, and new ones were created for various purposes during the Armistice. At one time during the Peace Conference I made a list of more than sixty such coordinating bodies in action.

The United States was represented on most of them. I was a member of twenty and chairman of half a dozen. It soon became evident that we must have coordination and unity of action among our American members. To attain this, I made the following recommendation to the President early in January 1919:

DEAR MR. PRESIDENT:

1. As you are aware, our Government has been represented in Europe upon various inter-Allied councils, relating to finance, food, shipping, and raw materials, war trade measures, etc. The purpose of these councils is rapidly changing and the American attitude toward them and the problems they represent must change. The matters involved are much interlocked and up to the time of the Armistice were co-ordinated through the Council [the American War Council] sitting under your chairmanship. Messrs. Hurley, Baruch, Hoover and McCormick are, or will soon be, in Europe. The working of these bodies still needs co-ordination by the heads of the departments concerned, who will be in Europe together with the chief representatives here of the departments whose heads are still in Washington.

2. This same group is essential in determination of policies to be pursued by our Government in the peace negotiations.

3. It is recommended that a council be set up, comprising Messrs. Hurley, Baruch, McCormick, Davis and myself under your chairmanship, to discuss and decide such joint policies as are necessary in both these phases and to co-ordinate it with the Peace Commission by inclusion of Colonel House, General Bliss, and Admiral Benson, Colonel House to act as Chairman in your absence or inability to find time.

HERBERT HOOVER

The President sent back the memorandum marked "Approved: W. W."

The Committee was appointed by the President, as suggested, and became known as the "President's Committee of Economic Advisers." Later Hurley returned to the United States and Robinson took his place. Four members of this body, including Baruch, McCormick and myself, had been members of the President's War Council in Washington.

Aside from its job of coordinating the American economic front, among the multitude of inter-Allied economic councils and boards, this Committee was often drawn upon by Mr. Wilson for advice in other important matters, as will be shown later in this narrative. Our meetings were generally informal and often held at mealtime. Minutes were seldom kept and so far as there is a record, it will be found mostly in McCormick's Diary.

The following background sketches of the experience and positions in Paris of the men on this Committee will be helpful in understanding the later chapters:

Edward M. House was for ten years the President's closest friend and adviser, both in politics and international affairs. He was a volunteer aide, holding no official position until he became a member of the Peace Delegation. He was a pleasing personality who moved quietly about his duties.

The Colonel had come out of the school of politics with great skills. He was a superb negotiator of the President's ideas and plans. As an adviser he was sometimes impulsive and given to compromise. In his relations with men he was seldom critical, but reserved his opinions for the confidences of his Diary, in which he wrote very frankly about almost everybody on the Paris staff.

I had known him ever since 1915, when he first came to Europe as an unofficial emissary of the President. He had supported me on all important occasions. I greatly regretted the breach which ultimately developed between the Colonel and the President.

Bernard M. Baruch had served with distinction during the war as Chairman of the War Industries Board. His major duty in Paris was as a member of the President's peace staff, participating especially in negotiations on the financial and reparations provisions in the Treaty. He was not only a fine gentleman and an able adviser with a great background of experience, but he had a sort of sixth sense. In meetings where many minds were participating, and getting nowhere, he would come up with a summation of the ideas and a plan which solved the problem.

Henry M. Robinson was a leading California banker, who had served in Washington and was a volunteer member of many of the boards and commissions during the period we were in the war, particularly in respect to shipping. While he represented the Shipping Board in Paris, the President brought him into the service of the Peace Delegation in many capacities. He was a man of most pleasing personality, of fine judgment, courage and great loyalties.

General Tasker H. Bliss was a great soldier who had served in responsible positions of command prior to the war. During the war he was for a short time Chief of Staff in Washington but in most of the war period was the American member of the Supreme War Council in Paris.

As a member of the American Peace Delegation during the Armistice, he was far more than a soldier. He was a statesman of high order with a profound knowledge of history. He had a penetrating mind and an ability to express himself vigorously and with courage.

Norman Davis had served ably in the Washington war administration in many capacities. In Paris he served the dual role of representative of the United States Treasury and as a member of the President's staff in negotiation of finance and reparations questions. He had a valuable doggedness in negotiation and a great capacity to debate against odds with imperturbable good humor.

Vance McCormick was probably the President's most intimate adviser in Paris aside from Colonel House. His normal occupation was that of a newspaper publisher. Formerly Chairman of the Democratic National Committee, he was an ardent political partisan and at times influenced the President in this direction. He had served during the war in Washington as Chairman of the War Trade Board with great ability. He was an amenable and cultivated man, who loved the social side of Paris life.

When he came to Paris to represent the United States in blockade matters, he was naturally unfamiliar with the forces in motion in Europe and required some months to appraise them thoroughly, which he did in time. Not having had extensive administrative experience or knowledge of Europe, he could not understand the problems with which I had to deal and often complained with good humor that I exaggerated my difficulties.

I have referred to the good fortune that McCormick kept a diary. No other of the American officials except Secretary Lansing, Colonel House, and Gordon Auchincloss, Colonel House's secretary, made such an intimate and continuous record. I could not find time to keep such regular notes but did dictate a few paragraphs daily on important interviews and my conclusions.

Before McCormick died, he directed that a copy of his diary be sent to me and often his entries threw important light on events during the peace negotiations.

I have every reason to remember all these men with gratitude.

The many inter-Allied economic organizations were finally coordinated into two major councils. Initially we started with the Council of Relief and Supply. This Council included Allied members and the American representatives were the President's economic advisers except House and Bliss. The Allies imported so many assistants into its meetings that there were often fifty persons in the room. This body became a "talk fest" and most American members dropped out whenever possible.

THE SUPREME ECONOMIC COUNCIL

I obtained the agreement of Lord Robert Cecil, who represented the British in such matters, to abolish this Council of Relief and Supply and substitute a more important organization to be known as the Supreme Economic Council, which would supervise and coordinate all inter-Allied economic agencies.

I drafted its "constitution" and President Wilson secured its adoption by the Council of Ten on February 8 with but minor changes.[1]

---

[1] The "constitution" was as follows:

    (1) Under present conditions many questions not primarily of military character which are arising daily and which are bound to become of increasing importance as time passes should be dealt with on behalf of the United States

On February 13, the President appointed the American members Baruch, Davis, McCormick, Robinson and myself.

THE SUPERIOR BLOCKADE COUNCIL

At the request of Vance McCormick, the President secured from the Prime Ministers approval of the creation of the Superior Blockade Council to coordinate several different agencies dealing with the problem of the blockade. This Council was composed of representatives of Great Britain, France, Italy and the United States; McCormick was Chairman. It was supposed to function under the Supreme Economic Council.

THE RELIEF AND RECONSTRUCTION OF EUROPE

Next to the Peace Conference itself, the most important American activity during the peacemaking and for some time afterward was the Relief and Reconstruction of Europe, under my direction. Mr. Wilson often referred to it as the "Second American Expeditionary Force to Save Europe."

Chroniclers of the President's work in Paris have mainly concerned themselves with the Peace Conference, its political struggles, its failures and accomplishments. But the activities of the Relief and Reconstruction are an important segment of any history bearing on Mr. Wilson. Its purpose appealed to his humane spirit, and to it he gave his constant personal attention. It also carried out important political missions aside from its major purpose.

In another memoir I expect to give a complete and fully documented account of this Second Expeditionary Force to Save Europe, but here I am concerned mainly with Mr. Wilson's re-

---

and the Allies by civilian representatives of these governments experienced in such questions as finance, food, blockade control, shipping and raw materials.

(2) To accomplish this there shall be constituted at Paris a Supreme Economic Council to deal with such matters for the period of the Armistice. The council shall absorb or replace such other existing interallied bodies and their powers as it may determine from time to time. The Economic Council shall consist of not more than five representatives of each interested government.

(3) There shall be added to the present International Permanent Armistice Commission two Civilian Representatives of each associated Govt. who shall consult with the Allied High Command, but who may report direct to the Supreme Economic Council.

The original of this document, in my handwriting, is in the Hoover Institution on War, Revolution, and Peace.

lationship to it. Some background is, however, necessary in order to understand that relationship.

Deterioration of food supplies and actual famine were the inevitable consequences of the war, because of the diversion of manpower to fighting, of manufacture of agricultural machinery to munitions, and of fertilizer chemicals to explosives.

The surrender of Germany and the other enemy empires was not due solely to the hammer blows of the Allied Armies but in a large measure to the fact that the whole of Europe, outside of the Allied and neutral countries, was in the midst of raging famine. Also the Allies and neutrals themselves were far more dependent on food and other supplies from overseas than they had been even before the war.

We of course knew the supply problems of the Allies and neutrals during the war; we also knew from our information services that the morale of the enemy countries was crumbling from lack of food, medical supplies, clothing and raw materials. But it was not until the Armistice had raised the curtain that the terrible plight of the people in Central and Eastern Europe came into full view. The prospect was even worse than after the Thirty Years' War, when one-third of the population of the continent of Europe is said to have died from starvation.

We were confronted with about 215,000,000 people of Central and Eastern Europe in acute famine, and another 185,000,000 people of the Allies and neutrals urgently in need of large imports of overseas supplies to survive.

With Mr. Wilson's approval I had made a survey of the potential supply of overseas food and the probable needs. I had estimated roughly that about 40,000,000 tons of overseas food were available and about 42,000,000 tons were needed. However, many nations, other than those in Europe, had to have supplies and we estimated that not more than about 30,000,000 tons would be available for Europe. Of the overseas supplies, the British and French had first call on those available from their dominions, which, however, furnished only a part of their needs. Thus, there was thrust on the United States the burden of almost all the supplies for the other nations in Europe.

Fortunately, the United States Food Administration, which I had directed with the constant support of Mr. Wilson, had in

1918 prepared for one of two alternative events: either the continuance of war until the new harvest of 1919 or, if the war ended, the famine which would inevitably follow. As a combined result of the patriotic efforts of our farmers, our guarantees of the prices they would receive and the reduction of consumption through the self-denial of the American people, we were ready at the Armistice to supply about 19,000,000 tons of food, or more than three times the maximum we had ever exported before the war. Together with some supplies dammed back by the ship shortage in Burma, Manchuria, Java and the Argentine, this tonnage had to keep all the European world alive until the harvest of midsummer 1919.

Because of the blockade and the diversion of industries to war production, the peoples of Europe had little ability to provide exports to pay for these supplies. Practically all channels of credit, except the governmental sources, had been exhausted by the war. The burden of furnishing loans or credit with which to pay for food and other supplies fell mostly upon the United States.

However, from any point of view, unless Europe could be fed, pestilence stopped and reconstruction started, there could be no peace made in Paris. The immensity of the undertaking of relief and reconstruction under Allied auspices can be illustrated by a few figures in round numbers:

Overseas food supplies for Europe coordinated	27,000,000 tons
Food supplied to the world from the United States	19,000,000 tons
Food supplies arranged by barter among Eastern European states	1,000,000 tons
Approximate tons of shipping employed monthly by the Relief and Reconstruction	2,000,000 tons
Coal distributed from mines supervised by the Relief and Reconstruction	45,000,000 tons
Mileage of railways administered by the Relief and Reconstruction	32,000 miles

The Relief and Reconstruction overseas supplies were financed in round numbers by:

Loans from the United States	$3,200,000,000
Loans from the major Allies	67,000,000
Loans from other nations, about	20,000,000
Total loans	$3,287,000,000

Overseas supplies sold for cash or goods from:

The United States	$216,000,000
The major Allies	138,000,000
Other nations—about	41,000,000
Total	$395,000,000
The United States contributed in charity* cash and supplies	$310,000,000

*This includes post-peace relief. The Relief and Reconstruction organization had no record of Allied charity but it was considerable, especially from British transportation.

Our work continued after the harvest of 1919, and before the end we had by organization of special canteens rehabilitated more than 15,000,000 dangerously undernourished children and provided supplies for a mass of waifs and orphans. We also fought a great battle against the sweep of 1,000,000 cases of typhus westward from the old Russian lines, all the way from the Baltic to the Black Sea.

I had brought only a few key men from the United States who were specialists in food matters. With the most helpful co-operation of General Pershing and Admiral William S. Benson, I recruited some 4,000 able Americans from our armed forces who were awaiting their return home. Many of them were "experienced old hands" from my previous organizations who had enlisted in the Army. Within a short time we had spread our organization over thirty-two countries and had included tens of thousands of nationals in our service.

We had the only connected telegraph system over all Europe, which I describe in a footnote at the end of this chapter. With this widespread organization, we were automatically the best source of political and economic information from everywhere in Europe. Therefore, I was frequently called upon for such data by the President, the Treaty committees, and the Big Four. I discuss in the next chapter the many political and economic missions assigned to us outside our regular duties.

This massive activity made it necessary for me constantly to get the President's approval for various undertakings, and his intervention with the Council of Ten and the Big Four. It required my meeting with him at least once a week, and in critical times we had daily conferences.

All this served as an extra drain on Mr. Wilson's vitality, but the results were a constant satisfaction to him, because my men — like those under General Pershing — never failed him at any point.

ORGANIZING THE RELIEF AND RECONSTRUCTION

To demonstrate many of the President's mental attitudes and actions, I must briefly relate the building up of my organization to handle these problems.

We had expected to deal with the question of relief and reconstruction after settlement of "the basis of peace" and Armistice agreements. However, in mid-October 1918, before the Armistice, the British, French and Italian Governments came to an agreement among themselves and then presented us with a detailed plan of organization whereby all the credit, food, raw materials, ships and coal of the Allied and Associated Powers would be pooled for a period of some years after the peace had been made. This pool was to be operated from London by a board of four directors, representing Britain, France, Italy and the United States, and a chairman without a vote. The board would be ruled by a majority. Thus, although the United States would make the major contribution, the effect would be a total domination of the American economy from Europe.

A great number of cables went back and forth. As an indication of the view which both the President and I took of this proposal, I give two typical messages exchanged before the Armistice:

7 November, 1918

DEAR MR. PRESIDENT:

Please find enclosed herewith a telegram which I am despatching to Mr. Cotton [the Food Administration's representative in Europe] in respect to the proposals for the world's food and shipping supplies. . . .

I believe this cable is in accord with the conclusions of our conference yesterday and I am wondering if you could see your way to despatch this same telegram to Colonel House, informing him that it has been sent to Mr. Cotton by myself and that it is with your authorization and, furthermore, if you could state to Colonel House that I will be leaving within the next few days for Paris. . . .

Yours faithfully,

HERBERT HOOVER

The cable approved by the President was:

7 November, 1918

To COTTON, LONDON:

For your general advice this Government will not agree to any programme that even looks like Inter-Allied control of our economic resources *after peace*. *After peace* over one-half of the whole export food supplies of the world will come from the United States and for the buyers of these supplies to sit in majority in dictation to us as to prices and distribution is wholly inconceivable. The same applies to raw materials. Our only hope to securing justice in distribution and proper appreciation abroad of the effort we make to assist foreign nations, and proper return for the service that we will perform will revolve around complete independence of commitment [to such a pool] . . . on our part. . . .

As to any intermediate action during armistice this can be handled as to its political aspects simply as a relaxation of blockade [and] under present arrangements as to coöperation in this matter. As to . . . feeding Austria, Bulgaria, Turkey, and Serbia, the efficient thing is to organize a duplication of Belgian Relief organization. Such machinery can determine the needs, arrange for the relaxation of blockade necessary, can find help from Allied Governments, can secure credits . . . [for] liberated Governments or municipalities or banks, [such organization] can operate [German and] Austrian and other shipping, can buy and sell and distribute food, and take independent action generally. . . .

The representation of the Allies in such commission could be proportional to the actual resources in food and money that they find for its support. Such a commission can operate with the Food Administration here directly in food purchases where they will be coördinated with other buyers and in case of purchases in other . . . [countries] can co-operate through existing agencies to avoid competition, thus the international disorganization outlined in your 35 [cable] will be avoided and above all the extension of the functions and life of Inter-Allied Food and Maritime Councils, either now or after peace, will be prevented.

We cannot consent to the delegation of neutral buying in the United States. . . . We must continue to act with entire independence in our commercial relations with all neutrals and Belgian Relief. I trust, therefore, you will in representing this Government discourage any attempts to carry out the proposals of your 35 [cable].

HERBERT HOOVER

This cable was also transmitted by the Secretary of State to

Colonel House, with the additional information that "The Department approves entirely the policy above set forth."

The President had the same attitude toward the organization of Relief and Reconstruction as he had maintained toward Allied demands concerning the American Army. He had insisted upon unified American forces under General Pershing, declaring that we would coordinate and cooperate with the Allies, but keep our single command of these resources. His general attitude is also indicated by his stipulation that we were not an ally but were an "associated power."

While this cable discussion was going on I had, with the President's authority, put under way the loading of over 500,000 tons of food and other supplies for the acute famine area in Eastern Europe. And the President gave directions placing at my disposal the large surplus of food, medical supplies and clothing accumulated by the Army and Navy in Europe in anticipation of continued war.

THE NEGOTIATIONS IN LONDON

Mr. Wilson asked me to go to Europe and arrange the organization to be set up with the Allies. I arrived in London ten days after the Armistice, on November 21, with a number of our expert Food Administration staff. Fortunately, Norman Davis, representing the Treasury, was with us. Hugh Gibson had been assigned to me by our State Department and Robert A. Taft accompanied me as legal adviser and Lewis Strauss as my secretary.

The next morning we went into session with batteries of European officials representing the various departments concerned. Despite our previous refusal they insistently demanded the adoption of the pool idea. Several points became evident. They feared that President Wilson would use our resources to force them into line with his peace ideas. As a matter of prestige they wanted all relief and reconstruction conducted solely in the name of the Allied and Associated Powers, and they wanted to use these controls over life and death for political pressure on the twenty-odd other nations involved in the Peace Conference. Our negotiations extended over weeks.

We Americans argued that such a huge administrative job could not be conducted by a board any more than the 300-mile-front battle which won the war could have been directed by a committee. We contended that there must be a single head of our proposed organization, responsible only to the Supreme War Council. We at once agreed to the creation of an Allied Council for overhead coordinative and cooperative purposes, with similar councils in each country. We argued that supposed unity of action for prestige purposes would only be a sham, as each supplying government had to take obligations from the receiving countries for future payment, and thus each country served would know immediately and exactly where help came from. We declared that the United States would not countenance the use of food, medicines and clothing for political pressures.

To prevent any impression that I might be seeking something for myself, I informed their leaders that my only purpose in Europe was to aid in setting up an effective organization; that I would not undertake any administrative job; that I had already given more than four years to war service; that I wished to rebuild my profession. I suggested that there must be an American in the position of leadership and that the ideal man would be one of the successful American generals in the war.[2]

The real difficulty underlying these discussions was the same conflict of fundamental Old and New World concepts which I have previously described.

The Allied nations' recovery from war hinged not only on maintaining "empire" but expanding it and increasing their power and prestige to do so. Their motive was empire first, and their bureaucracies thought only in such terms.

Aside from the use of relief and reconstruction for purposes of pressure and empire, an immediate problem with which I could fully sympathize confronted each of these peoples. The specters of impoverishment, unemployment and debt haunted them. The emotions of hatred and vengeance, with the resulting demand for reparations from the enemy, were at a feverish pitch among their people and clouded all problems of furnishing food and

---

[2] Hugh Gibson's Diary contains the following entry dated November 23, 1919:
"In the meantime he [Hoover] seems to have arrived at one decision which is that we must have unified control of food and relief work and that as we are to supply 60% of the food and 85% of the money an American should have the supreme command. He does not want to take it himself as he knows just how thankless a job it will be, but he thought there might be some American General who could handle it properly,—he had Harbord in mind."

other supplies to the enemy countries. But despite our sympathies with their difficulties and emotions, some aspects of their proposals had to be resisted.

Aware that the President could use America's economic power to compel acceptance of his "basis of peace," they did not believe our assurances of the purely humanitarian nature of the organization we proposed. They probably reasoned that if they had such powers, they would use them for political purposes. In any event Davis and I failed to convince them of the altruism of America's motives.

One unexpected source of obstruction of the proposals made by Davis and myself is indicated in a paragraph in Hugh Gibson's Diary from which I have omitted the names. He recorded:

> ——and other Americans have been raising hob with our plans over here by running to the British with advance dope about what we were thinking and planning. In several instances, too,——at least has taken upon himself to tell the British and French that the various provisions in our relief plan presented by the President did not emanate from him but were the machinations of Hoover. That of course has not made our task any easier. After we had stood about enough of it I was sent this morning to see the Secretary [Lansing had arrived in Europe]. . . . The Secretary waxed wroth. . . . [——was soon returned home.]

I finally went to Paris and laid the situation before Colonel House, who sent this cable to the President:

November 27, 1918

FOR THE PRESIDENT

Hoover arrived in Paris Tuesday morning. I am fully advised of and in agreement with his plans. . . . The chief problem presented is the difficulty of devising a plan which will not antagonize the Allies and particularly Great Britain and at the same time permit single American leadership in relief to the civilian populations of Europe. I am sure you will agree that American leadership is essential taking into account the fact that we are the most disinterested nation and the other allies are affected by local political interests. Further the supplies to be utilized for this purpose must in the main be obtained in the United States and will dominate American markets. . . . The matters that Hoover and I have discussed will not permit of delay in reaching a decision and accordingly I suggest that the views of the United States Government be presented in writing to the three Prime Ministers at their meeting in London. . . .

It is exceedingly important that I have your advices concerning this matter at the earliest possible moment.

EDWARD HOUSE

I have not given the text of the plan that Colonel House recommended in the preceding text, as the President's reply differed somewhat and became the controlling declaration of American policies. The President devoted four days to considering the Colonel's recommendations with his Cabinet. The reply came on December 1, 1918, directing House to transmit an identical message to each of the Foreign Ministers: Balfour, Pichon and Sonnino. As this message is expressive of Mr. Wilson's grasp and orderly mind, I give it in full:

PARIS, FRANCE
December 1, 1918

MY DEAR MR. BALFOUR:

The President has requested me to communicate to you for the consideration of your Government the following memorandum containing his views respecting the general question of furnishing relief to the civilian population of the European countries affected by the war:

"I have given much thought to the formulation of the most practical means of carrying into effect the resolution presented by Colonel House at the last meeting of the Supreme War Council at Versailles to the effect that the Supreme War Council in a spirit of humanity desired to coöperate in making available, as far as possible, supplies necessary for the relief of the civilian populations of the European countries affected by the war.

"In considering this matter, I have had consequently in mind the urgent necessity of the case and the fact that it is essential, in the working-out of relief of this character on a large scale, that there be a unity of direction similar in character to that which has proved so successful under French and British Chief Command in the operations of the Allies on the land and on sea respectively. I suggest that the Supreme War Council proceed along the following lines:

"In order to secure effective administration there should be created a Director-General of Relief whose field of activities will cover not only enemy populations, but also the whole of the populations liberated from enemy yoke and the neutrals contiguous to these territories.

"It is obvious that present inter-Allied administrative arrangements cover the Allied countries themselves and if the whole of the world's food supplies could be made available through sufficient shipping, there appears to be sufficiency to take effective care of these other populations provided that these supplies are administered with care, with economy, and with single direction.

"The one essential to this plan, in order that all world supplies may be brought into play, is that enemy tonnage shall be brought into service at the earliest possible moment. It would appear to me entirely just that the enemy shipping, in consideration of relief of enemy territory, should be placed in the General Food Service of all the populations released from the enemy yoke as well as enemy territory.

"I have carefully considered the suggestion made by Mr. Balfour to the Supreme War Council at the time the terms of armistice to be offered the enemy were under discussion, to the effect that the enemy should be required to place under the operation and control of the Allied Maritime Transport Council the enemy mercantile fleet in enemy and neutral ports. It appears to me that in practice there would be many embarrassments presented by this plan and that the principle should be maintained that this fleet be used as to its carrying capacity for purposes of relief and be under the direction of the Director-General of Relief. In order to secure its adequate operation, the Director-General should assign appropriate portions of this tonnage, first, for operations individually by Italy, France, and Belgium sufficient to transport the relief to actually liberated nationals of these nations. The administration of relief in the three above instances would then naturally fall entirely under the three Governments mentioned, and would not further interest the Director-General of Relief. Second: The remainder of enemy cargo tonnage, or such part of it as is necessary, should be placed under the operation of the British Ministry of Shipping and the United States Shipping Board in equal portions, these two institutions agreeing with the Director-General of Relief to deliver a quantity of cargo equal to the carrying capacity of these two fleets from such sources to such destinations as the Director of Relief may direct in supplying the balance of populations to be relieved. Third: The passenger tonnage, or so much of it as may be required by the United States Shipping Board, should be assigned to them, they giving the equivalent cargo capacity delivery to the Director-General of Relief. Under this plan it does not follow that enemy shipping would be employed directly in the transportation of this cargo, but that equivalent cargo should be delivered. This plan enables the use of enemy passenger tonnage in the transportation of the United States Armies homeward. This arrangement would in effect add materially to the volume of the world's shipping and release tonnage for the particular purposes of the individual countries.

"In the operations of the Director-General of Relief, he would of course purchase and sell foodstuffs to enemy populations and therefore not require financial assistance in this particular further than working capital. In the relief of newly liberated peoples such as Belgium, Poland, Serbia (including Jugo-Slavia), and Bohemia [Czechoslovakia], it will no doubt be necessary to provide temporary advances from the Associated Governments to these recuperating nationalities with which they can purchase supplies from the Director-General, such arrangements to be worked out by the Associated Treasuries. In some cases public charity may have to be mobilized.

"In the Director-General's dealings with neutrals they of course would provide their own shipping and financial resources, and probably some tonnage and food, either directly or indirectly, for the purposes of the Director-General, they acting under his direction and authorization as to supplies and sources thereof, the Director-General, of course, acting in these matters in coöperation with the blockade authorities of the Allies and the United States.

"In order to prevent profiteering, the Director-General must make his purchases directly from the respective food administrations of the Associated Governments where his supplies arise from their territories, and when purchasing in neutral markets he should act in coöperation with the established inter-Allied agencies.

"It is evident that after the Allies have supplied themselves from their own territories at home and abroad and the balance from other sources, the only effective source of surplus supplies available for relief lie to a minor extent in the Argentine, but to a vast preponderance in the United States. The Director-General will have a large command of American resources and markets and will require the individual support of the American people in saving and productive activities.

"Owing to the political necessity of American control over American resources and the greater coördination and efficiency to be obtained thereby, I am sure that you will agree with me that the office of Director-General of Relief must be held initially by the United States Food Administrator and in case of necessity by such a successor as may be nominated by me. I would suggest, however, that the policies of the Director-General should be determined by the Supreme War Council, to whom he should report, it being our united policies in these matters not only to save life, but also to stabilize governments.

"All these arrangements to be for the period of emergency and it is highly desirable for them to be liquidated as fast as practicable."

I shall be grateful to you if you will advise me as soon as practicable the views of the British Government concerning this matter.

Faithfully yours,

E. M. HOUSE

In the meantime, I had spent November 28 and 29 in Brussels in consultation with the Belgian Relief staff and the Belgian Ministry. The Belgians were insistent that they did not wish their supplies or their economy placed under any such control as that discussed in London, as to which they had received full advices from their Minister to Britain.

WE START RELIEF

Starvation among two hundred million people in the areas of acute need would not wait on debates over power politics. I concluded that after all the United States controlled its own destiny, and that the American people did not need permission from anybody to deliver food to hungry people. Our food ships were arriving. I decided that the President could get further with the Allied Prime Ministers than I could get with bureaucrats; and that I would go ahead with relief for the hungry, and await his arrival for any further discussions.

On December 10, I opened a headquarters in Paris. My authority to act stemmed from several sources. President Wilson had appointed me to organize the job. I was the United States Food Administrator, the Chairman of the United States Grain Corporation, the Chairman of the Sugar Equalization Board, the head of the Committee for all Food Purchases in the United States, and the Chairman of the Belgian Relief Commission. We had 500,000 tons of food afloat and, under the President's orders, we could call on Army and Navy surplus supplies and on the services of military personnel.

Despite the President's message to the Allied Governments their representatives ignored his views, and on December 13, the day before his arrival in Paris, presented me with the old pool proposals in even more extended form in a memorandum of over 5,000 words.

Meeting with the President on December 16, I described to him the fog of power politics which surrounded Paris and the starving people. I advised the President that the Allies had few resources other than the ships which the British could contribute. I advised him to go over the heads of the massed bureaucrats to the Prime Ministers, and insist upon his own plan.

My other business at this interview affords an illustration of the perception and quickness of action characteristic of Mr. Wilson, which always was my experience with him.

Neither the Food Administration nor the War Department could at this time, under the law, part with any food without being paid for it. The President had authority to make loans to the European nations who had fought on the side of the Allied and Associated Governments, with which my organization could be paid for food and the Army surplus. This authority did not extend to enemy governments, and thus excluded Austria, where, in Vienna, starvation on a mass scale threatened within ten days. Therefore, to enable me to start sending food to the city, I proposed that Mr. Wilson furnish the Food Administration with $5,000,000 from his National Security and Defense Fund, which he could dispose of at will. I had a cable drafted for him as follows:

December 16, 1918

Secretary of the Treasury:

Please pay at once to the U.S. Food Administration Grain Corporation five million dollars from my fund for National Security and Defense.

Woodrow Wilson

Without comment he marked it "Approved W. W."

We also had an acute situation in Serbia. I suggested that credit be extended to that country, which could be done under the law, and drew up for him a draft of a cable to the Secretary of the Treasury, authorizing payment to the Food Administration of

$35,000,000 as a loan for that government. Again without comment he marked this cable "Approved W. W."

I had tangled with the War Department over the destinations of our cargoes en route and gave the President a draft cable to that Department straightening the matter out. Also silently, he marked this "Approved W. W."

I took up with him the urgency of a special Congressional $100,000,000 relief appropriation by the Congress, because there was no other method of financing relief for many of the liberated states which had not participated with us in the war, and I had no funds for charitable purposes. From this appropriation I wanted to set up a system of rehabilitation of subnormal "children of famine" solely as an American enterprise under the American flag, and along the lines that we were already providing for 2,500,000 children in Belgium and Northern France. The President at once directed that the request be made to Congress by the administration in Washington. (The appropriation was made 60 days later.)

I also discussed with him the urgency of relaxing the blockade on food and gave to him a draft memorandum which he directed Colonel House to transmit on his authority to the Allied Governments. I give this memorandum in Chapter 11 relating to the blockade.

Upon the completion of these matters, I told Mr. Wilson that as soon as the organization for the Relief and Reconstruction was straightened out, and as soon as I had arranged for the Belgian and French Governments to take over the Belgian Relief, I wished to return home to try to revive my professional work.

He remarked, "You cannot leave me with this worry in the hands of some new man and expect me to make peace as well." No one could leave so cooperative and so burdened a man, and I replied, "All right, I will resign to my fate."

Mr. Wilson took up the Relief and Reconstruction organization problem directly with the Prime Ministers, and after the passage of a dozen documents by Colonel House, the President's plan of December 1 was adopted and my appointment as Director-General was announced on January 4. We set up an advisory body which was limited to "coordination and cooperation," and which, as I have stated above, was succeeded by the Supreme Economic Council.

There can be no appreciation of the burdens on the President without a summary, albeit a highly condensed one, of the problems with which he was required to deal personally in connection with the Relief organization.

SHIPPING

We were under continued difficulties in securing shipping for our work. We needed about 2,000,000 tons in motion all the time. We had agreed that the Allies would furnish about 1,500,000 tons and the American Shipping Board 500,000 tons. When the German cargo ships were secured, as they were belatedly (see Chapter 11), they were to be used for relief purposes. Our supply schedules up to mid-February had been met by the use of such ships as we could get and by the distribution of Army surpluses. Our troubles with American shipping began with loading for arrivals scheduled to take place after mid-February and in March. Edward N. Hurley, the Chairman of our Shipping Board, was an able administrator and a dedicated man, but thought that my organization should give way to American exporters anxious to recover their foreign trade.

On February 12, our New York office advised me that Mr. Hurley was assigning only 136,000 tons of shipping for February instead of 500,000. Therefore I was compelled to trouble the President, and he instructed me to inform Hurley in his name that he wanted the agreed tonnage assigned to us. But Hurley disregarded this and our assignments of tonnage were inadequate.

Then the President himself cabled to Secretary of War Baker and to Chairman Hurley:

> . . . The human, political and military issues that revolve upon any failure of delivery of this program are incalculable. I therefore desire that the Shipping Board shall find the tonnage necessary. . . .
>
> WOODROW WILSON

But our New York office cabled me:

> HOOVER:
>
> After joint conference War Department, Shipping Board, ourselves, Hurley states that maximum tonnage that can be allocated for relief shipments up to end of April is three hundred thousand tons deadweight. . . .
>
> FOOD ADMINISTRATION

I then wrote the President:

March 27, 1919

MY DEAR MR. PRESIDENT:

I have received the attached telegram ... in response to your direction to ... [Hurley] and the War Department that they should find this tonnage. ...

... I wish to say that I simply cannot take the responsibility for this situation unless this tonnage is provided. ... Every country that we have under relief is rumbling with social explosion. All the people in these countries are under drastic food regimes and to make a cut ... can mean only a total collapse.

Faithfully yours,

HERBERT HOOVER

Hurley made more promises, but as usual the pressure on him by the export traders was too great, and I was compelled again to address the President:

PARIS, April 25, 1919

MY DEAR MR. PRESIDENT:

I am extremely sorry to trouble you with ... matter of [such] lesser import than those with which you are faced.

You will recollect having sent a direction to Mr. Hurley to furnish the Relief Administration with 500,000 tons of shipping for [monthly] loading. ... Up to the present moment ... [we have] less than 220,000 tons ... [for April delivery]. This comes on top of the failure ... of loading in March, in which month we received only 200,000 tons. We are at present in the midst of a positive famine. ... I am only able to eke out ... by borrowing from other governments as against future replacements. ...

I feel that I have at least the right to inform you of my total inability to carry out the obligation that has been placed upon me, ... I have no desire to desert the post, but it does not seem to me fair that I should be given this responsibility and given assurances that would enable its execution, and then to be faced with this constant failure. When you consider that the American mercantile fleet delivered into Europe during the last days of the war nearly one million tons of commodities per month ... and when you consider the very considerable increase in our fleet, I think you will appreciate that I am not asking for the impossible ... in order to save Europe. ...

I then protested at the Shipping Board's furnishing American coal operators with shipping to Italy on the excuse of giving employment to American coal miners. I pointed out that

> ... in order to give $3.00 worth of employment in the United States, our Government is about to expend $35. The British have taken the obligation, [to coal Italy] and are performing their obligations. . . . It would occur to me that it . . . [would be] better to stem the tide of starvation in Europe. . . .

The Swem Papers show that the President, on April 28, wrote Henry Robinson, representing the Shipping Board in Paris:

> MY DEAR MR. ROBINSON:
>
> Will you not be kind enough to . . . in my name make the strongest representations to the Shipping Board. . . . It is evidently, I think, a case of the unwillingness of the Franklin Committee to divert ships from commercial routes which may promise large profits but in a matter of world exigency like this the Franklin committee should be made to yield and cooperate. With regard to the arrangements for shipping coal to Italy, . . . obviously this is not the time to further Italian industrial interests at the expense of feeding a distracted world. I am sure that you will agree with me in these matters.

The President also informed me verbally that he had taken care of this matter. Whatever that care was, it was more effective than our previous efforts. Mr. Hurley assigned me the ships.

We had less trouble getting shipping from the British. They were genuinely cooperative and no Presidential pressures on them were needed, although we had to fill their occasional deficiencies with neutral charters at the expense of the United States.

The French would not even provide ships for our overseas relief to their own people in the north of France.

However, as a result of these efforts in every direction, we managed to secure a combination of British and American ships, together with German refugee and chartered neutral ships, which did the job. Had it not been for our Army surplus and the President's insistence, the consequences would have been disastrous.

RAILWAYS

The fragmentation of the old empires of Austria, Russia and Germany into eleven new republics also fragmented their railway systems, river transport and sources of coal supply. On top of this, the Peace Conference was undecided about boundaries which affected both railways and coal. To make matters worse, the Italians had a quarrel of their own with Yugoslavia which still further upset food transportation and coal distribution. We were piling up food in the ports while the entire supply of fuel and transport in Eastern Europe was rapidly reaching the point of no return. The trouble was mostly with the Italian authorities.

After we had exhausted every device of persuasion and even threats, I finally had to seek aid again from the President:

PARIS, 12 February, 1919

DEAR MR. PRESIDENT:

The feeding of the . . . [Czechoslovakians, Austrians, Hungarians and Yugoslavians] all revolves around the use of port facilities and a single railway running out of Trieste. The Italians have taken such an attitude towards these other peoples that the operation of the railway is practically hopeless. . . . They have also stopped all communication through to Trieste. . . . They are apparently driving all of the other races than Italians out of Trieste . . . we have little reliable labor for discharging ships.

We have used every argument possible with the Italian authorities and there is in my view but one solution: that is, that the operation of such docks and railways as we need for feeding these interior people shall be placed under . . . the actual executive control [of our representative]. . . . I want to protest most strongly against any further Treasury advances to the Italian Government until this matter of fearful injustice is put right. If you approve, I will ask Mr. Davis to make it a condition of further advances with the Treasury that this situation shall be straightened out to my satisfaction.

Faithfully yours,

HERBERT HOOVER

The President's reply was:

PARIS, 14 February, 1919

MY DEAR HOOVER:

I think this may be a very useful piece of advice to give Mr. Davis in advising him how he is to handle this exceedingly important matter.

In great haste.

Faithfully yours,

WOODROW WILSON

However, this did not cure the Italian attitude.

After having wasted more time while people went appallingly hungry, I had to go back to the President again. Because he was in the United States at this time, the dispatch went through Secretary Lansing. A condensation of it is:

28 February 1919

FOR THE PRESIDENT:

Hoover informs us that since February first he has had large supplies of food at Trieste and has been strenuously endeavoring to obtain its distribution by railway inland to Jugo-Slavs and Czecho-Slovaks but . . . less than one-third the needed supplies have been moved during the month of February. The whole matter came to a head yesterday by, first, demand of the Italians for 100 engines and 2000 cars from the Austrians, which we understand has been acceded to under protest that Vienna will starve and it will certainly greatly cripple transport to Czechs as well as to Austrians; second, by action of the Italians on the 22nd instant of embargoing all traffic into and through Jugo-Slavia as a retaliation for supposed outrages by Jugo-Slavs on Italian subjects. This not only isolates Jugo-Slavs but cuts off principal railway into Austria and Czecho-Slovakia. . . . Jugo-Slav supplies are cut off. Hoover . . . protested . . . that the stoppage of American foodstuffs to starving people cannot be used as a political weapon. . . . The only possible solution seems to be for you to authorize us to notify the Italians that we do not propose to have foodstuffs used further as a political weapon in Southern Europe, and that we cannot be expected to continue financing Italian food supplies. . . .

LANSING

On March 3, the Assistant Secretary of State, J. C. Grew, sent me the following telegram:

PARIS, 3 March 1919

DEAR MR. HOOVER:

. . . President directs me to state that he approves of the action proposed. . . .

Yours sincerely,

J. C. GREW

On March 5, I asked Secretary Lansing to allow me to present the situation to the Council of Ten. Premier Clemenceau represented the French; Mr. Balfour the British; and Baron Sonnino the

Italians. The minutes show that I presented a detailed statement of the facts as to the piling up of food in the ports, the total inability of our local representatives to get cooperation from the different interior railway administrations, and the acute starvation resulting.

I presented a plan whereby my organization should be given a mandate to take over such rolling stock as we needed on the 32,000 miles of Eastern European railways; assemble it into special trains and operate them in priority over all other traffic without regard to frontiers; and guarantee to return all the rolling stock we used to its original owners.

The Italians, the French and the British agreed but demanded an inter-Allied board for this purpose. I was glad to have such support but stipulated that I should appoint the Chairman and his entire staff. When I presented this plan to the governments in Eastern Europe, they all consented and cooperated.

We established a southern division, comprising about 10,000 miles of railways connecting the countries dependent on the Adriatic ports, under Colonel W. B. Causey, a prewar railway man; and a northern division, comprising about 20,000 miles of railways mostly dependent on Baltic ports, under Colonel T. R. Ryan.

Prior to this setup, we had moved a maximum of 700 tons of food and supplies daily out of Trieste. Within 10 days we were moving 8,000 tons daily.

These railways were worn out by the war and in a desperate state. Their urgent requirement was new rolling stock. With the President's authority, my organization was able to secure some resources of this sort. About 1,500 German locomotives and 5,000 cars had been assigned to the American military authorities as a result of the Armistice demands on Germany. There was also a surplus of the rolling stock belonging to the American Army in France. It was useless to send the former and much of the latter back to the United States; therefore, on the President's suggestion General Pershing made most of it available to us. The equipment obtained in the Armistice agreement required no payments. I arranged with the United States Army Liquidation Commission to sell or "credit" considerable of their surplus rolling stock. The latter amounted to about 1,800 locomotives and 26,000 cars.

With the signing of the Peace Treaty we thought that we had called in all the American officers who were engaged in this transportation service. But months afterward I received a plaintive letter from a lieutenant at Bentschen, a German-Polish railway crossing, asking if he could not be relieved. He was still taking the numbers of all the cars that went each way and reporting them to our empty offices in Paris. He was undoubtedly the original forgotten man.

COAL

As I have noted, the fragmentation of the old empires had stifled coal production and distribution. Some of these states had been deprived of their coal fields, and production had broken down in those which had mines. There was no authority to command distribution to those countries which had no mines. In the operating mines, the miners were inefficient from hunger, and Communism was fast making progress. Coal also, became an instrument of power politics among these governments.

With Mr. Wilson's approval, I proposed, at a meeting of the Supreme Economic Council on April 27, 1919, that I should have a mandate to control the management and distribution of all coal mines in Eastern Europe. The Council agreed, subject to the usual appointments of the inter-Allied missions. I appointed a strong American chairman and his staff.

Upon General Pershing's recommendations, I chose Colonel Anson Congee Goodyear to take charge. In civil life he was both a coal operator and a railway man. Colonel Goodyear set up a staff of sixteen coal operators and engineers drawn from the American Army. With authority to shut off the flow of food, and especially because of his own cheerful personality, he did a magnificent job both in increasing production and better distribution.

PESTILENCE

We had long since been in battle with three of the Four Horsemen of the Apocalypse — Death, Destruction and Famine. Then came the Fourth — Pestilence.

Late in March 1919, word came to our Paris office that typhus was sweeping westward from all along the line of the old Russian western front. Committees to combat the menace had been organized in Poland, Czechoslovakia, Hungary, Austria and Yugoslavia, and they appealed to the Big Four for help.

Typhus is transmitted by lice. Its spread was stimulated by the scarcity of soap, since people necessarily ate the fats ordinarily used to make soap. And pestilence was intensified by debilitation from the lack of food, the destruction of homes and the filthy conditions in overcrowded hovels.

On April 4 I was called to a meeting of the Big Four, where they requested my advice. I suggested that pestilence was a matter for the Red Cross societies. They asked that I take it up with those organizations. After great delays and investigations both the American Red Cross and the League of Red Cross Societies at Geneva stated that they had neither staff nor resources to deal with it. The Big Four requested more advice. To get a better grasp of the situation, I convened a meeting in Paris of the Ministers of Health of several of the countries concerned. All this involved much delay in coping with this situation. Their reports indicated that there were possibly 1,000,000 cases, with mortality at that time of possibly 100,000 deaths per week.

I transmitted this information to the Big Four and recommended that the Allied Governments furnish the Red Cross societies or the Ministers of Health the monetary aid and equipment they needed. The Big Four took some time to decide on this. They finally overrode my protests that this was not my job and demanded that I organize it. Further delay was caused by search for a staff which knew about such a problem. I could find no available civilians. I then turned to the American Army Medical Corps, where Colonel Harry Gilchrist was recommended as the best man. Colonel Gilchrist and the staff he would need were scheduled to go home and wanted to go. All of this caused more delays. General Pershing was cooperative but needed official instructions from the President. I drafted the following letter to the General, which the President signed:

June 25, 1919

To the Commander-in-Chief of
the American Expeditionary Forces:

You will issue orders directing Colonel Harry L. Gilchrist, Medical Corps, U.S. Army, and such additional personnel, commissioned and enlisted, as he may select, to report to the Minister of Public Health, Poland, for duty in connection with the extermination of the typhus fever epidemic now raging in that country.

Woodrow Wilson

To which the President added:

DEAR GENERAL:

I hope this can be done, but sign the order subject to your approval.   W. W.

The General, under the law, had also to get the approval of the Secretary of War. I cabled Secretary Baker urging these appointments, to which he willingly responded. But there were more delays.

On July 16 General Pershing issued an order: "Colonel Harry L. Gilchrist, Medical Corps, with staff will report to Mr. Herbert Hoover, Paris."

The General cooperated fully and we ultimately obtained about 1,400 Army personnel of all ranks, including hundreds of efficient sergeants. I obtained the delousing equipment of the American Army. Also in their first installment were 1,500,000 suits of underclothes, 3,000 beds, 10,000 hair clippers, 250 tons of soap, and 500 portable baths. I further requested as a gift a large amount of anti-typhus equipment from the British, French and German Armies. They all responded generously. The Allies and the Germans furnished us free transportation and my organization arranged to cover the further expense out of the $100,000,000 Congressional appropriation.

We formed a line of battle in front of the typhus areas hundreds of miles long — a "sanitary cordon." With the aid of local police, traffic was stopped across this line except to persons with "deloused" certificates or with assured recovery beyond the infection stage. Then Colonel Gilchrist's staff, with the aid of the police and health authorities, gradually deloused, disinfected and reclad the people, village by village, in a general movement eastward.

In the midst of this operation the funds voted by Congress came to an end. But the President arranged for the Army personnel to stay on the job at Army expense. The Colonel and his men continued in this service until they were sure the fire was out — in other words, until the lice were dead.

On one occasion I sent Dr. Vernon Kellogg of my staff to the typhus front to find out what more our organization could do. He got inside the cordon, but then, when he was returning by automobile, a stern American sergeant, in spite of the Doctor's indignation, ordered him deloused, his hair cropped and his clothes baked. In the end, the Doctor's sense of humor triumphed over his indignation, and for many years he proudly exhibited his certificate.

Colonel Gilchrist and his men did a magnificent job and the Fourth Horseman of the Apocalypse was unhorsed — for a while.

CONTINUED CHILDREN'S RELIEF

The rehabilitation of children conducted with the $100,000,000 appropriation, was due to end by law on June 30, 1919. At this time we were only midway in our vital work of restoring these millions of youngsters. We could not bear the idea of deserting them and the tens of thousands of devoted women in fifteen countries whom we had organized for their care.

Therefore, on June 6, I wrote the President proposing a method of continuing the work. The important paragraphs of this letter shed light both on our organization of the work and Mr. Wilson's humane interest amid his other overwhelming duties.

DEAR MR. PRESIDENT: PARIS, 6 June 1919

As you are aware, under your approval I set up very early in this general relief work in Europe a plan and organization for special feeding of children sub-normal because of under-nourishment. In this matter, we defined sub-normal children as those already showing the disease effects of under-nourishment and therefore in a much worse state than what is usually considered in the United States as under-nourishment. It appeared at the time, and has since been demonstrated, that the furnishing of rough staples to large massed populations under the difficulties of distribution in weak governments was more or less a hit or miss as to whether the children, especially of the poor, would receive sufficiency of such staples. Furthermore, in order to bring them back to normal they required special types of food which no available finance could provide for the population as a whole.

I then described our organization of canteens conducted by committees of women, under experienced American supervision. We furnished free the special food, medical supplies and clothing. I stated our method of returning rehabilitated children to their homes. (We had already returned 2,500,000 such youngsters in Belgium and Northern France.) We had also returned many to their homes in Eastern Europe, but at the moment we had a load of about 3,500,000 children in the canteens. I continued:

. . . Some of the money has been found by public charity in the United States and locally; we have found some from the residue of the Five Million Dollar fund which you have placed at my disposal, and I have found some from the Hundred Million Dollar appropriation of Congress. We also have a contingent fund in the Grain Corporation which I will describe later, on which I am expecting to draw for some of this cost.

As you are aware, the Hundred Million Dollar appropriation ceases to be effective and will, in fact, be exhausted on the 30th of June and there seems little hope of getting this great mass of child life back to anything like normal for some months yet. . . . I feel that it must go on . . . [even] after the broad relief measures of Europe have been relaxed [by] . . . the harvest. I am, therefore, greatly concerned over the question of finance, as it represents an expenditure of . . . [three to four] Millions of Dollars a month.

In the course of our operations in Europe, we have been constantly faced with the possibilities of large losses if there should be a breakdown in the political situation . . . [from] the enormous stocks of food afloat and in warehouse. We have, therefore, in the sale of these foodstuffs, provided a small margin for insurance to cover such an eventuality, thus having gradually built up the contingent fund before referred to. We are approaching the end of our large shipping campaign, and I now have hopes that we will get through without such a loss. . . .

With the President's authorization, our organization had publicly declared to each nation under relief that neither the American Relief Administration nor the Grain Corporation would make profits out of the famine. I had set up agreements with each country concerned that this contingent fund would be applied to the children's work.

My letter continued:

> . . . It is obvious that no single country in Europe is going to obtain what its politicians want, and that there will be, until they awaken to more rational sense than most of them display at the moment, a tendency for them to blame the United States for failure to secure each and every one his objectives against the other.
>
> Beyond all this, of course, is the infinitely more important, intrinsic question of the saving of child life by such widely organized and wholesale methods as will meet the necessities of Europe at the present time.
>
> Faithfully yours,
>
> HERBERT HOOVER

The President returned this letter to me with the following note on it, in his own handwriting:

> MY DEAR HOOVER:
> I entirely approve the proposal you here make.
>
> WOODROW WILSON

The name under which we had carried on this work was the American Relief Administration. It was known to hundreds of millions of people all over Europe and was emblazoned, with the American flag, on the walls of every canteen. In order to continue the work with the same good will which we had already established we determined to set up its successor as a volunteer organization under the same name. The President approved.

I instructed the New York office of the Food Administration to set up a nonprofit corporation with a board comprising the leading men of my organizations and with a membership of any one of our American staff who wished to join. Almost all joined.

Under the President's authority, I transferred residual stocks or cargoes en route which belonged to the official American Relief Administration to this new organization, and also transferred to them the "margins." In addition we raised private funds by a drive in the United States in which we were supported by Mr. Wilson.

We continued this organization for over four years after the peace was signed. Before the end we had, with American charity, under the American flag, rehabilitated more than 15,000,000 dangerously undernourished children and cared for a mass of waifs and orphans.

And this was but one of the President's many extraordinary administrative burdens, as the next chapters will show.

OUR TELEGRAPH SYSTEM

On page 90, I stated that a description of our telegraph system would be found in a footnote at the end of this chapter.

For months after the Armistice the continued enmities throughout Europe and the Middle East blocked the restoration of complete telegraphic communications. The telegraph systems among the Allies were connected but censorship exercised by them greatly delayed messages. In the other countries a message had to be carried across the frontiers by an accredited person and started on its way all over again. It would have taken more than a week to get a message from Paris to Helsingfors or to Constantinople, even if we had maintained an agent at each frontier. The alternative was the courier service maintained by the Army, which was even slower.

It was imperative that my organization have quick communications service. Initially Admiral Benson provided us with radio service from major ports to our Paris office. But this was incomplete and the Navy had to go home. Therefore, I requested each of the governments in Europe, aside from the Allies and some neutrals, to assign two telegraph circuits to us. General Pershing directed the Signal Service of the Army to manage the system and they furnished "doughboy" operators at every essential point. In order to connect our Paris office with this system across France, General Pershing built a special line to his headquarters at Chaumont, where he was connected with the American Army in Germany. To allay all suspicions when I made my request to the governments, I stated that we would send all our message *en clair,* so that they could read them. However, this undertaking became embarrassing to our men, who needed to transmit confidential material and their private opinions of officials and things in general. At times they resorted to American slang dating as far back as the beginning of the Republic.

Later on, we allowed the press to use our system for *en clair* dispatches. Still later, the official representatives of the various nations in Paris secured agreement that they use the system with code messages to their governments. We charged for these services and used the receipts for the care of children.

10

THE PRESIDENT'S TROUBLES WITH PEACE
IN THE BACK BLOCS

The Australians had introduced the expressive term "Back Blocs" to describe all Europe and the Middle East outside of the Allied and neutral countries. This saved constant repetition of the names of some twenty nations which had declared their independence or set up constitutional governments — and also included was Communist Russia.

I have already described (page 87) the spread of our organization of Relief and Reconstruction. It extended over the Back Blocs, and when trouble arose in those quarters, we were called upon for information and assigned many missions outside our regular job. But beyond these demands was our need for aid from the President and, through him, from the Big Four, all of which greatly added to Mr. Wilson's burdens. A description of only a part of them will indicate the additional strains put upon him.

THE COMMUNISTS

One of the side problems which drained the President's vitality during the Armistice was the activities of the Communists who were busy spreading revolution over Central and Eastern Europe through Russian agents and financed by captured Czarist gold. To deal with such incidents chronologically would only confuse the reader and interrupt the narrative. Therefore, I discuss some of them according to the particular countries involved.

Communist Russia was a specter which wandered into the

Peace Conference almost daily. There was no unity among the Big Four on how to deal with it. In a footnote at the end of this chapter, I discuss the President's attitude toward the Communists in general. I may say here that he was opposed to every aspect of their manifestations.

On January 16, 1919, the Allies invited the Soviet Government to send representatives to a conference at Prinkipo, an island in the Sea of Marmora off the Turkish coast. The Communists toyed with the idea but demanded advance agreements. Several unofficial Americans visited Moscow and came back with various ideas for the President on how to make peace with the Soviet Government. All the offers by Communists to negotiate contained impossible advance stipulations.

During the Armistice all of the Allied and Associated Powers were involved in supporting attacks by "White" armies against the Soviet Government. In Siberia, the United States and Japan were supporting the White Army of General Kolchak. From the Black Sea, the British and French were supporting the White Armies of Generals Denikin and Wrangel. The Allies, including the United States, had taken Murmansk on the Arctic to prevent large stores of munitions, sent to aid the Kerensky regime, from reaching the Communists. Later the British supported a White Army under General Yudenich in an attack directed at Petrograd from the Northern Baltic.

The British and French exerted great pressure on Mr. Wilson for Americans to join in a general attack on Communist Russia. General Foch drew up plans for such an attack. Winston Churchill, representing the British Cabinet, appeared before the Big Four on February 14, 1919, and demanded a united invasion of Russia.

The President's attitude toward Churchill's proposal is indicated by a telegram from the *George Washington* during the first journey home. It is given in the Swem Papers as follows:

January 19, 1919

AMERICAN MISSION, PARIS:

Am greatly surprised by Churchill's recent suggestion. I distinctly understood Lloyd George to say that there could be no thought of military action and what I said at the hurried meeting Friday afternoon was meant only to convey the idea that I would not take any hasty separate action myself but would not be in favor of any course which would not mean the earliest practicable withdrawal of military forces. It would be fatal to be led further into the Russian chaos.

Not only was the President opposed to American participation in such a plan, but General Tasker Bliss, on February 26, circulated a strong note among the American Delegation opposing any such intervention. I agreed with General Bliss.

One paragraph in General Bliss's letter added some information on Allied intentions:

There is every reason to believe (it is quite evident from the statement made by Marshal Foch at the meeting of the Supreme Council yesterday afternoon) that a plan is in preparation for waging war on Russia as soon as peace is concluded with Germany. This plan contemplates the formation of a great army of Greeks, Rumanians, Czecho-Slovaks, Poles, Estonians, and others, under French direction, to fight Russia. It is perfectly well known that every nation in Europe, except England, is bankrupt, and that England would become bankrupt if she engaged on any considerable scale in such an adventure. I have reason to believe that such a plan could not be formulated except in the hope that the necessary assistance will be given by the United States. . . .

On March 26, after the President's return to Paris, he asked for a memorandum on my information and opinion on the Soviet problem. After I had drawn up the memorandum, it occurred to me that something constructive might actually be done about the problem, and I included my suggestion.

The more important paragraphs of the memorandum were:

March 28, 1919

DEAR MR. PRESIDENT:

As the result of Bolshevik economic concepts, the people of Russia are dying of hunger and disease at the rate of some hundreds of thousands monthly in a country that formerly supplied food to a large part of the world.

I feel it is my duty to lay before you in just as few words as possible my views as to the American relation to Bolshevism and its manifestations. These views at least have the merit of being an analysis of information and thought gleaned from my own experience[1] and the independent sources which I now have over the whole of Europe, through our widespread relief organization.

It simply cannot be denied that this swinging of the social pendulum from the tyranny of the extreme right to the tyranny of the extreme left is based on a foundation of real social grievance. . . . This situation was thrown into bold relief by the war and the breakdown. . . .

The Bolshevik ascendency or even their strong attempts so far are confined to areas of former reactionary tyranny. Their courses represent the not unnatural violence of a mass of ignorant humanity, who themselves have learned in grief of tyranny and violence over generations. Our people, who enjoy so great liberty and general comfort, cannot fail to sympathize to some degree with these blind gropings for better social conditions. . . .

I expressed the hope that in time the pendulum would swing back from this murderous tyranny, and continued:

Politically the Bolsheviki most certainly represent a minority in every country where they are in control. The Bolsheviki . . . [have] resorted to terror, bloodshed and murder to a degree long since abandoned even amongst reactionary tyrannies. . . . [They have] embraced a large degree of emotionalism and . . . thereby given an impulse to [their] propaganda comparable only to the impulse of large spiritual movements. . . .

. . . [There is danger] the Bolshevik centers now stirred by great emotional hopes will undertake large military crusades in an attempt to impose their doctrines on other defenseless people.

I expressed the fear that Communism might breed more wars but said that problem must wait. I stated that I had the most serious doubt that outside forces could do other than infinite harm, for any great wave of emotion must ferment and spread under repression, and I continued:

We have also to . . . [consider], what would actually happen if we undertook military intervention. We should probably be involved in years of police duty, and our first act would probably in the nature of things make us a party with the Allies to re-establishing the reactionary classes. It also requires consideration as to whether or not our people at home would stand for our providing power by

---

[1] I had practiced my profession for several years in many parts of Russia before 1914.

which such reactionaries held their position. Furthermore, we become a junior in this partnership of four. It is therefore inevitable that we would find ourselves subordinated and even committed to policies against our convictions.

In all these lights, I have the following suggestions:

First: We cannot even remotely recognize this murderous tyranny without stimulating actionist radicalism in every country in Europe and without transgressing . . . every National ideal of our own.

Second: That some Neutral of international reputation for probity and ability should be allowed to create a second Belgian Relief Commission for Russia. He should ask the Northern Neutrals, who are especially interested both politically and financially in the restoration of better conditions in Russia, to give to him diplomatic, financial and transportation support; . . . He should be told that we will raise no obstructions and that we would even help his humanitarian task if he gets assurances that the Bolsheviki will cease all militant action across certain defined boundaries and cease their subsidizing of disturbances abroad; . . . This plan does not involve any recognition or relationship by the Allies of the Bolshevik murderers now in control. . . . It would appear to me that such a proposal would at least test out whether this is a militant . . . [intent] upon world domination. If such an arrangement could be accomplished it might at least give a period of rest along the frontiers of Europe and would give some hope of stabilization. Time can thus be taken to determine whether or not this whole system is a world danger, and whether the Russian people will not themselves swing back to moderation and themselves bankrupt these ideas. This plan, if successful, would save an immensity of helpless human life and would save our country from further entanglements which today threaten . . . our national ideals. . . .

Faithfully yours,   HERBERT HOOVER

The President welcomed my plan because it would keep the Allied militarists in Paris busy debating for some time, and also because, if it succeeded, it would be of great value in saving human life and bringing stability to Europe.

The plan was a very faint hope. To carry it out, I needed some neutral person with a well-known name to head it. I telegraphed Fridtjof Nansen, the polar explorer, asking him to come to Paris from Norway.

Nansen had visited the United States during the war, seeking food for his country, and I had helped his mission as much as possible considering those difficult times. We had become friends. Nansen was a fine, rugged character, a man of great moral and physical courage. But when it came to venturing outside his sphere of life and mixing in international politics, he was paradoxically timid and hesitant. Nor did he have any affection for the British. When he was in America, I had found him very resentful of the British blockade. I had learned that the depth of his feeling came not only from the immediate blockade difficulties but from the starvation Norway had suffered through the British blockade during the Napoleonic wars. The fires of resentment had been kept hot all these long years by Ibsen's epic tragedy, which had burned into the mind of every Norwegian school child.

Through the Norwegian Prime Minister, I induced Nansen at least to come to Paris. When he arrived, I had the whole program ready, including the exact text of the documents to be exchanged.

But Nansen was frightened by the task. It was not until we got the Norwegian Prime Minister to press him again that he consented. In order to make the record complete, I here present the documents involved. The first document, which I drafted, was a letter to be addressed to President Wilson which Nansen signed:

PARIS, April 3, 1919

MY DEAR MR. PRESIDENT:

The present food situation in Russia, where hundreds of thousands of people are dying monthly from sheer starvation and disease, is one of the problems now uppermost in all men's minds. As it appears that no solution of this food and disease question has so far been reached in any direction, I would like to make a suggestion from a neutral point of view for the alleviation of this gigantic misery, on purely humanitarian grounds.

It would appear to me possible to organize a purely humanitarian commission for the provisioning of Russia, the foodstuffs and medical supplies to be paid for perhaps to some considerable extent by Russia itself, the justice of distribution to be guaranteed by such a commission, the membership of the commission to be comprised of Norwegian, Swedish and possibly Dutch, Danish and Swiss nationalities. It does not appear that the existing authorities in Russia would refuse the intervention of such a commission of wholly non-political order, devoted solely to the humanitarian purpose of saving life. If thus organized upon the lines of the Belgian Relief Commission, it would raise no question of political recognition or negotiations between the Allies with the existing authorities in Russia.

I recognize keenly the large political issues involved, and I would be glad to know under what conditions you would approve such an enterprise and whether such commission could look for actual support in finance, shipping and food and medical supplies from the United States Government.

I am addressing a similar note to Messrs. Orlando, Clemenceau and Lloyd George.

    Believe me, my dear Mr. President,
        Yours most respectfully,

                        FRIDTJOF NANSEN

The reply from the Big Four to Nansen, which I also drafted, ran as follows:

                            PARIS, 9 April, 1919

DEAR SIR:

The misery and suffering in Russia described in your letter of April 3rd appeals to the sympathies of all people. It is shocking to humanity that millions of men, women and children lack the food and the necessities which make life endurable.

The Governments and peoples whom we represent would be glad to co-operate, without thought of political, military or financial advantage, in any proposal which would relieve this situation in Russia. It seems to us that such a Commission as you propose would offer a practical means of achieving the beneficent results you have in view, and could not, either in its conception or its operation, be considered as having any other aim than the "humanitarian purpose of saving life."

There are great difficulties to be overcome, political difficulties, owing to the existing situation in Russia, and difficulties of supply and transport. But if the existing local governments of Russia are as willing as the governments and peoples whom we represent to see succor and relief given to the stricken peoples of Russia, no political obstacle will remain. There will remain, however, the difficulties of supply, finance and transport which we have mentioned, and also the problem of distribution in Russia itself. The problem of supply we can ourselves hope to solve, in connection with the advice and cooperation of such a Commission as you propose. The problem of finance would seem to us to fall upon the Russian authorities. The problem of transport of supplies to Russia we can hope to meet with the assistance of your own and other Neutral Governments whose interest should be as great as our own and whose losses have been far less. The problems of transport in Russia and of distribution can be solved only by the people of Russia themselves, with the assistance, advice and supervision of your Commission.

Subject to such supervision, the problem of distribution should be solely under the control of the people of Russia themselves. The people in each locality should be given, as under the regime of the Belgian Relief Commission, the fullest opportunity to advise your Commission upon the methods and the personnel by which their community is to be relieved. In no other circumstances could it be believed that the purpose of this Relief was humanitarian, and not political, under no other conditions could it be certain that the hungry would be fed.

That such a course would involve cessation of all hostilities within definitive lines in the territory of Russia is obvious. And the cessation of hostilities would, necessarily, involve a complete suspension of the transfer of troops and military material of all sorts to and within Russian territory. Indeed, relief to Russia which did not mean a return to a state of peace would be futile, and would be impossible to consider.

Under such conditions as we have outlined, we believe that your plan could be successfully carried into effect, and we should be prepared to give it our full support.

V. E. ORLANDO
D. LLOYD GEORGE
WOODROW WILSON
G. CLEMENCEAU

Nansen then sent a dispatch to Lenin on April 17, in which he quoted his letter to the Big Four and their reply, and continued:

I would be glad to hear from you in this matter at your earliest convenience.

I may add that the neutral organization which I propose offers its services in this cause without any remuneration whatever, but of course its expenditures in the purchase and transportation of supplies must be met by the Soviet Government.

Believe me, Sir,

Yours most respectfully,

FRIDTJOF NANSEN

I had arranged with the French to have this message sent to Moscow by radio from the Eiffel Tower Radio Station. However, in the meantime the French had concluded that Kolchak, Denikin, Wrangel or someone would defeat the Reds, and although Clemenceau had agreed to our proceeding, his Minister of Foreign Affairs, Pichon, protested violently at any action. After ten days with no reply from Moscow, I instructed my representative at The Hague to send Nansen's telegram again from the Dutch Radio Station. The Russians, on May 3, acknowledged its receipt through that station.

The Communists made full reply by radio on May 14. The message was picked up by the Denmark Station and sent to me. The Russian reply was a long and warm acceptance of the proposed relief but a violent refusal to stop fighting until they had won their objectives either by war or by negotiation. It also contained much comment upon the undesirable way of life of the Allied and Associated Powers. I believed the reply left a crack open and that much of it was for internal consumption. I wanted to pursue the question further, but in the meantime the French denounced the whole business in the press and so the effort died at no cost but words.

A month had been absorbed by these discussions and by this time the Paris pressures for an American attack on the Communists had eased up.

THE BALTIC STATES

Related to these Communist problems were the events in the Baltic States. The four of them — Finland, Estonia, Latvia and Lithuania — had thrown off the Russian yoke and set up representative governments. Each had been attacked by the Communists, through internal conspiracies or by armies or both. We started to provide them with food, medicine and clothes immediately after we got our organization under way. Thus we became eyewitnesses to their troubles, and at times actual participants, at which point we needed help from the President. Each of the new republics presented different problems.

After centuries of self-government, Finland's freedom had been eclipsed for a hundred years by Czarist annexation. When light came again, the Finns won their internal and external wars against the Communists so completely that they were not too much disturbed by that evil for over two decades thereafter. At the time of the

Armistice, however, they were within sixty days of complete starvation, for their usual supply of food from Russia had been cut off.

The Allies were continuing their blockade against Finland, including a prohibition of their ships to go to sea and restrictions on all financial transactions. We solved this in so far as food was concerned by ignoring it under Admiral Benson's assurances that no blockade could stop United States flagships from carrying food to starving people. To meet the Finns' emergency, we borrowed food from Sweden and Denmark by promising to replace it. The Finns had about $18,000,000 deposited in foreign banks or owed to them by the United States for sequestered funds, which they could not use under Allied restrictions. I arranged for the Grain Corporation to continue food and medical supplies on the security of these funds.

The Superior Blockade Council, through Vance McCormick, and the Supreme Economic Council, with support of all the American members, continuously fought for the removal of all these restrictions, but we did not succeed.

The solution for Finland was to obtain recognition of her independence by the Allies so that she could use her own resources. The French were the obstacle, as they believed that Communist Russia would some time collapse and that the Finnish question should be kept open to settle with the expected new Russian Government. I urged the President to raise the question in the Big Four and let me do the talking. He asked for the usual memorandum. It read:

26 April, 1919

MY DEAR MR. PRESIDENT:

I am wondering if there is not some method by which the recognition of the full independence of Finland could be expedited. They have now had a general election, they have created a responsible ministry: this ministry is of liberal character. There are many reasons why this matter should be undertaken, and at once.

The United States has always had a great sentiment for the suffering of the Finnish people, and their struggle over a century to re-gain independence.

By lack of recognition, they are absolutely isolated from . . . the rest of the world. They are unable to market their products. . . . They have ships without flags; have no right to sail the seas. They are totally unable to establish credits, although they have a great deal of resource, as no bank can loan money to a country of unrecognized government. They are isolated by censorship. Their citizens are not allowed to move as their passports do not run.

I then described the relief operation and the Finns' financial, trade and shipping situation, and continued:

> If ever there was a case for helping a people who are making a sturdy fight to get on a basis of liberal democracy, and are asking no charity of the world whatever, this is the case. I am convinced from our reports that unless Finland is recognized within a very short time . . . the present government cannot survive the difficulties with which it is faced. . . .
>
> Nor do I see why any half measures need to be taken in this matter. They have gone through every cycle that the world could demand in political evolution, to the point of an independent people, and I feel that they would long since have been recognized had it not been for the terrible cloud of other questions that surrounds the world. . . .
>
> Faithfully yours,
>
> Herbert Hoover

The President requested that I see Premier Clemenceau as to appearing before the Big Four. As always with me he was most cooperative. I did not need to appear with my prepared but short oration. He sent my letter to the Council of Ten and the President added to the urging in this note to Secretary Lansing on May 3:

> My Dear Lansing:
>
> I am pretty clear in my view that the case of Finland stands by itself. It never was in any true sense an integral part of Russia. It has been a most uneasy and unwilling partner and I think that action in regard to the recognition of the Finnish Government would not commit us or embarrass us with regard to the recognition of any other part of the former Russian Empire that might be separately set up. I am very keen for the recognition of Finland, as you know.
>
> Woodrow Wilson

The Council met the same day and agreed to recognition. But it was agreed by them that the decision should be kept secret until it could be announced simultaneously by all Governments.

A few hours after their decision was made, Rudolph Holsti, the Finnish representative in Paris, came to see me full of emotion and gratitude. He informed me that he had seen my letter and that both the French and the British had communicated to him confidentially what had been done.

As soon as the decision was made public, Colonel Logan of my staff telegraphed to Major Ferry Heath, the head of our organization in Finland, that recognition had been granted and added:

> The recognition of Finland has been brought about entirely by Mr. Hoover by his urgent and repeated representations to the various governments.

Heath's reply makes illuminating reading:

> You doubtless know that the news of England's recognition arrived three days prior to the news that we had also recognized Finland. Naturally, this resulted in a feeling of obligation towards England which was only partially dispelled by the tardy arrival of the news from the United States.

Our problems with the other three Baltic States, Estonia, Latvia and Lithuania, with their combined population of only 4,700,000, were unending.

Never has there been another instance of human emancipation under such appalling difficulties. Here were three non-Slavic tribes, probably somewhat related to the Finns and Hungarians who had settled this area in the dim past. They had been subjected over centuries alternately to German, Polish and Russian oppression. There was an alien aristocracy over them, made up of descendants from the original invasion of the German Baltic barons—the "Balts" —with a sprinkling of Russian overlords. In this top layer were the great landowners and industrialists. Yet over hundreds of years these races had shown extraordinary intellectual resistance to Germanization and Russianization. They had maintained their languages, their culture and the determination that freedom would come some time.

With the political explosion in Europe of the Communist Revolution and the Armistice, these races erupted into revolution, establishing representative government and personal freedom. Their individualism was such that the three states would not combine into one, although their racial affinities, aspirations, economic problems and future defense and independence all pointed to that necessity.

They were confronted with difficulties which to any but intrepid peoples would have been too much to contemplate. They were internally divided in their political ideas because, unlike the Finns, they had had no experience in self-government. When their political and social divisions came to light there were twelve to sixteen different political groups in each parliament, from Communism to rank autocracy and including religious and industrial groupings.

Two years before the Armistice, they had been invaded by the Germans—indeed they were annexed to Germany under the Brest-Litovsk Treaty between the Communists and the Germans. The Germans had created an army of occupation mostly of Balts and White Russians under German officers, with General von der Goltz in command. The Allies, at the Armistice, fearing general chaos if von der Goltz's army withdrew, stipulated that his army should stay there until the Allies settled their future. Von der Goltz's army lived by requisition, and every German and Balt common soldier had been promised a large landed estate.

Each of these three states was invaded by the Communists, and at times we were unable to supply food except to some coastal cities and irregular inland areas.

The meager Latvian Army was defeated by a Communist invasion on January 2, 1919. The Latvians managed to hold their southern provinces but Riga, the greatest city on the Baltic, was seized by the Communists. They kept such a tight hold on the place that our organization was able to glean only rumors.

This was the bewildering image which faced Mr. Wilson in the Baltic. Based on this sparse information, I sent a note on the situation to the Big Four on May 7, 1919, and followed it with a more ample statement to the President on May 9, recommending an immediate naval force in the Baltic ports, with other military assistance:

PARIS, May 9th, 1919

MY DEAR MR. PRESIDENT:

I feel the time has come when it is necessary to take some more definite action with regard to the situation in the three Baltic

States of Estonia, Latvia, and Lithuania. I enclose herewith a sketch map showing approximately the ethnological boundaries and at the same time the present military status.

The food conditions in these states are simply terrible. From a shipping, finance, and food point of view, we could overcome this if some kind of order can be established. We are gradually extending our distribution along the coastal fringe of the non-Bolshevik area, but even in such areas the hinterland is in a state of chaos due to Bolshevik invasions, with the resultant arson and slaughter. About one-half of the coast area is held by the Bolshevik, or is in such a state of anarchy as to make it impossible to send ships in. At Riga, for instance, the Red Army withdrew some days ago, leaving the town in the hands of a starving mob, among whose actions was to drive some twenty thousand bourgeoise women and children into an island in the bay, and the results are beyond all description.[2]

From a relief point of view, the situation is hopeless except... [for] a few coastal towns, unless we can have some sort of order and protection. The Germans, of course, occupy Lithuania, and some instruction must be given them to cease interfering with the development of the government there—for something must be established to succeed the German occupation.

The population in none of these states is Bolshevik. In many places they are putting up a good fight to try and establish their independence from the Moscow tyranny. They insist if they were given military supplies they require no other help to establish their boundaries and to maintain order, and our people concur in this opinion.

The problem seems to me as follows:

(a) To place enough naval strength (not large) in each of the ports to protect the relief of all the coastal towns;

(b) To furnish military supplies to the established governments so as to enable them to maintain order in the interior and to defend their borders....

The situation is one that is so appealing from every human point of view, that I am wondering whether or not it would be possible for yourself and the Premiers to set aside a short period, when the British and American naval authorities, who are familiar with this situation, could appear, together with myself on the food

---

[2] This note was incorrect in saying that the Communists had withdrawn from Riga. They were still on the job and doing their worst.

side, in the hope that some definite political and relief policy could be arrived at.

Faithfully yours,

HERBERT HOOVER

The President had my letter referred to the Council of Ten, apparently without reading it, and they came to the conclusion that a Committee should be set up to examine the situation. The Committee, of which I was a member, met on May 13. It reported:

That the maintenance of order was a necessary condition of the distribution of food-stuffs in the Baltic provinces;

That the present position in Lithuania and Latvia, by which the maintenance of order was entirely in the hands of the German forces, was extremely unsatisfactory and should in any case not continue long;

That as the despatch of Allied troops to the Baltic Provinces was out of the question, the only alternative was the organization of such native forces and volunteers from outside as might be obtainable.

Therefore, the Committee decided that a military mission under British command should be organized for the purpose of advising the three Baltic Governments on organization, equipment and training of local military forces for defense against the Bolsheviks and for the retirement of the Germans from their territories.

The Committee also recommended that a credit of £10,000,-000 be placed at the disposal of the Baltic States by the Allied and Associated Governments to enable them to pay the Allies for necessary equipment and supplies for which securities were to be given.

I had no confidence that this would meet the situation in Riga and again recalled my letter of May 9 to the President, to which he replied on May 21 with the following suggestion:

PARIS, 21 May, 1919

MY DEAR HOOVER:

I read with deep interest and concern your letter of the ninth of May about the situation in the Baltic Provinces, and yesterday had an opportunity to read it to the other members of the "Council of Four." Mr. Lloyd George suggested that I request you to have a conference with Admiral Hope, or anyone else who represents the British Admiralty here, in order to ascertain whether it was feasible from a naval point of view to carry out the programme you suggest. If the programme were adopted, it would, I suppose, necessarily be the British Navy that executed it, and we would very much appreciate a memorandum from you as to the result of your conference with the British Admiralty.

Cordially and sincerely yours,

WOODROW WILSON

I discussed these questions with Admiral Hope and urged that naval destroyers be sent at once.

The Allied Military Mission without naval forces arrived in the Baltic States on May 26. In the meantime (no doubt with the President's approval), Admiral Benson sent his destroyers into the ports where we were placing our supplies.

But from this point on the troubles of the three states differed.

Estonia was the smallest of the three Baltic States, about half the size of Indiana, and it had a population of some 1,100,000, of whom about half were farmers. The Russian Red Army invaded the country in December 1918, but an improvised army of mainly Estonian peasants assisted by some Finnish, Swedish, White Russians and Latvian volunteers, defeated the Communists in February 1919. Our men reported that George Washington's army at Valley Forge was better clothed, better fed and better armed. There can be no doubt of their courage. One Estonian division had casualties of 50 per cent in a single action. But they held their country.

We were now able, with the support of Admiral Benson, to organize their relief efficiently. A note of true Americanism sounds in one of Lieutenant John Thor's reports. He had charge in Reval, and related that upon the arrival of our ship, the S.S. *Lake Dancey*, the captain asked for a field for his crew to determine whether the sailors or the firemen had the better baseball team. Thors marked out a field and decided that he would charge the Estonians admission to this strange performance. He borrowed a band from the town and obtained full publicity in the press. Our sailors and firemen donated cigarettes to be sold for 1.50 marks a pack—say 25 cents—a reduction of about 80 per cent of the current price. The band, cigarettes and baseball game all proved a huge success. After the performance, Lieutenant Thors found that the receipts amounted to 3,200 marks for the Children's Relief.

Latvia was far more trouble to us.

Karlis Ulmanis had been elected its provisional President. He was one of the unique figures to emerge in the war years. He had been sent to an uncle in a mid-West state when ten years old, had been educated at the state university, and had taught economics in American high schools. Shortly before the war he had returned to Latvia to take care of his mother, and was caught in the Russian Army draft. Probably more than any one other man his devotion to freedom was responsible for the independence movement in these three Baltic States.

I have already related that his Government had been driven out of Riga by the Communists. However, on March 1, 1919, he staged a revolt against the Communists at Libau in South Latvia and again pulled his Government together, setting up headquarters in that city. We supplied him with food, but a mixed German-Balt-White Russian Army, under a German adventurer named von Stryck, seized Libau in an attempt to take all three Baltic States. Ulmanis had to flee again, this time to Sweden. Our men suspended food distribution for a few days to see what would happen next. On April 20 von der Goltz of the Balt Army issued a proclamation announcing that he had nothing to do with the overthrow of the Latvian Government. The adventurers fled, whereupon our men resumed distribution in that area.

Because there were intolerable delays in the action proposed by the Council of Ten, which in fact only began to function in July, and because I had had further information about the horrors, in Riga, I decided to take personally the responsibility of action. I instructed Colonel James Logan, Chief of our Military Contact Division, to get in touch with von der Goltz and persuade him to occupy Riga with his Balt Army and the remnants of the Latvian Army in the area. Since it was the duty of von der Goltz's Army under the Armistice terms to preserve order in the Baltic States, and since he was alive to the barbarities in Riga, which involved many Balts, we surmised that he would not be averse to taking action.

Von der Goltz's Army took parts of the city on May 22.

On May 21 our staff assembled a train of forty carloads of food from Libau and started it toward Riga under Lieutenant Harrington, with two sergeants and half a dozen doughboys. The train reached a point ten miles from the city. Beyond that the tracks had been torn up.

Lieutenant Harrington set his doughboys to recruiting labor and repairing tracks while he went ahead into Riga, and he was able to get some food into the city on May 24.

I later repeated to Mr. Wilson the story of this action, which I had from one of Harrington's sergeants. When Harrington arrived at Riga, fighting in the suburbs was still going on and there were many dead from starvation and battles in the streets. Harrington did not quite know how to take hold of the situation, and inquired if there were an American Consulate. There was. He sent a sergeant, who found a small American flag nailed to the door and a type-written notice in Lettish and vigorous English warning all comers to stay away — signed "The Acting Consul of the United States of America." The sergeant had some difficulty in raising anybody, but finally a girl peeked through a crack and, seeing his uniform, threw the door wide open — and broke into tears. She was the Consulate stenographer, an American of Lettish birth, who had stood by the ship when the Consul had been forced to leave upon the German occupation. She pulled herself together quickly when told that the Americans had a trainload of food at the edge of the city and wanted to find some civilians in authority. She knew whom to get and managed it as if she had been the very mother of Riga itself. She herself was very thin and hungry, and the sergeant assumed the duty of caring for her.

Mr. Wilson's remark upon hearing this narrative from me was: "We need a lot of Harringtons and his sergeants at home."

One of Admiral Benson's destroyers accompanied one of our cargo ships into Riga, where it arrived amid great rejoicing.

The history of the Communists' doings in Riga from January to May 1919 has never been adequately told in English. A Latvian Soviet Republic had been set up, originally under Lettish and Finnish Communists. My staff reported that the prisons were opened and the dregs of Riga — once a city of a million people — were turned loose. Together with the Communists, they looted every store, every house. The people were left without food except at exorbitant prices. The banks and public institutions were plundered. Literally hundreds of innocent people were executed daily without trial in a sadistic orgy of blood of which the world has known few equals. Clergymen, doctors, teachers, young girls were taken to prison and mowed down by machine guns. On many days as many as 1,000 were executed. Deaths from starvation and other causes were so many that coffins could not be provided, and bodies by the hundreds were dumped into trenches.

My organization was soon to experience another kind of trouble, but from the other side. A Balt colonel, placed in charge of the city by von der Goltz, set up a military court, made up mostly of Balts, to find and try those guilty of executions under the Red regime. There were men on this court whose wives, sons and daughters had been among the executed. At once a White Terror replaced a Red Terror, with another round of executions. Our men not only protested, but asked me to protest. I had no particular authority in the matter, but I sent a telegram to Colonel Groome, who was en route to take charge in Riga:

> . . . The Germans alone are responsible for this white terror which succeeded the red terror. . . . As soon as you get to Reval see the . . . [German] military commanders, communicate to them my views and secure from them a definite assurance that the Riga incidents will not be repeated. Tell them plainly that you are directed by me to see that these unlawful and inhumane acts do not occur. . . . The American people will not lend their support for an instant . . . to any movement which would countenance such actions.
>
> HOOVER

The Balt Court then limited its executions mostly to proved criminals.

Ulmanis now returned to Riga and, with food behind him, set up a provisional government again. But at this point a war developed between the Balts and the Letts. Colonel Groome with Lieutenant Harrington succeeded in arranging an armistice and brought various elements together into a coalition under Ulmanis against the Communists.

On June 28, the day the Peace Treaty was signed at Versailles, the citizens of Riga, Libau and other towns came, with their children, in parades of thousands to the offices of our organization. They sent grateful messages to President Wilson. They came bearing flowers, with bands playing "Yankee Doodle," their idea of our na-

tional anthem; but they brought also tears and prayers of thanksgiving.

Lithuania was about the size of West Virginia, with a population of approximately 2,000,000. The Lithuanians had declared their
independence soon after the Armistice. Shortly thereafter they were
invaded by the Soviet Armies, but a ragged force of 25,000 peasants
defeated the Russians. Our food supplies gave strength to the new
republic.

EPILOGUE TO THE BIRTH OF THE FOUR BALTIC STATES

Over the years after the peace and prior to 1938, I had received
invitations from a score of countries in Europe to become their
guest as a mark of appreciation for services in the First World War.
These included Finland, Latvia, Estonia and Lithuania. In response to these invitations, in January 1938 I spent a few days in
Finland, Latvia and Estonia, where great courtesies were shown me.

I found that the four Baltic States were enjoying the highest
standard of living of any place in Europe. Their ambitions for
representative, constitutional governments of free men had not, except in Finland, been altogether successful. The multitude of fac-
tional political parties in the Parliaments of the three states had a
few years previously produced governmental and economic chaos,
and before my visit they all had Fascist governments, with mild but
resolute dictators. Ulmanis had been voted out of power by his un-
manageable Parliament, but was now again in control.

In 1940 the three minor Baltic States were seized by the Communists. Ulmanis was taken to Russia a prisoner and there put to
death in prison. Under Communist domination of these three states,
there again began a horrible era of liquidations, deportations to
Siberia and colonization of Russians on seized farms.

The restoration of these states to Western civilization may
come again some day. Races whose mores have survived a thousand
years of foreign oppression do not easily perish.

HUNGARY

We were faced with five revolutions in Hungary while trying
to feed its people. We did not trouble President Wilson about the

first one, which was the Hungarians' declaration of an independent republic.

The second revolution, however, presented problems to the President and the Big Four. Béla Kun, a Hungarian, while a prisoner of war in Russia had joined the Communists and had been especially indoctrinated for service in Hungary. He was sent to Budapest with a supply of gold to organize a revolution. His conspiracy succeeded and on March 22, 1919, he made himself dictator. He inaugurated a Red Terror, confiscated all property, and sadistically executed more than 2,000 persons without semblance of trial.

Because of these events the Big Four imposed a tight blockade on Hungary. Prior to the revolution my organization had set up our usual system for the rehabilitation of famine-debilitated children, the food supplies in this case being paid for by the Hungarian National Bank from its gold reserves. At the moment of Béla Kun's seizure of power, we had a trainload of food en route for this purpose. The French officials in charge of the blockade refused to allow the train to pass, although we had arranged that the distribution to children would be continued under our organization.

Here again I had to appeal to the President for help. He arranged that Clemenceau give the proper orders—and we continued the feeding of the children.

On April 15 I transmitted to the President the following telegram from Captain Gregory:

> Trains of food recently held up by the French arrived yesterday Budapest. Created most favorable feeling for Americans as demonstrating their integrity in carrying out their engagements, more particularly among the anti-Bolshevik labor element in Budapest.

The problems of my organization with Béla Kun were however much wider than this. He controlled our railway connections to the surrounding states, and unless they were to starve, we had to secure some cooperation from him. Our staff proposed an agreement with him by which we would continue to operate our trains over Hungarian lines and, in turn, we would sell him food.

On April 15, 1919, I addressed the President:

DEAR MR. PRESIDENT:

I regret the necessity to trouble you to secure the approval of the three premiers to a short statement that I desire to make to the Hungarian Government by way of premise to the completion of certain negotiations with them vital to the relief of Central Europe.

After explaining the situation, I continued:

. . . If we put Hungary on precisely the same food basis as the other states, we shall lose our control of the situation in the surrounding states. We have ample indication that the restraining influence that we hold on these governments is effective but if the disturbing elements in Austria, Czecho-Slovakia, Jugo-Slavia, etc., consider that they will be as secure as to food supplies after disturbance [Communist revolutions] as before, our present potentiality to maintain the status quo of order is lost. Furthermore, there are no doubt difficulties in the minds of some of the Allied Governments. . . . Therefore, in order to avoid these various pitfalls, I propose to complete the negotiations with the Hungarian Government as to transportation and supply of food with the preliminary announcement on the following lines:

The proposed economic arrangement with the Food Administration as to railway transportation and food supplies for Hungary is provisional and purely humanitarian and has no relationship to the settlement of any political questions.

That the Associated Governments do not at present intend to accord the same consideration to Hungary as they are according to liberated countries and German Austria today. To these latter countries they are sending a constantly increasing flow of food supplies for the purchase of which the Allied Governments are voluntarily providing the necessary finances. So far as Hungary is concerned, the Associated Governments will for the present only advance food supplies for such services and funds as may be acceptable to the Food Administration. . . .

The matter is of urgent character and it is impossible for anyone to agree on the political issue involved except yourself and the three premiers. Any amount of discussion between the members of the bodies in which I sit cannot possibly result in other than a reference to yourself in the end. . . .

The President replied the same day in his own handwriting as follows:

MY DEAR HOOVER:

The Four this morning approved the enclosed plan and I beg that you will proceed with it.

W.W.

I transmitted to the President, at his request, day-by-day accounts of Béla Kun's progress which I received from the well-informed Chief of our mission in Vienna, Captain T. T. C. Gregory.

Béla Kun was a busy man. He seized the remaining gold reserves in the National Bank. He mobilized a small army under the command of General Boehm and officers of the old regime and invaded a part of Czechoslovakia. He bought some arms from Italian Army officers[3] with gold, and in his spare time used some of the gold to subsidize a Communist conspiracy in Vienna.

At the President's suggestion, the Big Four requested my views on the "confused situation." I recommended that, in addition to the blockade, they make a declaration of Allied policies on Hungary that would give the Hungarians opposed to Kun some hope of their nation's future. They did not think this wise at that moment. On the other hand, on July 10, they requested General Foch to prepare a plan for an Allied invasion of Hungary in which he proposed an American contingent.

President Wilson had returned home and Undersecretary of State Frank Polk had succeeded him as our representative on the Big Four. To him I protested the use of American troops for such a purpose. I urged my previous plan, stating that Kun's support was weakening, as had been demonstrated by the resignation of General Boehm and his escape to Austria.

On July 26 I was called to a meeting of the Big Four, and again recommended a declaration of Allied policies which would give some hope to the Hungarian people. The Big Four asked me to draft such a declaration. I did so. It stated:

> The Allied and Associated Governments are most anxious to arrange a Peace with the Hungarian People and thus bring to an end a condition of things which makes the economic revival of Central Europe impossible, and defeats any attempt to secure food and other supplies for its population. These tasks cannot even be attempted until there is in Hungary a Government which represents its people, and carries out in the letter and the spirit the engagements into which it has entered with the Associated Governments.

---

[3] Being advised of this transaction by Captain Gregory, I protested it at a meeting of the Supreme Economic Council, to the chagrin of the fine, honest Italian members of that body. They investigated, secured the gold and subsequently handed it to me to feed Hungarian children.

None of these conditions are fulfilled by the Administration of Béla Kun; which has not only broken the Armistice to which Hungary was pledged but is at this moment actually attacking a friendly and Allied Power [Czechoslovakia]. With this particular aspect of the question it is for the Associated Governments to deal on their own responsibility. If food and supplies are to be made available, if the blockade is to be removed, if economic reconstruction is to be attempted, if peace is to be settled it can only be done with a Government which represents the Hungarian people and not with one that rests its authority upon terrorism.

Polk told me that the President had approved the draft, and it was issued on July 26.

Six days later, on August 1, after 100 days of government, Béla Kun was overthrown by the trade-union leaders, who brought about a revolt in his army. Kun fled by plane; some of his assistants committed suicide. A Government largely of trade-union leaders assumed power and the Republic was reestablished. This was Hungary's third revolution.

At this juncture the Rumanian Army began an invasion of Hungary "to right their wrongs," and on August 5 occupied Budapest. They promptly began looting the city in good old medieval style, including the food in our canteens and the children's hospitals.

Coincident with the occupation by the Rumanian Army, on August 5 another revolution took place with the help of the Rumanian Army. The Archduke Joseph, with eleven gendarmes and Rumanian machine guns directed at the government building, seized power and arrested the trade-union Ministry. A cry arose from all the liberated countries in Eastern Europe to Paris, "The Hapsburgs are coming back."

Premier Clemenceau received a letter from the Archduke on August 8. In it he accused the trade-union Ministry of including some of Kun's supporters, and stated his program to be "to crush Bolshevism." He asked for a closer association with the Allied Governments. I was away on an inspection trip to Poland. Upon my return on August 19, I was again requested to attend a meeting of the Big Four.

The minutes of the meeting show that I gave the Council detailed information on the plundering by the Rumanian Army (including the testimony of two American eyewitnesses of their taking sixteen wagonloads of American food from the hospitals—as a result of which eleven children died).

Premier Clemenceau handed me the Archduke's letter of August 8 and asked me how we should deal with him.

The minutes record the following:[4]

> As to the Archduke's usurpation, he [Hoover] would like to call attention to . . . a sidelight on the situation. The *coup d'état* by which the Archduke Joseph's Government had been installed was not entirely a Hungarian affair, Rumanian troops had surrounded the meeting place of the Ministry and had turned their machine guns on the building in which they were sitting. This event had had an immediate repercussion throughout Poland and Eastern Europe and the Bolshevists were making much of it and claiming that the Alliance was trying to re-establish reactionary government in its worst form. This had done more to rehabilitate the Bolshevist cause than anything that had happened for a long time. . . . If things were allowed to continue as they were, the old . . . [regime] would be well established in ten days and the Allied and Associated Powers would have to be prepared to see the House of Hapsburg begin to re-establish itself throughout all its former dominions. He [Hoover] could only suggest that the Council should instruct its representatives in Budapest to call the Archduke before them and say that his Government could never be accepted or recognized. Such action might induce the Archduke to step aside and invite the social democrats to form a coalition government.

I was asked to draft such an instruction, which I did with zest, and presented it at the afternoon session. There was some hesitation about adopting it for fear that it was too direct and that the Archduke would defy the Big Four. I suggested that he could be given the impression that the Allies had armies of several million men and that his Rumanian military support was a weak reed. Finally, rather than act through the Allied Commission of four generals which the Big Four had established in Budapest, I was directed to send the telegram over my organization wires to Captain Gregory, who was then in Budapest, for delivery in person, with such verbal instructions as might expedite matters. The telegram in part read:

> The Allied and Associated governments . . . are most anxious to conclude a durable peace with the Hungarian people, but they

---

[4] Minutes of the Meeting of the Heads of Delegations. 21 August 1919. H. D. 35.

feel that this cannot be done while the present Hungarian Government is in power. That Government has been brought into existence, not by the will of the people but by a *coup d'état* carried out by a small body of police, under the protection of a foreign army. It has at its head a member of the house of Hapsburg, whose policy and ambitions were largely responsible for the calamities under which the world is suffering, and will long suffer. A peace negotiated by such a Government is not likely to be lasting, nor can the Allied and Associated Governments give it the economic support which Hungary so sorely needs. . . .

In the interests, therefore, of European peace the Allied and Associated Governments must insist that the present claimant to the headship of the Hungarian State should resign, and that a Government in which all parties are represented should be elected by the Hungarian people. The Allied and Associated Powers would be prepared to negotiate with any Government which possessed the confidence of an Assembly so elected.

On the following day, August 23, I received over our telegraph system a reply from Captain Gregory, expressed in the effective American slang in conformity with *en clair* language:

Archie on the carpet at 7 P.M.
Went through the hoop at 7:05 P.M.

We translated the message into proper terms and sent it to the Council then in session. When the messenger handed it to Premier Clemenceau, he also showed him the original telegram. Clemenceau at one time had been a reporter on a New York newspaper and had no difficulty understanding it. He claimed it for his own as a "memento of the war."

An angry queen brought down the curtain on this episode. After I reached New York in mid-September 1919, a 1,200-word letter reached me from the Queen of Rumania. The letter was written wholly in longhand and the ink itself spluttered her indignation over the report which I had furnished the Big Four about the actions of the Rumanians in Budapest. Today the letter is a collector's item.

AUSTRIA

Béla Kun had moved so far along with his Communist conspiracy in Austria that the Austrian Government reported to my staff that they expected a serious outbreak on May Day (1919). With the

President's approval I authorized the Austrians to placard Vienna with a statement from me to the effect that any such action would jeopardize the city's already sparse food supply. No disturbance took place.

These were by no means all of the President's burdens resulting from the activities of the Communists. I discuss others in relation to Germany in the next chapter.

Outbreaks of Jewish Persecution in Poland

Late in May 1919, reports of brutal treatment of Jews in Poland were spread in the press. These reports naturally injured the Polish cause in the United States. Preliminary information from my staff did not confirm the whole of the press story, but did indicate that there had been some bad incidents. I wrote the President about it and suggested that I might get Prime Minister Paderewski to ask him to appoint an American committee to investigate the situation, which would also be a signal for these outbreaks to stop. Mr. Paderewski readily agreed, and I received the following note from the President:

3 June, 1919

My Dear Hoover:

I have received the request of Mr. Paderewski to which you refer in your letter of the second and I am going to try to act upon it for I have the deepest interest, as you have, in assisting Poland in every way and amongst other things in this troublesome question of the treatment of the Jewish people.

Woodrow Wilson

The President appointed Henry Morgenthau, Sr., Chairman, General Edgar Jadwin, and Congressman Homer Johnson. They quieted both the persecutions and the exaggerated reports.

Armenia

Probably Armenia was known to the American school child of 1919 only a little less than most other countries. The association of Mount Ararat and Noah, the staunch Armenian Christians, who were massacred periodically by the Mohammedan Turks and the Sunday-school collections during decades to alleviate their miseries—all cumulated to impress the name of Armenia on the American mind.

With the Communist Revolution the Caucasian States of Armenia, Azerbaijan, and Georgia declared their independence and established themselves as Republics. They were at this time protected from Communist invasion by the White Armies under General Denikin, operating to the north of them.

Russian Armenia had a native population of about 1,500,000, but some 400,000 to 500,000 refugees poured in upon them from Turkish Armenia, to the south, as a result of Turkish persecution designed to drive them out of Turkey. In addition, the Georgians had no great love for the Armenians and the Azerbaijanians were very unfriendly.

The only access to Russian Armenia was by a branch from the railway line between Batum and Baku, which was controlled by Georgia. After the Armistice the British landed troops to protect their oil supplies over this railway.

Some background of our relief operations in Armenia is necessary to understand our calls for Presidential help. Until the appropriation of $100,000,000 by Congress, my organization had no funds for Armenian support. Under the law, they could not qualify as belligerents against the Central Powers. The American Near East Committee, headed by Arthur Curtiss James and Cleveland Dodge of New York, had been operating for many years to aid the Armenians generally. With the Armistice, they launched an appeal for public support for a fund of $30,000,000, to which, at their request, we gave warm support. The Near East Committee informed us that they could finance themselves. As I welcomed any one who could help, I dismissed the subject from my mind.

But on February 22, 1919, Howard Heinz, our organization representative in Constantinople, reported that the Committee's funds were proving inadequate. As our $100,000,000 appropriation was now available, I directed him to ship food, medical and clothing cargoes to the Near East Committee.

In late March, however, Heinz received most disturbing reports as to the inability of the Committee to manage the Armenian situation, and dispatched Major R. Stoever of his staff to investigate. Major Stoever's report was so appalling that I telegraphed Colonel William N. Haskell, who was in charge in Rumania, to send Captain Joseph Green of his staff, together with adequate assistants, to Armenia as quickly as possible.

Further reports confirmed Major Stoever's that tens of thousands of Armenians were dying of starvation and typhus, and confirmed reports of cannibalism.

With Major Green's arrival in Armenia in May, together with our cargoes, we hoped that the worst was over. In any event, we were delivering every pound of food which could be transported over the railways. Then Green was met by a demand from the Georgian Government, which held up our trains and insisted upon a toll of 2,000 tons of food per month.

If anyone wants material for a treatise on human woe, intrigue, war, massacre, incompetence and dishonesty, he can find ample source material in the mass of reports from our American officers on Armenia.

The British now gave us notice that they were withdrawing their military contingent from Georgia.

On June 20 I wrote the President:

> Our people estimate that there are already 200,000 deaths from starvation and that unless we can have a rigid control of this railway under the British authorities and unless we can stop the piracy of the Georgian Government, and unless we can have no interruption by military change, we shall certainly lose another 200,000 lives.
>
> I do not wish to burden you with the heart-breaking details of the whole Armenian situation. The daily reports that we have, not only through all our own agencies at work here but as well through the British . . . , are of the most appalling that have yet developed out of the war. I need only mention that the eating of the dead is now general. We have large stocks of foodstuffs lying in Batoum and I am confident that everything has been done both on our part and on the part of the British authorities that could have been done . . . , but these interruptions can mean nothing but total breakdown.
>
> With the arrival of harvest about the end of August, the situation will be much ameliorated [owing to our provision of seed grain].
>
> If it were possible for you to discuss this matter with your colleagues it might be that some arrangement could be made that the . . . [removal of troops] could be delayed and that the British authorities could take a more emphatic and rigid control of the railways than they now hold, and that emphatic notice be given the Georgian Government. . . . The matter is of the most urgent order.
>
> Faithfully yours,
HERBERT HOOVER

On June 27, I made an additional request in a letter to the President. After pointing out that my funds would end on July 1, I suggested:

> That a single temporary resident Commissioner should be appointed to Armenia, who will have the full authority of the United States, Great Britain, France and Italy in all their relations to the de facto Armenian Government. . . . His duties . . . [should be] to supervise and advise upon various governmental matters in the whole of Russian and Turkish Armenia, and to control relief and repatriation questions pending the determination of the political destiny of this area.
>
> In case the various Governments should agree to this plan, immediate notification should be made to the de facto Governments of Turkey and of Armenia of his appointment and authority. . . . He will be appointed to represent . . . [our new] American Relief Administration and the Committee for Relief in the Near East, . . .
>
> I assume that the personnel of this Mission would be necessarily comprised of [American] army and navy officers who would retain their rank and emoluments and I understand from the . . . [Committee] for the Near East that they would be prepared to supply such funds as were required for incidental expenses until such other arrangements could be made.
>
> Faithfully yours,
HERBERT HOOVER

The President arranged that the Big Four agree in principle to this plan.

As Major Green and his staff badly needed a rest, on July 3 I wrote Secretary Lansing, proposing the appointment of Colonel William N. Haskell as High Commissioner, and again asked that something be done about the Georgian Government:

PARIS, 3 July 1919

DEAR MR. SECRETARY:

> In respect to the authorization of the acceptance in principle by the Heads of State that an American should be selected to represent the various Powers so far as may be at the de facto Government of Russian Armenia, and to take entire charge of the relief measures in that quarter, I beg to say that we suggest the approval of Colonel William N. Haskell. Colonel Haskell has had charge of the relief measures in Rumania for some months.
>
> I would be glad if the Council . . . could see their way to

pass the following resolution and to put into effect the instructions to various Allied agencies there:

Colonel W. N. Haskell, U.S.A., is appointed by this Council to act as High Commissioner to the de facto Government of Russian Armenia on behalf of the United States, British, French and Italian Governments, it being understood that Colonel Haskell will be coincidentally appointed to take full charge of all relief measures in Russian Armenia by the various relief organizations operating there. All representatives of the United States, British, French and Italian Governments in Armenia, Georgia, Azerbaijan and Constantinople are to be at once instructed to co-operate with and give support to Colonel Haskell.

I attach hereto telegrams from our staff in Armenia which I earnestly present for your consideration, and I wonder whether, in dealing with the Armenian situation, the [Supreme] Council . . . would not agree to each Government's despatching the following telegram to their representatives at Tiflis and Batoum for communication to the Governments of Georgia and Azerbaijan:

We understand that the Georgian Government is making demands for portions of the food supply shipped to the Armenians as a consideration for transportation, and is otherwise interfering with the transport of food into Armenia. We wish to have it strongly emphasized to these de facto Governments that any such action or any failure of earnest support in transportation of food to Armenia will, to say the least, entirely prejudice their case in any decisions as to their political future.

Faithfully yours,
Herbert Hoover

The President and the Big Four agreed to my proposals. The life of my Congressional appropriation had ended on July 1; so to bridge over until new Armenian support could be found I ordered several cargoes en route to Europe to proceed to Batum and also assigned our remaining Constantinople stocks. Colonel Haskell had to find substitutes for Major Green's men. As usual, he was aided in this task by General Pershing.

On July 13, Premier Clemenceau issued the following statement:

Colonel W. N. Haskell, of the United States Army, has been designated by the Supreme Council of the Allied and Associated Powers, under date of July 5, 1919, to fulfill in Armenia the functions of High Commissioner, in the name of the Governments of the United States of America, the British Empire, France and Italy. It is understood that Colonel Haskell will be at the same time charged with all measures tending to aid Armenia, with the assistance of the various aid societies operating in the region. All the American, British, French and Italian representatives in Armenia, Georgia, Azerbaijan and at Constantinople will immediately receive instructions to lend aid and assistance to Colonel Haskell.

CLEMENCEAU
The President of the Peace Conference

We had more trouble with Armenian relief, but it did not involve the President, who had then returned to the United States.

After the arrival of the Colonel the prestige of his position began to take effect. He obtained arms for the ragged Armenian Army from the British and soon had established order and stopped attacks from the surrounding states. From voluntary gifts, and with aid from a special Congressional appropriation supported by the President, we managed to furnish adequate supplies to the Colonel. We incidentally arranged for the migration of numbers of Armenian boys and girls to the United States in our returning ships and otherwise.

Having ended the dreadful famine, and with a good crop assured and the Armenian Government strengthened, Colonel Haskell and his staff came home in mid-1920. Matters were proceeding smoothly when, in July 1921, the Communists annexed Armenia, and its tragedy continued in a new setting.

THE PRESIDENT'S ECONOMIC ADVISERS

I have, in the previous chapter, related the appointment of the Committee of Economic Advisers, comprising Messrs. Baruch, Davis, McCormick, Robinson and myself, together with General Bliss and Colonel House.

To indicate further the burdens imposed on the President aside from the task of making peace among forty-seven nations, I may cite a few instances from the operation of this Committee. The Committee kept no formal records and McCormick's Diary is about the only written account of these incidents. Here is his entry of January 31, 1919:

...The President informed me he had heard from reliable sources the Allies want to pool the total expense of the war and have us pay our proportionate share of the whole. This, of course, is not to be considered, and the President was considerably exercised over this proposal and wanted me to tell the other "advisers" not to get mixed up in any of their committees by discussing this subject at this time; but we were to confine ourselves only to our own . . . financial or other problems in which the enemy countries are involved, thereby keeping clear of embarrassing discussions which have nothing to do with Germany.

In early April a question arose as to America continuing its representation after the peace on the sixty-odd inter-Allied councils, commissions or committees which had been created before or after the Armistice to deal with current economic questions. The President's economic advisers recommended that inasmuch as we would have neither staff nor appropriations after the peace, we should end the entire connection at that time.

Another problem arose to plague us concerning the multitude of commissions and committees which were being created in the Treaty. On April 11, I addressed the President, giving my views on this situation:

I don't see how we can remain in these [treaty] enforcement commissions . . . exacting the political objectives with the military strength of the United States as a background.

I have the feeling that revolution in Europe is by no means over. The social wrongs in these countries are far from solution and the tempest must blow itself out, probably with enormous violence. Our people are not prepared for us to undertake the military policing of Europe while it boils out its social wrongs. I have no doubt that if we could undertake to police the world and had the wisdom of statesmanship to see its gradual social evolution, we would be making a great contribution to civilization, but I am certain that the American people are not prepared for such a measure and I am also sure that if we remain in Europe with military force, tied in an alliance which we have never undertaken, we should be forced into this storm of repression of revolution, and forced in under terms of co-ordination with other people that would make our independence of action wholly impossible.

Faithfully yours,

Herbert Hoover

The President replied as follows:

PARIS, 15 April 1919

MY DEAR MR. HOOVER:

I am very much impressed by your objection to the United States continuing to supply members to the various commissions which are to be set up under the Peace Treaty and am ready to say at once that I agree with you.

I am afraid that we cannot escape membership on the . . . Commission on Reparation because that commission will undoubtedly need an umpire, and I am afraid we must take the necessary risks in that matter. But with regard to most of the others, you may be sure I shall fight shy.

With warm appreciation of your letter,

Cordially and sincerely yours,

WOODROW WILSON

On April 23 Prime Minister Lloyd George addressed a long letter to the President, proposing a plan to provide Europe with working capital after the Peace Treaty was signed. The plan called for a joint guarantee by the United States, Britain, France and Italy of six and one-half billion dollars of German, Austrian and Hungarian bonds, the proceeds to be used to rehabilitate European industry after peace. The President referred the matter to his Committee of Economic Advisers. We rejected the whole idea for various reasons, one being that the Reparations Committee had already determined on an immediate payment of five billion dollars of reparations from the enemy to the Allies, or just about equal to this proposed loan. In other words, we, who would receive no reparations, would be participating in providing working capital for these countries to replace the drain of working capital caused by the reparations.

An entry in McCormick's Diary for April 24 reports:

At 10.00 went to meet Hoover at Davis' room to discuss new proposal of British for international bond issue to relieve financial distress in Europe and to use U.S. credit to guarantee bonds of bankrupt nations.

We advised the President to have nothing to do with the proposal.

Two days later Lloyd George proposed another financial plan to the President, whereby all Allied debts would be consolidated, with the United States participating in their joint guarantee. McCormick's Diary on April 25 records its fate:

> All advisers busy today discussing new financial scheme of British to consolidate debt and have all Allies guarantee interest and principal. That means the United States would guarantee all the bankrupt nations. The more the plan is studied the less enthusiastic our people become. It is the same old game they have been working on all through the conference, to get the United States to underwrite their debts. We will have to help but I don't believe in quite that way.

Lloyd George had still another idea which he proposed to Mr. Wilson. On June 13 McCormick's Diary records:

> ... I was called upon the phone and told the President wanted to see economic advisers at 10.00 A.M., before the 11.00 o'clock meeting of the Big Four, now the Big Five, as the Japanese joined Council this morning. When we, that is, Baruch, Hoover, Davis, Lamont and I, arrived the President told us Lloyd George was arguing importance of Allied control of all purchases of foodstuffs, otherwise prices would get too high and European countries ruined. President, of course, opposed to principle, but wanted our opinion and practical arguments against same. We strongly advocated no price control and no Inter-Allied combination. The President said he thought Allies would do collective buying in any event and wondered how we could break it. Baruch and I did not think it would last as it would defeat itself. Hoover said that Lloyd George should be told that if they attempt to control and lower food prices the production would fall off seriously, and he feared the result. The President said Lloyd George never argued from real hard facts, but depended on his eloquence. He said he made him mad by intimating we were not willing to join because we wanted higher prices for our food. He said he and Lloyd George had a hot argument and Lloyd George later apologized for his insinuation. . . .

In late June, McCormick told me that the President had informed him that Lloyd George had still another financial idea, that the Prime Minister now wanted to pool the total expenses of the war. Mr. Wilson was much exercised and wanted all of us to oppose it.

At the request of the "advisers" I sent a note to the President expressing their views—all negative.

I may state here that the President's committee of advisers were not adverse to organized financial aid for Europe after the peace. We considered that such action must be set up by Congress and planned by the regular departments in Washington with no previous commitment by the President. This approach the President approved.

Note. President Wilson never tolerated Communism. Aside from many incidental statements strongly denouncing it during the Armistice period, probably the best formulated statement of his views appeared a year after Versailles in a dispatch from Secretary of State Bainbridge Colby to the Italian Ambassador on August 10, 1920. The President at this time had passed the worst crisis of his illness, and Secretary Colby some years later informed me that he had gone over the draft of this message paragraph by paragraph with the President and that some of the expressions in it were introduced by the President.

The purpose of this note was to express the American Government's position on Communism and I need quote only a few sentences:

. . . the Bolsheviki . . . an inconsiderable minority of the people, by force and cunning seized the powers and machinery of government and have continued to use them with savage oppression to maintain themselves in power. . . .

It is not possible for the Government of the United States to recognize the present rulers of Russia. . . . This conviction . . . rest upon . . . facts, which none dispute . . . that the existing regime in Russia is based upon the negation of every principle of honor and good faith, and every usage and convention, underlying the . . . structure of international law. . . . The responsible leaders of the regime have frequently and openly boasted that they are willing to sign agreements and undertakings with foreign Powers while not having the slightest intention of observing such undertakings. . . . They have not only avowed this as a doctrine, but have exemplified it in practice. . . . Responsible spokesmen of this Power . . . have declared . . . that the very existence of Bolshevism in Russia . . . must . . . depend upon . . . revolutions in all other great civilized nations, including the United States, which . . . overthrow. . . . their governments and set up Bolshevist rule in their stead. . . .

. . . the Bolshevist Government [has] . . . extensive international ramifications through the Third Internationale . . . which is heavily subsidized by the Bolshevist Government . . . [and has] for its openly avowed aim the promotion of Bolshevist revolutions throughout the world. . . . There is no room for reasonable doubt that such agents would receive the support and protection of any diplomatic agencies the Bolsheviki might have in other countries. Inevitably, therefore, the diplomatic service of the Bolshevist Government would become a channel for intrigues and the propaganda of revolt. . . .

. . . There can be no mutual confidence . . . if pledges are to be given and agreements made with a cynical repudiation of their obligations already in the mind of one of the parties. We cannot recognize . . . the agents of a government which is determined and bound to conspire against our institutions; whose diplomats will be the agitators of dangerous revolt; whose spokesmen say that they sign agreements with no intention of keeping them. . . .

11

WOODROW WILSON'S ORDEAL OF THE
FOOD BLOCKADE ON EUROPE

An immense added burden was inflicted upon President Wilson through continuance of the blockade on Central and Eastern Europe, whose 300,000,000 people were struggling to live and get on their feet.

Article XXI of the Armistice Agreement provided that:

> The existing blockade conditions set up by the Allied and Associated Powers are to remain unchanged.

The stated reasons for this provision were to maintain political control of the Continent until peace was made.

I had obtained through the President the following slight modification of this article:

> The Allies and the United States contemplate the provisioning of Germany during the Armistice as shall be found necessary.

The entire American group in Paris, from the President down, considered a rigid blockade utter folly because it created unemployment, prevented economic recovery and fertilized Communism.

The idea of a blockade to force a political objective or to punish by starvation was a horror to most Americans. Until we arrived in Europe, it had never occurred to any of us that the wartime blockade of food, medical supplies and clothing would be continued against the neutrals and the newly liberated countries or in violation of the indirect promise made to Germany.

Soon after my arrival in Europe in November, I sent members of my staff to Germany to investigate the situation. These men found that the food shortage was worse after the Armistice than before; that the new Republic could neither keep the farmers from hoarding food nor hold in check the bootlegging of food to those who could pay; and that their rationing was breaking down. Worse still, my men reported a general reduction in the weight of the population, actual starvation in the lower-income groups in the cities and such debilitation of millions of children that only stunted minds and stunted bodies could result. A mass of statistics was collected to confirm these conditions.

My staff also reported that the Republic was growing weaker from "Spartacist" uprisings; that machine guns were firing in the streets of several cities; and that there was real danger of a revolution on one side from the militarists and on the other from the Spartacists (Communists), both working on the emotions of the hungry people.

In a meeting with the President two days after he had arrived in Europe, I presented to him the blockade situation and suggested that Colonel House should address the Prime Ministers upon the effects of the food blockade and gave him a possible draft for such a letter. In the House Papers there is the following note from the President to Colonel House and a copy of the proposed letter with the President's statement of approval.

15 December, 1918

MY DEAR HOUSE:

The enclosed is the result of my conference with Hoover this evening. Would you be willing to communicate this paper to the Allied Governments, as you conveyed the original note about the relief administration to which this refers?

Affectionately yours,

WOODROW WILSON

In this proposed letter I reviewed the arrangements of the United States Food Administration with the Allied Governments during the war; the great stimulants to production which we had applied with their full approval; the huge surpluses we had prepared for possible continuation of the war; stated that with the Armistice the Allies would naturally wish to obtain their food supplies from the cheaper stocks which had been dammed back in remote countries for lack of transportation; and then continued:

> Viewing the world's food situation as a whole, there is manifestly no surplus, even of American production, if the import of food into enemy neutral and liberated countries were released upon a normal scale. There would in fact be a shortage in many commodities.

> This increase in food production in the United States is therefore still of the highest importance, for it becomes the supply through which the very life of many countries must be sustained, and the American people wish it used in a sympathetic manner for these purposes.

> These foodstuffs, however, cannot at present reach many of these new areas freely, where they are so sorely needed, because of the blockade restrictions of many descriptions. The surpluses of American supplies are backing up and many of them are perishable and there is thus created a very threatening economic situation.

> The present situation, therefore, is one of two-fold character:

> *First.* With literally hundreds of millions of underfed human beings in the world, the spoilage and waste of a large quantity of food in the United States cannot for a moment be entertained, either by the American public or by the Allies. Many of the American surpluses are of perishable character, and instant action is necessary to prevent waste as well as hunger.

> *Second.* There must be instant expansion of marketing of American surpluses or there will be a great financial reaction in the United States. A review of the very large stocks now held and the large amount of banking credit advanced against these stocks creates a situation of the utmost danger. Any failure to find solution to this situation . . . would possibly precipitate financial difficulties in the United States, which would injure the hope of continued economic assistance to the Allies for a long time to come.

> No guarantees of any character have ever been at any time required to produce foodstuffs for . . . the American people and all guarantees have been solely for the purpose of creating surpluses for the European Allies. These guarantees not only apply to the existing food supplies but also extend to next year's wheat crop.

> Our present surpluses, however, in wheat, flour, barley, rye, pork products, condensed milk and cotton seed oils are above the indicated demands of the Allied Governments between now and the next harvest. . . .

Therefore, I am directed to inquire if you will not recommend to your Government:

(a) That all restrictions upon neutral trading be at once removed in these commodities;

(b) That no objection be raised by the Allied Governments to direct or indirect sale and transportation to enemy countries or to the necessary financial transactions involved.

[Following in Wilson's handwriting, pencil]

The president has directed me to present these recommendations as matters of the utmost urgency and the key to many settlements which are to be presently attempted.

Approved

W. W.

On December 20 the President requested that I give him a memorandum on the political situation in Germany. Its essential paragraphs were:

PARIS, 20th December, 1918

DEAR MR. PRESIDENT:

Soon after the Armistice, you took one or two occasions to make clear that the maintenance of order in Germany by the German people was a prime requisite to ... peace, and that the necessity of feeding Germany arose not only out of humanity but out of its fundamental necessity to prevent anarchy. . . .

As you are aware there is incipient or practical Bolshevist control in many of the large centres. There is also a Separatist movement in progress amongst the German States, arising somewhat from fear of Bolshevism. . . .

The saving of the German people would be absolutely hopeless if the normal . . . distributive function and food control should cease, as it certainly would under a Bolshevist regime.

Again a political Separatist movement amongst the German States would produce the same situation that we have in the old Austrian Empire, where some sections of the Empire have a surplus of food and by practical embargoes are creating food debacles in other centres. We must maintain a liquidity of the existing food stocks in Germany . . . or the situation will become almost unsolvable. . . .

It would appear to me therefore that some announcement with regard to the food policies in Germany is critically necessary, and at once. If that announcement could be made something on the line that the United States and Allies could only hope to solve the food difficulties in Germany until next harvest through the hands of a stable government based on an expressed popular will, and a hint be given that the Allies cannot anticipate furnishing the food assistance to Germany through the hands of Bolshevist elements, it would at once strengthen the situation in Germany and probably entirely eliminate the incipient Bolshevism in progress, and make possible the hope of saving their food situation....

Yours faithfully,

HERBERT HOOVER

With the backing of the Colonel's letter to the Prime Ministers and the support of the President himself, on December 22 I laid before the Inter-Allied Blockade Council in London, a definite plan of action:

1. That food, and medical supplies should move freely to the liberated countries and the neutrals.

2. That the neutrals should be permitted to trade food to the enemy countries for goods which were noncompetitive with those of the Allies;

3. That, when shipping and finance measures were settled with the Germans, such supplies should be free to them subject only to quantity control required by any world shortage of food.

The Council approved this relaxation of the blockade on December 24. The neutrals were notified of this relaxation by the Council and I informed the American business world. A number of contracts were at once signed between American firms and the neutrals for the sale of food, which in turn they could trade with the Germans.

A VERY UNHAPPY INTERLUDE

However, a devastating repudiation of this agreement came on December 31. Without consulting me, the Allied blockade authorities reversed their decision and clamped a tight blockade anew on all Europe. They went further and repudiated all their contracts to purchase food from the Food Administration's enormous surplus we had built up for the contingency that the war might go on.

The friendly Italian representative on these bodies informed us that the action had been taken at the initiative of the British "as a measure to reduce world food prices in the interest of all mankind."

Our warehouses were already overloaded and a flood of grain and food animals was coming hourly to the processors in the United States. With no European outlet, the processors would be unable to continue buying at the guaranteed prices.

As this action was the work of the lower echelons of bureaucrats in London, I determined to combat it on the same bureaucratic level without troubling the President more than was necessary. I did suggest that he urge the dangers on the Allied Prime Ministers if he had an opportunity.

To meet the situation, I first consulted Admiral Benson, in command of our fleet in European waters, as to the Allied right to stop American flagships en route with food for starving people in Eastern Europe. The Admiral's language was more explicit than polite, but the sum of his remarks was that no American flagship carrying food to famine-stricken people would be stopped by anybody, blockade or no blockade. The Admiral went further and placed one of his vessels, usually a destroyer, in each of the principal ports where we were landing, with a naval officer to assist in port matters.

To relieve our overcrowded warehouses, I instructed the Belgian and North of France Relief Commissions and the Food Administration's Grain Corporation to buy, transport and store supplies in neutral ports in Europe against the inevitable world shortage of food.[1] These supplies would be badly needed sometime.

I met with the French and Italian Food Ministers and stated that if they no longer needed food from the United States, I would notify our Treasury to cancel its advances for their food purchases. These two countries at once restored their orders, and to be sure of future supplies they ordered more. By mid-February the pressures of the farmers' shipments to the central markets had relaxed. We had held our guarantees, but at the cost of many sleepless nights for our Washington and New York staffs and myself.[2]

---

[1] The Grain Corporation was a wholly government-owned agency of the United States Food Administration, set up for the purpose of stimulating production, stabilizing prices, guaranteeing prices to our farmers and marketing our war surpluses in an orderly way.

[2] To those interested I recommend the following:

Frank M. Surface, *The Grain Trade during the World War*, The Macmillan Company, New York: 1928.

Despite the promise made in the Armistice Agreement, and despite every American effort, the food blockade on Germany was continued for four months after the Armistice. I deal with this subject somewhat extensively as it demonstrates not only an additional worry for the President but also the wide divergence between the American and Allied points of view.

This four months' delay of food to Germany was a most insensate, wicked action. People can take philosophically the hardships of war. When the fighting is over, they begin to bury the past as part of the fight. But when they lay down their arms and surrender in the belief that they may have food for their women and children, and then find that this instrument of attack upon them is maintained—then hate but slowly dies.

It was a crime in statesmanship against civilization as a whole. It sowed dragon's teeth of war which two decades later again enveloped most of mankind. But no one who reads the documents and records of the time will ever charge that crime against President Wilson and America. Yet we in the United States have had to suffer from this infection of revenge and bitterness which for a generation poisoned international life.[3]

The British gradually came around to the American point of view, but the French continued their obstructionist tactics. Although this obstruction was both exasperating and destructive of the possibilities of ultimate world peace, I often wondered what the attitudes of the American people would be if they had been twice, within the recollection of the living, invaded by a more powerful, ruthless, destroying, plundering enemy. Would we then have been willing to make sacrifices in the hope that our invaders could be brought to cooperate in building peace for mankind? However, in this case, it seemed to us Americans that the course was clear—that we must build on the one hope of supporting the new Republic of Germany. The only alternative was Carthage.

Frank M. Surface, *American Pork Production in the World War,* A. W. Shaw Company, New York: 1926.

Also, I have prepared a memoir covering this subject with further documentation.

[3] For full documentation on this subject, see *The Blockade of Germany after the Armistice, 1918-1919. Selected Documents of the Supreme Economic Council, Superior Blockade Council, American Relief Administration, and Other Wartime Organizations,* selected and edited by Suda Lorena Bane and Ralph Haswell Lutz, Stanford University Press, Stanford, Calif.: 1942.

The protracted debate and negotiations had another disagreeable aspect. The Americans who advocated the feeding of the Germans were not doing so out of any affection for the German militarists, who had been guilty of the greatest brutalities. It wounded us deeply that the French should assert that we were pro-German or would promote German interests ahead of theirs.

Before leaving to make some addresses in Italy, on January 1, 1919, the President requested a memorandum from me on the whole subject of the food blockade. The memorandum was written prior to the devastating action by the Blockade Council the day before, and therefore it is not mentioned. A few paragraphs are indicative of its tenor:

PARIS, January 1

DEAR MR. PRESIDENT:

In a broad sense, there is no longer any military or naval value attaching to the maintenance of the food blockade of enemy territory. Its retention may have political value in the right settlement of ultimate political issues, but its immediate incidence requires ... consideration. . . .

The problem of sustaining life and maintaining order in enemy territories revolves primarily around the problem of food supplies and secondarily around the gradual re-establishment of commercial life. . . .

I then sketched some of the background and the problems involved, including the need for the Germans to hand over to us their merchant ships in order to carry relief supplies, and I concluded:

A relaxation of commodity, finance, shipping, and corresponding blockades is the only measure that will protect the situation against the evils which may arise from actual hunger. Even a partial revival of the ordinary activities of life within enemy territories will tend powerfully to check rising Bolshevism and the stabilizing of governments.

It is not proposed that these measures proceed to the abandonment of [the whole] blockade prior to peace, but that certain agreed tonnage, agreed commodities for import and export; agreed avenues of credit operations and agreed channels of trade and communication must at once be established.

HERBERT HOOVER

To this statement the President added in his own handwriting:

To these conclusions I entirely agree.

W. W.

On January 10, Vance McCormick, Chairman of the American War Trade Board, arrived in Europe to sit in on blockade matters.

At the first meeting, on January 12, of the Supreme Allied Council of Supply and Relief I proposed that, subject to the Germans handing over the refugee ships, they should receive an installment of 200,000 tons of breadstuffs and 70,000 tons of fat products, with further supplies later. No action resulted and McCormick and I, supported by General Bliss, urged upon the President when he returned to Paris that these matters should receive immediate attention from himself and the Prime Ministers. The President arranged for a hearing before the Council of Ten on January 13.

At the meeting I sat in a small chair behind the President's right shoulder. Vance was behind him to the left. Allied officials likewise sat in chairs behind their Prime Ministers. In order to coach our champions in the debate, we had to poke our heads out from behind. This conducting of a synthetic debate by the bobbing of heads was a little difficult. However, the President made a strong presentation.

The minutes of the meeting state:

PRESIDENT WILSON expressed the view that any further delay in this matter might be fatal as it meant the dissolution of order and government. They were discussing an absolute and immediate necessity. So long as hunger continued to gnaw, the foundations of government would continue to crumble. Therefore, food should be supplied immediately, not only to our friends but also to those parts of the world where it was to our interest to maintain a stable government. He thought they were bound to accept the concerted counsel of a number of men who had been devoting the whole of their time and thought to this question. He trusted the French Finance Department would withdraw their objection (to the use of German gold or other securities to pay for food) as they [the Allies] were faced with the great problems of Bolshevism and the forces of dissolution which now threatened society.

The French Minister of the Treasury, Louis-Lucien Klotz, objected, arguing that German securities and gold should first go for reparations, and he indicated that the United States or Britain should make loans to the Germans with which to buy their food. As Congress had specifically prohibited any loans to enemy states, it was impossible to do this even had we been so inclined.

> The President . . . urged that, unless a solution for the immediate situation could be found, none of these debts would be paid. The want of food would lead to a crash in Germany. The great point, however, was this, that the Associated Governments have no money to pay for these supplies. Therefore Germany must pay for them, but if they were not paid for and supplied immediately there would be no Germany to pay anything.

The Council resolved that the food supplies must be sent into Germany and directed that the details of payment and transfer of their refugee merchant ships be settled immediately by conferences with the Germans.

Such conferences were held periodically during January and without results, owing to the obstructionist tactics sometimes of the British and always of the French, under one excuse or under another.

As we were getting nowhere, I sent a note to the President on February 1:

PARIS, 1 February 1919

MY DEAR MR. PRESIDENT:

Mr. McCormick will be sending to you the three resolutions which we are most anxious should be gotten through the Supreme War Council at its meeting on Monday or Tuesday. As you know, I have been advocating these points now for nearly two months and . . . and I see no hope of attaining any results except through strong intervention on your part. . . ,

... We have no justification in humanity or politics in debarring neutrals from buying all the food they wish for their own consumption now that we have . . . [sufficient] supplies. The blockade on Mediterranean countries has no purpose whatever, except to serve detailed selfish interests. All these measures impose a much larger burden on relief than would be necessary if all these people could produce and trade . . . where they may in food.

There is so much obstruction that I despair even getting it past the Supreme War Council unless world opinion is brought to bear, and I would like to have you advise me whether you do not think it is desirable for me to disclose to the press, the nature of these resolutions that you will propose, and I am sure there will be a reaction from the whole neutral world and a reaction from the United States in your support. . . .

Faithfully yours,

(Signed) Herbert Hoover

The President's reply was:

Paris, 3 February 1919

My Dear Mr. Hoover:

I dare say it would be serviceable to discuss these matters with the press as you suggest, but how can you when the French press is so carefully censored by the Government that everything is excluded which they do not wish to have published. You could probably get it in the English and the American papers but could you get publicity for it anywhere else?

Cordially and faithfully yours,

Woodrow Wilson

The President asked for a further memorandum on the three resolutions McCormick and I had proposed. On February 4, with McCormick's approval, again I went over the same ground. A few paragraphs from my letter are indicative:

Dear Mr. President:

. . . There is no right in the law of God or man that we should longer continue to starve neutrals. . . . That is the object of the first part of the . . . resolution.

. . . The French, by obstruction of every financial measure that we can propose . . . in the attempt to compel us to loan money to Germany for this purpose, have defeated every step so far for getting them the food which we have been promising for three months. The object of the second part of the . . . resolution . . . is to . . . find some channel by which the Germans can help themselves by trade with neutrals and South America. . . .

The object of the third resolution is to allow the people bordering on the Mediterranean to get into production and trade with all their might and by so doing not only revive their commercial life but also to a large degree supply themselves with food and other commodities and thus take a large part of the burden of relief from the back of our government.

There is no possibility that with all the restrictions on trade taken off . . . the old Empire of Austria could ever resurrect any military importance. At the present time, we are actually furnishing food to points in old Austria at the expense of governments [which] could be taken care of by private individuals if they could revive their foreign credits. . . .

I have worked consistently since arriving in Europe on the 25th day of November to secure these objects and I have to confess that although they have been accepted in principle in first one department and one government after another, they are constantly defeated by one bureaucratic and special self-interest after another . . . and I can assure you that the blockade against neutrals and the Southeast is being used today for purely economic ends. . . .

I realize that there is still some political importance in maintaining the blockade against Germany within certain limits, but it does not apply to the rest of Europe. I can see no hope of securing the removal of these restrictions except by a direct and strong intervention through yourself and mandatory orders given by the Supreme War Council.

. . . I am confident that no action is possible except of a mandatory character from the top.

Faithfully yours,

HERBERT HOOVER

Meetings of Allied delegates with the German Delegation were held at Spa Belgium, on February 6, 7, and 8, but they served only as backdrops for further obstruction.

McCormick's Diary for February 11 contains the following entry:

. . . Long, windy meeting afterwards on blockade relaxation. French seem to block every effort in this direction. . . .

Inasmuch as a recitation of the Conference arguments, resolutions, counterresolutions, speeches and reports would take volumes, I can better depict this battle by again quoting from McCormick's Diary:

February 17

... Attended first meeting Supreme Economic Council at Ministry of Commerce. Clémentel presided. Klotz, Loucheur for France, Lord Robert Cecil, Sir John Beale for Great Britain, Crespi and Ciesa for Italy, Hoover, Norman Davis and self for the United States. ... Discussed relaxation of blockade; did not get anywhere. Crespi said would not agree to any relaxation unless Great Britain or United States helped finance food for his distressed country. Meeting getting hot over Crespi's statements so Lord Robert adjourned meeting. Lord Robert very angry at Crespi's hold up game. ...

At a meeting on March 1, Mr. McCormick recorded:

Meeting of Supreme Economic Council at Minister of Commerce office. Trying to put through financial plan for permitting Germany to buy food. French blocked every plan. England and America dread consequences, as we seem living on a volcano. Two hundred million people not producing in the world and many hungry. ...

There were still more conferences, and finally, in early March, the Germans refused to turn over their useful merchant ships (about 2,700,000 tons including the Austrians', many in neutral ports) unless they had a guaranteed monthly supply of food until their next harvest. They were prepared to pay for it from their own gold reserve (totalling about $600,000,000). They stated that if they were to make a new agreement of some kind at the end of every month or starve, they might as well have it over with and let the Allies face the consequences.

The state of affairs at this time is indicated by an entry in McCormick's Diary on March 5:

... French still blocking food deliveries to Germany. Situation there alarming. Cables all show state of revolution. Americans in Germany being attacked. My opinion we are living on top of a volcano; if relief not immediate, bound to have trouble and will affect France. English fully alive to situation and fighting hard with us to better conditions. French agree but don't help and really hinder whenever possible.

In the meantime I settled upon a plan with Lord Robert Cecil, which we decided to present to the Council of Ten on March 8. I do not cumber this account with its long text, as its essential features developed in the subsequent debate. However, the plan included German payment for food with hire of their ships, acceptable commodities or gold; the immediate transfer of their merchant ships and an undertaking that if they kept the Armistice Agreements they would be assured a stipulated monthly supply of food, as far as supplies permitted, until the following August.

On the evening of March 7, Prime Minister Lloyd George asked me to see him to discuss the situation. With him was General Plumer, Commander of the British Occupation Army in Germany. General Plumer was in a state of emotion rare for a British soldier. He announced to me in tragic tones that Germany must have food. That was no news to me. What he said later on, however, was helpful. He said that the rank and file of his army were sick and discontented and wanted to go home because they just could not stand the sight of hordes of skinny and bloated children pawing over the offal from British cantonments. His soldiers were actually depriving themselves to feed these kids. Plumer added that the country was going Bolshevist. I supported all his arguments.

After Plumer left, Lloyd George demanded to know why I did not send in food. He said that I had been appointed to that job and that the Council had authorized it on January 13. Not often do I lose my temper. But this was too much. I was also weary from constant obstructionism by day and constant work by night. In my explosion I reviewed the British lack of cooperation since I had arrived in Europe, the ruin which would have come to our farmers by the repudiation of contracts and the reimposition of the blockade on December 31. I stated that we had in consequence been forced to store hundreds of thousands of tons of food in neutral ports, much of it highly perishable. I pointed out that the British Navy, since the Armistice, had viciously prevented the Germans from fishing in the Baltic, which had been one of their food sources all during the war. I recited a list of cities in Germany which had already gone Communist (Spartacist). I handed him a telegram from our staff representative stating that machine guns were chattering in Berlin streets at that very moment. I added a few points about starving women and children after a nation had surrendered in order to get food for them, and added that no honest man could read the promises of the Armistice without a blush. I said that the Germans had not had a ton of food in the four months since that promise. I recalled that during these months I had been warning of the steady advance of the Communists among a hungry people and of the weakening of the new German representative government. I expressed my opinion that the Allies were on the point of having nothing better to make peace out of in Germany than they had in Communist Russia.

Lloyd George was a humane and overworked man. He had been helpful to me on many vital occasions over the previous four years. I immediately regretted this outbreak, apologized for it and was about to leave when, to my surprise, he mildly inquired if I would deliver "parts of that speech" to the Council of Ten. I said that I would be delighted to do so, but that it would carry much more weight if it came from him. He asked if I would give him some notes on what had happened and what I proposed, which I did on the spot. When I returned to my room and put on paper what I had said, I promptly came to the conclusion that most of my explosion must be eliminated and so I prepared some notes in softer terms for the next day.

President Wilson was then in the United States, and thus not able to attend this March 8 meeting of the Council. The Americans were represented by Secretary Lansing, Colonel House, General Bliss, Messrs. McCormick, Baruch, Davis, Robinson and myself. The British were represented by Prime Minister Lloyd George, Lord Robert Cecil, J. M. Keynes and others. The French were represented by Premier Clemenceau, Foreign Minister Pichon, Finance Minister Klotz, Commerce Minister Clémentel, Marshal Foch and others. The Italians were represented by Baron Sonnino, Minister of Food Crespi, and others.

This meeting was a real occasion. The Big Three and Secretary Lansing sat in judgment on higher seats at the end of the room, with the different national groups scattered below. Since we Americans were regarded as fanatics in our opposition to most parts of the blockade, McCormick and I, prior to the meeting, had arranged for Lord Robert Cecil to present the ideas in the memorandum to which Cecil and I had agreed.

A long and heated debate ensued among the British, French and Italians. The published minutes are wholly inadequate, no doubt because the shift of languages and rapid-fire questions and reply confused the stenographers, but enough was recorded to suggest what took place.

The French Minister of Finance, Klotz, objected to some immaterial matters, but finally again disclosed his real thesis. The French would not lift the blockade unless somebody would furnish Germany food on credit. He charged the British with desertion and charged both the Americans and the British with trying to get the German gold and thus deprive France of her just reparations.

Clémentel, for the French, objected to any continued assurance of food for the Germans until the next harvest. He wanted a terminable, monthly ration and a limit on the amount of gold which could be used by the Germans to pay for food.

The minutes state that:

MARSHALL FOCH held that Clause 3 [of my memorandum] created a somewhat dangerous situation, since the Allies thereby bound themselves to supply food to the Germans until September 1st, unless, as stated in Clause 8, hostilities were renewed. Consequently, that Clause had the effect of disarming the Allies, who would be obliged to start hostilities should any difference arise with Germany, since, as long as the Clause remained, pressure could not be exerted by the fear of withholding food.

Mr. LANSING enquired what was the connection between the subject under consideration and the military situation.

M. CLEMENCEAU replied that at the present moment the Allies possessed a method of applying pressure to Germany, without appeal to arms, but if the Clause suggested were accepted, the only method of exerting pressure would be the renewal of hostilities.

I entered the debate at this point. The minutes give a wholly garbled account of my statement.

The gist of what I said was unemotional. I reviewed my previous dealings with Allied agencies concerning the German blockade and then continued from the notes I had prepared as follows:

The cold facts of the situation are: The Germans had been promised food at the Armistice; her women and children were starving when she surrendered; no food had been furnished her in the four months of winter; many of the German ships were in neutral ports and can not be obtained without her cooperation; the amount of gold or securities required were not one per cent of the sums [to be] levied in the reparations; the United States Congress, in its legislation authorizing loans and gifts to the Allies and liberated countries to supply them with food, had been adamant against any loans or credits to the former enemies; that we [Americans] had already supplied the Allied and liberated states with loans and credits to buy food amounting to ten times the amounts involved in the German transactions; that we could scarcely be charged with a lack of generosity; and finally that the political and social situation in Germany was such that if continued, the peace-making efforts of the Allies would be washed up within another sixty days.

Lloyd George provided the emotional spark in his answer to the Klotz, Clémentel and Foch arguments. The minutes record that he said:

> . . . the Preliminary Terms of Peace would shortly be presented to Germany, and if Germany refused to accept those terms, that would put an end to the armistice. But, when that happened, the Allies would be quite entitled to decide not to advance into Germany and to exert the necessary pressure by the stoppage of food supplies. Consequently, the only two contingencies when food pressure might be required, had been duly provided for. The Conference was therefore not parting with any potent weapon. On the other hand, he wished to urge with all his might that steps should at once be taken to revictual Germany. The honour of the Allies was involved. Under the terms of the armistice the Allies did imply that they meant to let food into Germany. The Germans had accepted our armistice conditions, which were sufficiently severe, and they had complied with the majority of those conditions. But so far, not a single ton of food had been sent into Germany. . . . [Their] fishing fleet had even been prevented from going out to catch a few herrings. The Allies were now on top, but the memories of starvation might one day turn against them. The Germans were being allowed to starve whilst at the same time hundreds of thousands of tons of food were lying at Rotterdam, waiting to be taken up the waterways into Germany: These incidents constituted far more formidable weapons for use against the Allies than any of the armaments it was sought to limit. The Allies were sowing hatred for the future: They were piling up agony, not for the Germans, but for themselves. The British troops were indignant about our refusal to revictual Germany. General Plumer had said

that he could not be responsible for his troops if children were
allowed to wander about the streets, half starving. The British
soldiers would not stand that, they were beginning to make com-
plaints, and the most urgent demands were being received from
them. Furthermore, British Officers who had been in Germany
said that Bolshevism was being created, and the determining factor
was going to be food. As long as the people were starving they
would listen to the argument of the Spartacists, and the Allies by
their action were simply encouraging elements of disruption and
anarchism. It was like stirring up an influenza puddle, just next
door to one's self. The condition of Russia was well known, and
it might be possible to look on at a muddle which had there been
created. But, now, if Germany went, and Spain: who would feel
safe? As long as order was maintained in Germany, a breakwater
would exist between the countries of the Allies and the waters of
Revolution beyond. But once . . . [the] breakwater was swept away,
he could not speak for France, but trembled for his own country. The
situation was particularly serious in Munich. Bavaria, which once
had been thought to represent the most solid and conservative part
of Germany, had already gone. He was there that afternoon to
reinforce the appeal which had come to him from the men who
had helped the Allies to conquer the Germans, the soldiers, who
said that they refused to continue to occupy a territory in order
to maintain the population in a state of starvation. Meanwhile the
Conference continued to haggle. Six weeks ago the same arguments
about gold and foreign securities had been raised, and it had then
been decided that Germany should be given food. He begged the
Conference to reaffirm that decision in the most unequivocal terms,
[that] unless this people were fed, if as a result of a process of starvation enforced by the Allies, the people of Germany were allowed to
run riot, a state of revolution among the working classes of all
countries would ensue with which it would be impossible to cope.

Clemenceau replied to Lloyd George, the essential paragraphs
in the minutes being:

> . . . he had already said, he was ready to give the food, whether
> promised or not. On the other hand, his information tended to
> show that the Germans were using Bolshevism as a bogey with
> which to frighten the Allies. If the Germans were starving, as
> General Plumer and others said they were, why did they continue
> to refuse to surrender their [merchant] fleet? The Germans certainly
> did not act as if they were in a hurry, and it was curious that a

people who was said to be so hard up for food should appear to be in no hurry to assist in obtaining it by giving up their ships. No doubt very pitiable reports were being received from certain parts of Germany in regard to food conditions; but those reports did not apparently apply to all parts of Germany. . . . In his opinion, the Germans were simply trying to see how far they could go; they were simply attempting to blackmail the Allies. To yield to-day would simply mean constant yielding in the future. . . .

In his opinion Marshal Foch should be instructed to meet the German Peace Delegates at Spa, and to tell them that the Allied and Associated Powers refused to argue or to discuss matters concerning the accepted clauses of the armistice. The Germans had promised to surrender their mercantile fleet, and immediate compliance must be demanded. The Germans could at the same time be told that food would be sent, but the conditions of Article 8 of the Armistice of 16th January, 1919, must in the first place be fulfilled. It was essential that no signs of weakness should be displayed on the eve of the settlement of other large territorial, military and economic questions. The Germans must not be given any advantage to-day that might give them the impression that the Allied Powers could be intimidated and made to yield. Therefore, in his opinion Germany should be asked point blank: "Are you or are you not going to execute the conditions set forth in Clause 8 of the Armistice?" If his proposal were accepted, the position of the Great Powers would be extremely strong and promises to supply food could then safely be made.

Marshal Foch had made an objection which he (M. Clemenceau) considered to be very strong, but a slight amendment of the text would easily put that matter right. In regard to the manner of payment, he would be prepared to waive his objection to the ear-marking of gold for the purpose, provided he knew that the Germans would work for their food. This was not an unreasonable request, and it would be found to be in agreement with the teachings of Christianity. In conclusion, he could not too strongly urge his view that the Germans should be made thoroughly to understand that the Allies would allow no nonsense in regard to the minute observance of the terms of the clauses of the Armistice. As soon as the Germans recognized this fact, he felt sure his colleagues, M. Loucheur, M. Klotz and M. Clémentel, who were ever ready to be guided by feelings of humanity, would easily arrive at an agreement in regard to the supply of food to Germany, and the payment therefor.

The discussion turned onto the French proposals, which would weaken the plan. Lloyd George, becoming annoyed, said to Klotz:

> ... on January 13th exactly the same speeches had been made by M. Klotz and he had then been overruled by the Supreme War Council. M. Klotz should ... submit to the decisions then given by the Supreme War Council.
>
> Nothing had, however, been done during those two months, and now the question had been brought up for discussion with all the old arguments. He would not have raised the matter, but for the fact that during the past two months, in spite of the decision reached by the Supreme War Council in January last, obstacles had continually been put in [Mr. Hoover's] way, with the result that nothing had been done. He appealed to M. Clemenceau to put a stop to these obstructive tactics; *otherwise M. Klotz would rank with Lenin and Trotsky among those who had spread Bolshevism in Europe.*

Colonel House intervened, saying:

> ... that it always made him unhappy to take sides against France. But the American Delegates had told him that they had gone to the utmost limits to meet the wishes of the French and unless Clause 4 were accepted practically as it stood, it would have no value.
>
> M. CLEMENCEAU exclaimed that his country had been ruined and ravaged; towns had been destroyed; over two million men had lost their lives; mines had been rendered unworkable; and yet what guarantees had France that anything would be received in payment for all this destruction? She merely possessed a few pieces of gold, a few securities, which it was now proposed to take away in order to pay those who would supply food to Germany; and that food would certainly not come from France. In a word, he was being asked to betray his country and that he refused to do.

Finally the tempers of the occasion abated and an agreement was reached based upon the memorandum proposed to Lord Robert Cecil by myself. The meeting with the Germans was arranged for March 13.

THE BRUSSELS MEETING OF MARCH 13–14

The meeting with the Germans at Brussels took place on March 13–14. A typical British admiral, Sir Rosslyn Wemyss, presided. He was a tall, dignified and determined man. The American Delegation comprised five members, with myself as Chairman. Henry Robinson represented the Shipping Board, Thomas Lamont the Treasury, Hugh Gibson the State Department, and the fifth was Lewis Strauss, my secretary at that time. The British had twelve delegates headed by Admiral Wemyss. The French had nine delegates headed by a general appointed by General Foch. The Italians had three delegates. The Belgians had two delegates—Emile Francqui and an associate. The Germans sent fourteen delegates headed by Edler von Braun, with whom I had dealt during the Belgian Relief and whom I had found to be a straightforward man. The twenty-three Allied Delegates sat on one side of a long table, the fourteen Germans on the other.

Emile Francqui, my colleague in Belgian Relief, and I sat together. He was visibly moved with satisfaction upon hearing the very Germans of whom we had so often asked concessions for the Belgians now on the other side of the table, asking us for food. In after years he developed this incident into a great and thrilling conversational drama.

The agreements with the Germans were long and technical. They provided for an assurance of 300,000 tons of cereals and 70,000 tons of fat monthly if the world supplies permitted, payment to be in acceptable foreign securities and via the hire of the German ships. The Germans were to be permitted to export certain commodities, and any balance needed to pay for food was to be gold, and was to be deposited in the National Bank of Belgium at my disposal as the Director General of Relief, except those payments for food furnished by the British. All available ships were to be handed over as rapidly as physically possible.

I gleaned some humor out of persuading the Admiral to agree that the Germans might keep their fishing boats and fish in the Baltic. However, he could not stand the idea of the Germans fishing in the North Sea. Although the German fleet had now been scuttled and lay at the bottom of the sea, he was loath to allow the Germans any freedom of the seas. We compromised by letting the Germans buy North Sea fish from the neutrals without including it as a reduction from the monthly food program.

The delays in opening this crack in the food blockade as promised in the Armistice had many terrible consequences. A host of innocent people had died of starvation. Had the Allies stuck to the original decision of December 24 on our proposal to relax the blockade by opening trade between the neutrals and Germany, much food would have flowed into Germany and less gold would have been required. When the crack was opened, the crisis in Germany was such that little payment could be made in trade, and practically the whole sum was paid in gold. The French received fewer reparations than would have otherwise been the case.

But there was a loss to the Allies far greater than this. The German people could not forget the continuation of the food blockade—in negation of the promise of the Armistice—and they used it to poison the minds of the peoples of the world.

We moved some 200,000 tons of food into Germany in ten days, and the dangers of Communist revolution considerably abated. My organization and our associates, the British and neutrals, provided a total of more than 1,270,000 tons of food and medical supplies for Germany, and we handled over $325,000,000 of German gold.[4]

When the door for food to Germany opened, I found hatred still so aflame in some sectors of the British, French and American press that, on March 21, I issued the following statement:

WHY WE ARE FEEDING GERMANY

From the point of view of my Western upbringing, I would say at once, because we do not kick a man in the stomach after we have licked him.

From the point of view of an economist, I would say that it is because there are seventy millions of people who must either produce or die, that their production is essential to the world's future and that they cannot produce unless they are fed.

From the point of view of a governor, I would say it is because famine breeds anarchy, anarchy is infectious, the infection of such a cesspool will jeopardize France and Britain, will yet spread to the United States.

From the point of view of a peace negotiator, it is because we must maintain order and stable government in Germany if we would have someone with whom to sign peace.

From the point of view of a reconstructionist I would say that unless the German people can have food, can maintain order and

---

[4] Some of the gold was paid in French coins which the French had paid to the Germans in the indemnity exacted by them after the Franco-Prussian War fifty years before.

stable government and get back to production, there is no hope of their paying the damages they owe to the world.

From the point of view of a humanitarian, I would say that we have not been fighting women and children and we are not beginning now.

From the point of view of our Secretary of War, I would say that I wish to return the American soldiers home and that it is a good bargain to give food for [the use of] passenger steamers on which our boys may arrive home four months earlier than will otherwise be the case.

From the point of view of the American Treasury, I would also say that this is a good bargain, because it saves the United States enormous expenditures in Europe in the support of idle men [in our Army] and allows these men to return to productivity in the United States.

From the point of view of a negotiator of the Armistice, I would say that we are in honor bound to fulfill the implied terms of the Armistice that Germany shall have food.

Let us not befog our minds with the idea that we are feeding Germany out of charity. She is paying for her food. All that we have done for Germany is to lift the blockade to a degree that allows her to import her food from any market that she wishes and in the initial [stages] . . . we are allowing her to purchase emergency supplies from [our] stocks in Europe, at full prices.

Taking it by and large, our face is forward, not backward on history. We and our children must live with these seventy million Germans. No matter how deeply we may feel at the present moment, our vision must stretch over the next hundred years and we must write now into history such acts as will stand creditably in the minds of our grandchildren.

The "crack" opened in the blockade, by which a monthly ration of food was allowed into Germany, was by no means the end of the battle of the blockade.

Unemployment was enormously widespread over all Central and Eastern Europe. President Wilson and all his advisers had urged earnestly, from the day we arrived in Europe, that reconstruction and peace required some relaxation of the ban on imports of raw materials and the export of manufactured goods as the road to stability upon which peace could be built.

The adamant determination of the Allies that they must hold

on to the blockade weapon to force compliance with political demands, until peace was signed, reduced our American efforts concerning the blockade to opening "cracks" for some country or for some commodity.

The Allies had one justification for their attitudes which Americans respected. They contended that they had a right to recover their export markets and their employment in advance of the former enemy countries. The record shows that Americans respected this contention, and that the "cracks" were adjusted to it.

There were endless meetings of the Superior Blockade Council, the Supreme Economic Council and the inter-Allied committees where these matters were discussed, and there were endless appeals to President Wilson for help in the Council of Ten or the Big Four.

It is not my purpose here to dip deeply into this record. Mr. McCormick's Diary illuminates the battle, and a few quotations will suffice.

Among others, the blockade was one of the terrible handicaps to the development of freedom and economic life of the four newly liberated Baltic States.

At a meeting on March 15, McCormick pressed for relief for these little countries. The entry in his Diary of that date reveals:

> ... Italy still misbehaving—trying to block everything until she gets her own needs cared for—also insisting upon carrying out of London treaty by which she was brought to enter the war. . . . Italy apparently trying to break up creation of Jugo-Slavia. . . . U.S. tried to free Poland, Esthonia, Lettland and Lithuania from further blockade restrictions owing to importance of resuming normal life to discourage Bolshevism. Great Britain withheld approval. . . . Afraid some trade advantage hoped for by Great Britain. Can see no other reason. . . .

Another entry in the Diary on March 19, in respect to the Baltic States, reports:

> Meeting of Blockade Council. Still struggling to get relaxation for Poland and Baltic provinces of old Russia. British still blocking —trade reasons—pretending military. . . .

The minutes of the Superior Blockade Council of March 20 record that it was agreed "that reasonable quantities of commodities should be permitted to reach Estonia," and recommended it "to the Supreme Economic Council for appropriate action."

The Supreme Economic Council, at a meeting on March 24, recommended this to the Council of Ten. On March 28 they recommended it to the Big Four. The next day the resolution was revised to include Latvia and Lithuania, and started all over again. On April 7 the Supreme Economic Council again agreed. But on April 28 the Council of Ten suspended all trade with these Baltic States "because of recent political developments."

On June 4 the Supreme Economic Council determined:

> . . . That for the present . . . food shipments could be made to Latvia and Lithuania, although other commodities could not, for the present, be shipped to these countries.

This was one of our few gleams of humor as we had been supplying these states with food, medical supplies and clothing since January.

As to the blockade of the other countries, McCormick records on April 9:

> Supreme Economic Council 10:00 o'clock. . . . Had a good scrap over relaxation of blockade and difficulties of communication all over Europe choking trade and commerce, causing idleness and making Bolshevists. Think we made some progress. . . .

At a meeting of the Supreme Economic Council on April 21, a general discussion took place concerning the continuation of the blockade of commodities other than food. The discussion accurately reflected the situation five months after the Armistice. According to the minutes, I made the following statement on behalf of the American members:

> . . . It was their view then and now that the blockade, in preventing the population of Germany from returning to productivity and employment, could only stimulate social disorder and undermine the possibilities of Peace. That . . . the only hope of reparation to the Allies . . . was by the earliest possible return to productive labor. . . . The American Delegates wished to emphasize the fact that they would not be a party to any proposals which would damage the interest of France, but they felt that in adopting the principle which they had adhered to . . . they were doing France the best service of which their Government was capable
>
> Replying to the suggestions of the French Delegates . . . [delegate Hoover] felt that a review of what had been accomplished

under the relaxation of the blockade [other than food] would make
but a meagre showing due to the amount of mechanical restriction
that had been placed around every effort . . . that it was impossible
for credit and trade to revive so long as these restrictions existed;
that the total result was to draw a stream of gold out of Germany.
They further stated that it was the view of the Government of the
United States that there [could be] . . . no question of blockade
measures after peace. . . .

The French at this point blamed the delay in supplies to Germany on the Americans because it was they who would not agree
to furnish such supplies on American credit. In answer I again described our point of view.

> . . . They [the Americans] had held from the beginning that the
> only basis of food supplies should be the exchange of products, and
> that the employment involved in their production was of equal im-
> portance politically and economically with the supply itself; that
> from the American point of view the French financial proposals
> meant only a further increase in the burden of credit already as-
> sumed by the United States, . . . that in this connection they [the
> Americans] had recently prepared an estimate showing that during
> the present harvest year the United States will have supplied Europe
> with foodstuffs to the value of . . . two-and-one-half billion dollars,
> for which it will have received in payment only four hundred million
> dollars in goods or securities; that there was an absolute limit to the
> amount that can be drawn from any bank.

The French delegates, speaking on behalf of their Government
stated:

> That while fully realising the desirability of a speedy return
> to normal conditions, they were unable at the present time, in view
> of the proposed early presentation of the terms of the Preliminaries
> of Peace to the Germans at Versailles, to concur in any proposals
> which would result in a further relaxation of the Blockade restric-
> tions on Germany.

On this same day (April 21) the President handed me a memorandum from an important British official, advocating a reorganization of the Ebert Ministry in Germany to include Communist (Spartacist) members, and suggesting various devices to secure acceptance of the Treaty. The correspondence illustrates the confusions of

the times, increased by the danger from the Communist specter. The President asked for my opinion of these proposals and I gave him the following:

21 April 1919

DEAR MR. PRESIDENT:

I enclose you, herewith, memorandum on the note which you handed me today with regard to the situation in Germany. I have put it in the form of a memorandum in case you wish to hand it to your colleagues for their edification.

Faithfully yours,

HERBERT HOOVER

My memorandum analyzed the foolishness of these proposals, then added:

. . . We cannot fail to again mention what we consider is one of the absolute fundamentals to constructively handle this situation. You and all of us have proposed, fought and pleaded for the last three months that the blockade on Germany [in addition to food] should be taken off, that these people should be allowed to return to production not only to save themselves from starvation and misery but that there should be awakened in them some resolution for continued National life. The situation in Germany today is to a large degree one of complete abandonment of hope. The people have simply lain down under the threat of Bolshevism in front and the demands of the Allies behind. The people are simply in a state of moral collapse and there is no resurrection from this except through the restoration of the normal processes of economic life and hope. We have for the last month held that it is now too late to save the situation. We do think, however, that it is worth one more great effort to bring the Allied countries to realize that all the bars on exports and imports should be taken down without attempts to special national benefits; that the Germans should be given an assurance that a certain amount of ships and working capital will be left in their hands with which to re-start the National machine.

We feel also from an American point of view that the refusal of the Allies to accept these primary considerations during the last three months leaves them with the total responsibility for what is now impending.

We do not believe that the acceptance of any possible treaty is very probable under present conditions, and we feel certain that the hope of reparation is gradually being extinguished by the continued use of the noose. We do not believe the blockade was ever an effective instrument to force peace; it is effective, however, to force Bolshevism.

To this the President replied:

MY DEAR HOOVER:

Thank you warmly for your letter of yesterday enclosing your memorandum on the situation in Germany apropos of the British memorandum which I handed you. It will be very serviceable to me indeed.

Cordially and faithfully yours,

WOODROW WILSON

McCormick records on May 5:

. . . At 10:30 met with Supreme Economic Council. Had the pleasure of showing to Council how France, who has been insisting upon maintaining the blockade against Germany, has been shipping carloads of cotton and wool materials into Germany through Alsace Lorraine. I had the goods on them from our representatives in the border and it created quite a stir in the Council. . . .

The American attack on the blockade as a whole did not let up for a moment until the Peace Treaty was signed. During May and June the Supreme Economic Council met ten times. The Superior Blockade Council met thirteen times. The other inter-Allied councils, boards and commissions had hundreds of meetings. At practically every meeting the Americans, and sometimes the British, urged the relaxation of the blockade on some country or with respect to some commodity. Minor relaxations were obtained, but any comprehensive major action was either opposed or delayed by the French. The net effect was not only the stifling of production, but the steady economic degeneration of Europe.

In a later chapter I deal further with the use of the blockade to pressure the Germans to accept the Treaty terms. Despite all our efforts, the blockade per se was not removed until the ratification of the Peace Treaty by Germany on July 7, 1919.

All through these efforts we were compelled to seek President Wilson's advice and authority constantly, thereby adding further to the heavy load he bore. His concern over the blockade was profound, his prediction of its ugly results accurate. He never spared himself in his efforts to lift it.

12

WOODROW WILSON ESTABLISHES
THE LEAGUE OF NATIONS

While the burdens on the President, shown in the last three chapters, were exhausting enough for any one man, his major job was to make peace. This gigantic task had two quite separate focal points:

First was the establishment of the League of Nations to preserve lasting peace.[1]

Second was the framing of the Treaty with Germany, as distinguished from the Covenant of the League, by which the pattern of peace would be set with the other enemy states. And it was also to establish the independence or relationships and the territorial possessions around the world of forty-seven other nations.

To clarify what happened at the Peace Conference, I shall discuss these two focal points separately and I shall refer to them as the *League* and the *Treaty*.

It must be remembered that on November 4, 1918, the Allies

---

[1] Plans to preserve peace by the collective action of nations were not new in the world. During the previous 500 years there had been nine of them under various names and with various methods. Some of their methods included arbitration, judicial decision and even action by arms against an aggressor.

The first really concrete agreement among nations for collective action came at the Congress of Vienna in 1814. It started with the Holy Alliance and gradually developed into the Concert of Europe. This was not an institution but rather a practice. The Great Powers came together at critical dangers of war and generally arrived at settlements. The United States joined in two such meetings in Europe. The Concert had played a real part in keeping the world free from world-wide wars between 1814 and 1914.

accepted all of the President's "Fourteen Points and the subsequent addresses," except freedom of the seas, as the basis of peace.

There can be little doubt that the President considered the establishment of the League of Nations as his primary goal, for through this agency he was confident that mistakes and maladjustments in the Treaty could in time be solved and controversies settled.

I need not record in detail the devotion of the President to this exalted idea. He gave his first public statement in respect to it over a year before we entered the war. Former President William Howard Taft and former Secretary of State Elihu Root interested him in an association that they had formed and named the *League to Enforce Peace.*[2] On May 27, 1916, President Wilson addressed a meeting of this association in which he gave it strong support. Some of his statements were:

> . . . Our own rights as a Nation, the liberties, the privileges, and the property of our people have been profoundly affected. We are not mere disconnected lookers-on. . . . We are participants . . . in the life of the world. The interests of all nations are our own also. We are partners with the rest. What affects mankind is inevitably our affair as well as the affair of the nations of Europe and of Asia. . . .
>
> . . . Only when the great nations of the world have reached some feasible method of acting in concert when any nation or group of nations seeks to disturb those fundamental things, can we feel that civilization is at last in a way of justifying its existence. . . .
>
> . . . the nations of the world must in some way band themselves together to see that right prevails as against any sort of selfish aggression; . . . I am sure that I speak the mind and wish of the people of America when I say that the United States is willing to become a partner in any feasible association of nations formed in order to realize these objects and make them secure against violation.

---

[2] It is of interest to record that Senator Henry Cabot Lodge, subsequently the major enemy of the League, contributed the following assurance of support to the idea of this association:

"But I do not believe that when Washington warned us against entangling alliances he meant for one moment that we should not join with the other civilized nations of the world if a method could be found to diminish war and encourage peace." See *Proceedings of the First Annual National Assemblage of the League to Enforce Peace*, May 26–27, 1916, p. 165.

I need not repeat the President's urgings of such international action in five of his 38 "points," enumerated in Chapter 4. Partly as a result of his dedication to the plan, considerable amount of research and preparation of possible provisions for the Covenant of the League had already been undertaken in the United States and Britain. The Papers of Charles L. Swem, the President's Secretary, show that as early as March 23, 1918, Mr. Wilson himself drafted a constitution for the League, writing twenty paragraphs in great detail. On April 5, 1918, he wrote a letter to a friend discussing some aspects of the League. The Papers of Colonel House show that in July 1918 the President directed David Hunter Miller, an able student of foreign affairs, to join with the Colonel in development of the Covenant. And the Colonel records that in August 1918 the President rewrote these drafts.[3]

As any publication of the constantly changing drafts might lead to confusion and destructive criticism over details, the President requested there should be no disclosure of the texts. He carried a draft of his own to Europe.

In the meantime the British had been working on a draft under Lord Robert Cecil and General Jan Smuts, Prime Minister of the South African Union. When the President reached Paris, the two groups decided that the first step should be to obtain from a plenary session of the Peace Conference an acceptance of the principle of the League; that it should be an integral part of the peace treaties with the former enemies; and that a special commission should be appointed to draft the Covenant.

This major step was taken on January 25, 1919 after a particularly eloquent address by the President to the plenary session. The more important passages are:

... We have assembled for two purposes — to make the present

---

[3] The Colonel seemed to think he and Miller wrote the original draft of the Covenant. Aside from the above actions of the President prior to their assignment, the President had before him a British draft as to which, according to Swem, he wrote the British Ambassador on July 3 as follows:

MY DEAR MR. [AMBASSADOR]:

I have received with your kind note of July 3 the interim report drawn up by a committee appointed by his Majesty's Govt. to consider the question of a league of nations. I have given it a hurried examination but will take the liberty of going over it more carefully and of communicating through you at a later date if I may my deliberate comments upon it.

Pray express to your govt. when you have the opportunity my appreciation of their courtesy in letting me see this report.

settlements which have been rendered necessary by this War, and also to secure the Peace of the world not only by the present settlements but by the arrangements we shall make in this conference for its maintenance. The League of Nations seems to me to be necessary for both of these purposes. There are many complicated questions connected with the present settlements which, perhaps, cannot be successfully worked out to an ultimate issue by the decisions we shall arrive at here. I can easily conceive that many of these settlements will need subsequent reconsideration; that many of the decisions we shall make will need subsequent alteration in some degree, for if I may judge by my own study of some of these questions they are not susceptible of confident judgments at present.

It is, therefore, necessary that we should set up some machinery by which the work of this Conference should be rendered complete. ... It will not suffice to satisfy Governmental circles anywhere. It is necessary that we should satisfy the opinion of mankind. The burdens of this War have fallen in an unusual degree upon the whole population of the countries involved. ... We are bidden by these people to make a peace which will make them secure. ...

It is a solemn obligation on our part, therefore, to make permanent arrangements that justice shall be rendered and peace maintained. This is the central object of our meeting. Settlements may be temporary, but the actions of the nations in the interest of peace and justice must be permanent. We can set up permanent processes. We may not be able to set up permanent decisions. ...

In a sense, the United States is less interested in this subject than the other nations here assembled. With her great territory and her extensive sea borders, it is less likely that the United States should suffer from the attack of enemies than that many of the other nations here should suffer; and the ardor of the United States, — for it is a very deep and genuine ardor — for the Society of Nations is not an ardor springing out of fear and apprehension, but an ardor springing out of the ideals which have come to consciousness in the War. . . . Therefore, the United States would feel that her part in this war had been played in vain if there ensued upon it merely a body of European settlements. She would feel that she could not take part in guaranteeing those European settlements unless that guaranty involved the continuous superintendence of the peace of the world by the Associated Nations of the World.

Therefore, it seems to me that we must concert our best judgment in order to make this League of Nations a vital thing — not merely a formal thing, not an occasional thing, not a thing sometimes called into life to meet an exigency, but always functioning in watchful attendance upon the interest of the Nations, and that its continuity should be a vital continuity; that it should have functions that are continuing functions and that do not permit an intermission of its watchfulness and of its labor; that it should be the eye of the Nation to keep watch upon the common interest, an eye that does not slumber, an eye that is everywhere watchful and attentive.

. . . [The] representatives of the United States support this great project for a League of Nations. We regard it as the keystone of the whole program which expressed our purpose and our ideal in this war and which the Associated Nations have accepted as the basis of the settlement. . . . This is the keystone of the whole fabric, we have pledged our every purpose to it, as we have to every item of the fabric. . . . We are here to see, in short, that the very foundations of this war are swept away. . . . And nothing less than the emancipation of the world from these things will accomplish peace. . . .

I hope, Mr. Chairman, that when it is known . . . that we have adopted the principle of the League of Nations and mean to work out that principle in effective action, we shall by that single thing have lifted a great part of the load of anxiety from the hearts of men everywhere. . . . I am merely avowing this in order that you may understand why, perhaps, it fell to us, who are disengaged from the politics of this great Continent and of the Orient, to suggest that this was the keystone of the arch. . . .

The principle of creating the League and its incorporation as an integral part of the Treaty was adopted unanimously. A subcommittee of fourteen delegates was appointed to draft the Covenant. The President was chosen Chairman. The most helpful members were David Hunter Miller, Colonel House, Lord Robert Cecil and General Jan Smuts. There were successive drafts out of which the final text was gradually developed.

In one of my meetings with the President at this time in connection with the Relief and Reconstruction, he asked if I had seen a draft and if I had any suggestions regarding it. I replied that it seemed to me that the proposed machinery of the League with its

Council, Assembly and Secretariat, the right of members to bring before the League any danger to peace and the provisions for the League to examine, report, arbitrate and conciliate, develop judicial action, and denounce a nation as an aggressor was all admirable.

I added that it seemed to me that a Covenant going that far would meet the prayers of most thoughtful people. I was doubtful, however, whether an organization so revolutionary and so young could successfully carry the burdens imposed by Article X, which guaranteed the boundaries of all the signatory nations, or the provisions for economic and military sanctions in case of aggression. I mentioned that the Concert of Europe had been dominated by the Great Powers, as would be the League, and by moral and diplomatic pressures had prevented widespread wars for one hundred years without so definite an organization as that proposed for the League.

The President listened amiably and replied that the Concert of Europe had failed, its great test being this war, and that much stronger action was necessary to prevent such a disaster in the future.

Upon returning to the Crillon Hotel I made a note of this conversation and repeated it to Colonel House. He replied that the President considered Article X and the provisions for coercion to be the heart of the League. He observed also that the President was a descendant of Scottish Covenanters and a believer in the provisions for force in the Constitution of the United States as the great symbol for action.

As my own job of Relief and Reconstruction was sufficiently engrossing and arduous, and not being charged with the responsibility for formulating the Covenant, I dropped the subject—although I was not convinced.[4]

The President submitted the draft of the Covenant of the League to a plenary conference of the delegates on February 14, 1919. After reporting that the draft had been unanimously accepted by the fourteen nations represented on the subcommittee, he read

---

[4]The draft had been put in print. I received my copy from Secretary Lansing, we both having apartments at the American headquarters in the Crillon Hotel. At this time Lansing was explosive in his opposition to Article X and the coercive provisions in the Covenant.

the text. I do not give the details, as the draft was subsequently amended. But it is appropriate to repeat parts of the accompanying address by the President:

> . . . It was obvious throughout our discussions that, although there were subjects upon which there were individual differences of judgment, with regard to the method by which our objects should be obtained, there was practically at no point any serious difference of opinion or motive as to the objects which we were seeking. . . . We felt that in a way this Conference had entrusted to us the expression of one of its highest and most important purposes, to see to it that the concord of the world in the future with regard to the objects of justice should not be subject to doubt or uncertainty; that the cooperation of the great body of nations should be assured from the first in the maintenance of peace upon the terms of honor and of the strict regard for international obligation. . . . The result was reached unanimously. . . .

He then described the method of the League's organization by which an Executive Council of eight members was to be appointed —four to be permanent, representing the Great Powers, and four to be elected by the body of delegates, representing all member nations of the League—together with a permanent Secretariat. He also described the right of every member nation to invoke action in case of controversies likely to cause war; the initial action of the League to consist in investigation of the facts, arbitration and conciliation and rallying world public opinion. The President declared at one point:

> Armed force is in the background in this programme, but is is in the background, and if the moral force of the world will not suffice, the physical force of the world shall. But that is the last resort, because this is intended as a constitution of peace, not as a League of War.
>
> . . . this document . . . is not a straightjacket, but a vehicle of life. A living thing is born, and we must see to it that the clothes we put upon it do not hamper it, — a vehicle of power, but a vehicle in which power may be varied at the discretion of those who exercise it and in accordance with the changing circumstances of the time. And yet, while it is elastic, while it is general in its terms, it is definite in the one thing that we were called upon to make definite. It is a definite guarantee of peace. It is a definite guarantee

by word against aggression. It is a definite guarantee against the things which have just come near bringing the whole structure of civilization into ruin. Its purposes do not for a moment lie vague. Its purposes are declared and its powers made unmistakable.

It is not in contemplation that this should be merely a League to secure the peace of the world. It is a League which can be used for cooperation in any international matter. That is the significance of the provision introduced concerning labor . . . .[In] the picture which I see, there comes into the foreground the great body of the laboring people of the world, the men and women and children upon whom the great burden of sustaining the world must from day to day fall, whether we wish it to do so or not; people who go to bed tired and wake up without the stimulation of lively hope. These people will be drawn into the field of international consultation and help, and will be among the wards of the combined Governments of the world. . . .

. . . there is an imperative article concerning the publicity of all international agreements. Henceforth no member of the League can claim any agreement as valid which it has not registered with the Secretary General . . . and the duty is laid upon the Secretary General to publish every document of that sort at the earliest possible time. . . .

The President also spoke of the proposed mandates over the areas stripped from the German, Austrian and Turkish Empires (with which I deal more extensively in Chapter 14), and continued:

. . . this document . . . is at one and the same time, a practical document and a humane document. There is a pulse of sympathy in it. There is a compulsion of conscience throughout it. It is practical, and yet it is intended to purify, to rectify, to elevate. . . .

Many terrible things have come out of this war . . . but some very beautiful things have come out of it. Wrong has been defeated. . . . The miasma of distrust, of intrigue, is cleared away. Men are looking eye to eye and saying: 'We are brothers and have a common purpose. We did not realize it before, but now we do realize it, and this is our Covenant of fraternity and of friendship.'

The draft had been prepared under great pressure of time and, despite the President's persuasive and glowing words, some of the provisions brought forth some criticism from the members of the Senate and some of the delegates to the Conference.

The day after its acceptance by the plenary session the Presi-

dent left for the United States to attend to executive business arising out of the closing session of Congress and to explain the League
Covenant to the American public and to the Senate Foreign Relations Committee.

He arrived in Washington on February 25 and two days later
gave a dinner at the White House for the members of the Senate
Foreign Relations Committee and the House Foreign Affairs Com-
mitte. All but three of the thirty-seven members were present. No
secrecy was imposed and no record kept, except that the questions
asked of the President and his replies were reported in the press.

Secretary of Agriculture Houston gives the following account
of the meeting:

> A number of the Republican senators, not including Lodge,
> who refused to state his objections, pointed out what they regarded
> as defects, including the omission of express recognition of the
> Monroe Doctrine, the failure to provide specifically that the
> League should not act on domestic matters, that there was no ex-
> pressed statement of the right of a nation to withdraw, and that
> the right of Congress to determine peace and war was not suffi-
> ciently safeguarded. The President listened patiently to these ex-
> pressions and gave assurance that their views would be met.

On March 4, 1919, immediately following this meeting, Senator Lodge offered a resolution in the Senate signed by thirty-seven
Senators. The essential sentences of this resolution are:

> The Constitution of the League of Nations in the form proposed
> to the Peace Conference should not be accepted by the United
> States. . . .
> That the negotiations on the part of the United States should
> immediately be directed to the utmost expedition of the urgent
> business of negotiating peace terms with Germany . . . and that
> the proposal for a League of Nations should be then taken up for
> careful consideration.

There was no consideration of the resolution by the Senate,
now about to adjourn, and the document became generally known
as the "Round Robin." Of the thirty-seven Senators who signed it,
all were Republicans, but fourteen Republican members of the
Senate did not sign.

There was a great deal of bitterness among some of these Senators, aside from the chronic attitude of Lodge. Many had supported the President during the war and were still smarting from his partisan statement in the Congressional campaign made four months previously, and from his failure to give substantial representation to the Republicans in the American delegation at Paris.

Nevertheless, a number of the Republican Senators who signed the Round Robin favored the Covenant subject to some changes. Some of the changes they wanted were mentioned in a letter from Democratic Senator Hitchcock to the President:

March 4, 1919

MY DEAR MR. PRESIDENT:

A number of republican Senators who signed Lodge's manifesto on the league of nations constitution will, in my opinion, vote for it nevertheless if it is a part of the peace treaty. A still larger number will give it support if certain amendments are made. The following I would mention as likely to influence votes in the order given:

First, a reservation to each high contracting party of its exclusive control over domestic subjects.

Second, a reservation of the Monroe doctrine.

Third, some provision by which a member of the league can, on proper notice, withdraw from membership.

Fourth, the settlement of the ambiguity in Article 15.

Fifth, the insertion on the next to the last line of first paragraph of Article 8, after the word "adopted," of the words "by the several governments."

Sixth, the definite assurance that it is optional with a nation to accept or reject the burdens of a mandatory.

I wish you a safe journey.

Yours truly,

G. M. HITCHCOCK

While the President was in Washington, his American staff in Paris, under Secretary Lansing, Colonel House and General Bliss, had been working on the Treaty. A storm blew up from a report that they and the Allies had engaged in a "conspiracy" to divorce the Covenant from the Treaty with Germany. This was probably based on rumors which freely flowed from the secrecy of the negotiations. But the President was misled by someone and was obviously disturbed.

On March 4, the day before he sailed again for Europe, he made a vigorous address supporting the League at a meeting in New York presided over by former President Taft. It included the following passage:

> ... and when that treaty comes back, gentlemen, on this side you will find the covenant not only in it, but so many threads of the treaty tied to the covenant that you cannot dissect the covenant from the treaty without destroying the whole vital structure. The structure of peace will not be vital without the League of Nations, and no man is going to bring back a cadaver with him.

When the President returned to Paris on March 14 somebody fed him with further accounts of the "conspiracy" to separate the Covenant from the German Treaty, along with accusations against Colonel House. According to Mrs. Wilson, the President, in a good deal of anger, issued a further statement to the press, insisting upon the inclusion of the Covenant in the Treaty with Germany. As a matter of fact, Colonel House and Secretary Lansing had been directing the American delegation and the Conference toward the preparation of a preliminary treaty, a project agreed upon with the President prior to his departure for home. These proceedings are discussed in a later chapter.

I can myself offer evidence that House was not engaged in any such "conspiracy." Daily during the President's absence it was necessary for me to have constant contact with the Colonel over my Relief and Reconstruction matters, especially the blockade questions as to which a major action was taken by the Council of Ten, as shown in Chapter 11. My contacts with the Colonel were increased by the fact that my apartment in the American headquarters at the Crillon Hotel was not far from his. We often talked of the progress of the treaty making and House had told me that he was opposed to separating the Covenant from the Treaty.[5]

Secretary Lansing, however, told me that he thought separation of the Covenant from the Treaty might help ratification; that

---

[5] This "plot" received its major airing in the publications of Ray Stannard Baker, the President's press chief in Paris. As the charges persisted, Lord Balfour, at House's request, sent him a memorandum on July 17, 1922, dealing with Baker's statements in great detail, and destroying every one of the allegations. It was not made public until 1927. See Charles Seymour, *The Intimate Papers of Colonel House*, vol IV, pp. 364–365. Houghton Mifflin Company, New York: 1928.

the opposition to the Treaty, as distinguished from the Covenant, would arise from the Americans of German, Hungarian, Irish, Bulgarian and possibly Italian descent, whereas they would not be opposed to the League if the two were separated. Be this as it may, there was no "conspiracy."

After the President's return to Paris, he and his colleagues continued to work on the Covenant. There were sessions of the League Subcommittee on March 22, 24 and 26. In these meetings Mr. Wilson sought substantial amendments to the Covenant to meet Senate demands. Also, he was showered by Messrs. Taft, Root and others with suggestions for proposed amendments, many of them similar to those outlined by Senator Hitchcock. They were all seeking a document that might better satisfy the Senate and their own views. However, none of the amendments that were adopted reached the heart of the opposition—which was Article X and the coercive provisions. The revised Covenant was agreed upon by the Conference Subcommittee on April 12.

The battle to secure Allied adoption of the Subcommittee's report, however, was by no means over. It was only by a series of compromises of many of the great principles enumerated in his "basis of peace" that the President got approval of the revised Covenant.

After these compromises the Covenant was completed and issued to the public on April 27. It was approved by a plenary session of the Conference on April 28. But we shall soon see that Woodrow Wilson had paid a high price for it.

13

WOODROW WILSON'S ORDEAL OF
SECRET NEGOTIATIONS

In the sixty days of the President's first visit to Europe, he had received stupendous acclaim from the European people. He had established the major principles of the League and had secured agreement for its inclusion in the Treaty with Germany by the unanimous vote of the Conference. He had formed the organization of Relief and Reconstruction, under American direction and on a nonpolitical basis, against the solid opposition of the Allies. He had defined American opposition to the tight blockade on Europe, with its economic degeneration, and had paved the way for some relaxation of it as to food. With the esteem of all Europe and warm good wishes for his return, it seemed at the time of his departure for New York that he had only to come back for a few weeks to this friendly atmosphere and complete a few remaining items to reach his final triumph.

One suggestion of the dissension to come marred the picture. Mrs. Wilson states that, before he left for the United States on February 14, Mr. Wilson had considered asking for Secretary of State Lansing's resignation because of his lack of enthusiasm for the League. He did not do so but appointed Colonel House as the effective head of the American Delegation.

But while the President was in Washington, his troubles began. There were the Senate demands for amendments to the Covenant. His confidence in his staff at Paris was upset by the false report of a "conspiracy" to separate the Covenant from the Treaty.

Even more disturbing, during his absence from Paris, the Allied Prime Ministers began to develop new attitudes about which the American Delegation in Paris kept him informed. By cable he was told of the French demands for the creation of an independent Republic of the Rhineland, their demands for Syria, the British demand for most of the other Arab States, and the Italian demands for all the possessions promised in the secret Pact of London.

It is desirable to record in some detail what actually was happening in Paris while the President was in the United States.

By a resolution in the Council of Ten on February 12, 1919, two days before the President's departure, it had been agreed by the President, Lloyd George, Clemenceau and Orlando that there should be a preliminary treaty with the Germans. The resolution was specific on the military terms, saying:[1]

> . . . Detailed and final naval, military, and air conditions of the preliminaries of peace shall be drawn up at once by a Committee to be presided over by Marshall Foch and submitted for the approval of the Supreme War Council; these, when approved, will be presented for signature to the Germans, and the Germans shall be at once informed that this is the policy of the Associated Governments.

The work of the Council was slowed down by an attempt by a Communist on February 19 to assassinate Premier Clemenceau. He was grievously wounded. Also Prime Minister Lloyd George had left Paris to spend some time in London on British domestic problems.

On February 22 Mr. Balfour, the British representative, introduced a resolution calling for the setting up of subcommittees to formulate drafts upon the subjects to be incorporated in it. The minutes of this meeting quote Colonel House as saying:[2]

> Mr. House said he was very glad to see that the Conference intended to bring about as soon as possible a Preliminary Peace . . . He had always felt that delay could only be favourable to Germany, and the longer the signing of Peace were postponed, the more chance would there be of circumstances becoming less favourable to the Allies. In regard to the two proposals now before the Con-

---

[1]United States Department of State, *Papers Relating to the Foreign Relations of the United States,* [The Paris Peace Conference, 1919], vol. III, United States Government Printing Office, Washington: 1943, p. 1005.
[2]*Ibid.,* vol. IV, p. 87.

ference, very severe military terms would have to be imposed on the Germans. And, he thought, the Germans would be more inclined to accept those conditions if, at the same time, the whole Peace Terms were made known to them. . . .

The minutes show a great deal of desultory argument, and in the end subcommittees were instructed to bring in draft provisions by March 8 for consideration by the Council. These drafts were to cover the questions of reduction of enemy forces to a peace basis; to delineate the boundaries of enemy and liberated states; to make disposition of certain colonies and possessions; to determine the total of reparations and the time in which they were to be paid; and to agree on economic controls over Germany. As there was already a committee on the League and a preliminary draft covenant, this subject was not discussed.

When the drafts for the preliminary peace were presented, Premier Clemenceau decided that any adoption of them must be deferred until President Wilson's return.

While returning to Europe on the *George Washington* the President anticipated what he would meet on arrival and formulated some ideas of what he would do about it. The Swem Papers contain his replies to questions from his associates aboard the ship. Swem was addicted to writing shorthand notes and quotes the President as saying:

"I have just had a cable from Colonel House. Lloyd George and Clemenceau held a meeting the other day in London at which House was not able to be present . . . but I gather that these men have agreed on a definite programme. Apparently they are determined to get everything out of Germany they can, now that she is helpless. They are evidently planning to take what they can get frankly as a matter of spoils, regardless of either the ethics or the practical aspect of the proceeding. They have not attempted to determine among themselves what they think they are entitled to or what Germany may be able to pay, but they favor the naming of a commission to fix exactly what Germany has got today and the appointment of another commission to apportion this among the Allied Governments. Now, we are absolutely opposed to any such plan. A statement that I once made that this should be a 'peace without victory' I believe holds as strongly today in principle as it ever did. Because it is impossible in this day to make a peace based upon indemnities; it must be a peace of justice to the defeated nations or it will be fatal to all the nations in the end.

"If they insist upon this sort of programme, I shall be compelled to withdraw my commissioners and return home and in due course take up the details of a separate peace. But, of course, I don't believe that that will come to pass. I think that once we get together, they will learn that the American delegates have not come to bargain, but will stand firmly by the principles that we have set forth; and once they learn that that is our purpose I believe we shall come to an early agreement."

How did he expect M. Clemenceau to "line up" with him on the general issues of the peace, he was asked.

"I really do not know," he replied. "I am told that Clemenceau once said that 'General Pershing is the stubbornest man I know, and I am saying that knowing Mr. Wilson, the President of the United States.' But I think we shall get along very well. I expect to find the individual heads of the Allied delegations more willing to join hands with us than with any of the other delegations. Italy I know would prefer to treat with the United States than with France or England on most questions, and I think that generally holds true of the others. If this turns out to be the case, it will be only a matter in the preliminary conferences of our standing 'pat' on our interpretation of the principles which have been accepted and attempting to accommodate the other delegations one by one, which will prevent any sort of combination of powers against the United States."

What would probably be the English programme at the conference, he was asked. . . .

"England in agreeing to the Fourteen Principles written into the Armistice is in the paradoxical position of submitting to the principle of disarmament and simultaneously announcing through her spokesmen that she means to retain naval supremacy.... If England holds to this course at the conference, it is tantamount to admitting that she does not desire permanent peace, and I will so tell Lloyd George. I'll do it with a smile, but it will carry its point. . .

"Militarism is no different on sea than it is on land. The suggestion which has been made that the American and British navies act together as the sea patrol of the world is only another form of militaristic propaganda. No one power, no two powers, should be masters of the sea; the whole world must be in on it. It must be definitely set forth in the treaty that no one nation or group of nations can say what shall or shall not be done on the high seas. It should be left to a league of all the nations to declare a blockade or override international law for the purpose of retaliating upon a power which threatens the peace of the world, but this power should not be vested in any single nation or combination of nations. The sea is a free highway. . . .

. . . This is not going to be a game of grab. Everybody, we hope, is going to get justice. . . Everybody isn't going to be satisfied. Italy, for instance, has an entirely different idea of what she is entitled to under the principles of the Armistice than those whose opinion I must accept feel that she is entitled to. For myself, I am frankly disposed to go as far as possible in accommodating Italy. I am counting upon her to be found on the side of the United States in most matters of dispute. We may need all the 'allies' we can get in the line. . . .

The President also discussed the problems of German colonies and evidenced his opposition to any incorporation of German Austria into Germany: Swem notes that:

In one of his many talks on the trip, he disclosed the plan of procedure he had in mind for the operation of the conference . . . .

"*I favor a small council composed of the Premiers of England, France, Italy and myself,* which would examine and collate the details of the proposed treaty, much as the Foreign Relations Committee of the Senate works, and later submit these propositions to a conference of all the belligerent powers. I would not have all the business of the conference submitted for consideration to the combined delegations of all the powers, or even to the complete delegations of the larger powers. Twenty-five or thirty delegates in one room mulling and quarrelling over the details of a treaty would be a criminal waste of time, if anything at all could be done by such a method. The purpose we have in mind can, I believe, be just as satisfactorily, and certainly more expeditiously, carried out by having the tentative proposals prepared in advance of the full meeting by a selected few, these proposals to be submitted for discussion and ratification by all the delegates. *This would involve secret conferences, exactly as confidential questions are discussed by the Foreign Relations Committee, but so far as the final gathering of the commissioners is concerned, the debate would be fully open to the public.*"

Colonel House met the President on the arrival of the *George*

Washington at the port on March 13. Mrs. Wilson's book may well be quoted:

> . . . My husband and Colonel House talked on while I waited in my adjoining stateroom. It was after midnight . . . when I heard my husband's door open and the Colonel take his leave. I opened the door connecting our rooms. Woodrow was standing. The change in his appearance shocked me. He seemed to have aged ten years, and his jaw was set in that way it had when he was making super-human effort to control himself. . . .

Mrs. Wilson asked: "What is the matter? What has happened?"

> "House has given away everything I had won before we left Paris. He has compromised on every side, and so I have to start all over again and this time it will be harder. . . . His own explanation of his compromises is that, with a hostile press in the United States expressing disapproval of the League of Nations as a part of the Treaty, he thought it best to yield some other points lest the Conference withdraw its approval altogether. So he has yielded until there is nothing left."
> . . . he threw back his head. The light of battle was in his eyes. "Well," he said, "thank God I can still fight, and I'll win them back or never look these boys I sent over here in the face again. They lost battles.— but won the War, bless them. . . .

Back in Paris, the President at once put into action his idea, expressed on the *George Washington,* of direct and secret negotiations between himself and the Prime Ministers with no one present but interpreters. This now became the Supreme Council, or the Big Four. The sessions lasted for many hours each day and Colonel House was not included at this time. The records of these conversations are very imperfect, and different versions do not agree. In any event, Woodrow Wilson went into battle for his ideas.

Unfortunately by the secrecy of these discussions the President had disarmed himself of his greatest weapon—appeal to the great world public that regarded him as the rightful leader of the crusade for the emancipation of mankind. The President up to this time certainly had not fully realized the dynamism of European emotions which controlled their statesmen, nor the age-old forces which dominated them. There were several meetings of the Big Four in which the demands of the Allies were soon unfolded.

At this moment also the President's American Delegation went into the background. He no longer had full confidence in House and Lansing. Bliss was seldom supposed to advise and then only on military questions, and this record will show that his advice was often disregarded. White was a symbol for Republicans and seldom knew what was going on. The President was going it alone.

Even if Mr. Wilson had not been alerted by ominous news from his own delegation, and at these meetings, he was to find full alarm in two "secret" documents circulated to the major peacemakers.

On March 25 Lloyd George issued a long memorandum[3] demanding a treaty of moderation with Germany. The "moderation" lay mostly in an insistence that there should be no dismemberment of Germany and in modest reparations. He advocated a "guiding principle" that in all states so far as humanly possible the different races should be unified, thus excluding many annexations by the new Eastern European states of the territory of other races. Lloyd George also described the many dangers of the spread of Bolshevism. He advocated early admission of Germany to the League and that the United States should join in a military alliance with Britain and France, guaranteeing France against future German aggression.

On March 31 André Tardieu, Clemenceau's man Friday, drew up Clemenceau's answer to these proposals, representing the French point of view. In his book he states that he pointed out that Germany had already surrendered all of her navy, a large part of her merchant ships, all of her colonies, and her foreign markets. He denounced "appeasement" of Germany; favored the strengthening of the small states by inclusion of Germans; advocated the reduction of the size of the German state to military impotency; and pointed out that otherwise the future security of France would be jeopardized.

Nowhere in these documents was there any reference to the "Fourteen Points and the subsequent addresses." Nowhere does Tardieu mention the League of Nations. Parts of these "secret" documents appeared in the press and it became obvious that the terms of the treaty with Germany were to be dictated by the "Old Tiger."

This intrepid old Frenchman personified all the emotions and

---

[3]The full text of Lloyd George's memorandum can be found in Francesco Nitti, *The Wreck of Europe*, The Bobbs-Merrill Company, Inc., Indianapolis: 1922, pp. 91–101.

sufferings of the French people. Twice in his lifetime he had witnessed German hobnailed boots on French soil. Constantly in his mind's eye were German brutalities, destroyed French homes, the dead and injured, the widows and orphans. In this last aggression the Germans had left behind about 1,400,000 French dead and 740,000 seriously wounded and they had taken 400,000 French prisoners. The Old Tiger had no confidence that Germany had gone through any spiritual transformation either by defeat or by the Reichstag revolution against the Kaiser and the militarist group. Nor did he have any faith in President Wilson or his "Fourteen Points and the subsequent addresses."[4]

I had breakfast each morning with the principal members of my staff. Each time there were present some of our leaders from somewhere in Europe. Our organization was made up of able men of all professions—lawyers, doctors, engineers, historians, economists, and career men from our military and foreign services. They were in contact with the peace delegations in Paris. Since we were absorbed in the progress of the peacemaking, the news we received was discussed every morning. When we received the two "documents," detailed above, we concluded that between them this would be a Punic peace.

On April 3, after about two weeks of this malignant atmosphere, the President's doctor, Admiral Grayson, announced that Mr. Wilson had a severe attack of influenza and would be out of action for some days, and that Colonel House would take his place in the meetings of the Big Four. The President's trouble was not the flu but a much more painful matter, being an infection of the prostate and bladder. I am able to make this statement on the authority of Dr. Albert R. Lamb, who, although not Mr. Wilson's doctor, was physician to the American Mission and in constant contact with Admiral Grayson.[5]

---

[4]See Chapter 16.

[5]This was given to me in a personal communication on July 4, 1957.

Some historians have contended that this illness impaired his clarity of mind and his vitality. Some even consider his stroke five months later as being connected with it.

I do not accept these views. This record will show that his subordinates transacted many important measures after this time. But though he was a very tired man, his mind and judgment were clear. He was sometimes impatient, which I could readily understand. In my world of smaller responsibilities, I sometimes reached the point when I could almost bite the devoted men of my own staff.

Vance McCormick records in his Diary on April 3:

> Davis and I went to President to report. Found him in bed with a bad cold at 6:00 P.M., very tired and I know discouraged. Allies acting like the devil. We are proposing most liberal terms and French particularly unreasonable. . . . He is at a loss to know what to do if impasse continues. Disgusted, threatened to go home as he must call Congress in May. I really pitied him as they are trying to make him the goat and he is powerless to fight publicly in the open because it would only help Germany by showing serious discord among the Allies.

Mrs. Wilson herself, in her *Memoir*, gives the best account of the stirring events that came in the wake of her husband's illness.

> Under this terrific strain of work and anxiety a more robust man might have broken. But had not a severe attack of grippe laid him low the fight would have gone on without respite. When the dread disease struck there was little reserve to fight with. He was too ill to rise from his bed. . . .
>
> More days of tense anxiety. Getting better, the President insisted on knowing what had gone forward while he had been incapacitated. Alas, his absence had been taken advantage of again. The news that came to him was so grave we trembled for the effect on him. But the spirit was stronger than the flesh, and instead of causing a relapse it stiffened his will. Silently I sat beside his bed, knowing that he was formulating his course. At length he said: "I can never sign a Treaty made on these lines, and if all the rest of the delegates have determined on this, I will not be a party to it. If I have lost my fight, which I would not have done had I been on my feet, I will retire in good order; so we will go home. Call Grayson for me, please."
>
> When Admiral Grayson came in the President said: "Grayson, I wish you would send word to Captain McCauley that I want the *George Washington* put in shape at once for my return home as soon as you think it is safe for me to make the trip."

The President's call for the *George Washington* was issued on April 7 and quickly became public knowledge. But there was far more background to that action than the impulse of a sick man.

Colonel House records in his Diary on April 5:

> I went in and out of the President's [sick] room at various

intervals so as to keep him informed as to the progress we were making. . . . I suggested to the President today that in the event there was no agreement by the end of next week . . . he draw up a statement of what the United States is willing to sign in the way of a peace treaty and give the Allies notice that unless they can come near our way of thinking, we would go home immediately and let them make whatever peace seems to them best. My suggestion was to do this gently and in the mildest possible tone, but firmly.

Colonel House notes in his Diary of Sunday, April 6:

I went to Versailles to lunch, but I had hardly gotten there before the President telephoned he would like to see me at four o'clock. He had our fellow Commissioners there and we discussed at great length the best possible means of speeding up the Peace Conference. It was determined that if nothing happened within the next few days, the President would say to the Prime Ministers that unless peace was made according to their promises, which were to conform to the principles of the Fourteen Points, he would either have to go home or he would insist upon having the conferences in the open. In other words, to have Plenary Sessions with the delegates of all the smaller powers sitting in.

General Bliss wrote to Mrs. Bliss on April 7:

In the afternoon the American Commission had a two hours' conference with President Wilson at his house. We all agreed that there should be no more secret conferences of the "Big Four" but that the President should tell his colleagues that they must at once come to time, or to insist on having all points of difference openly discussed in the Plenary Conference. I think things will come to a crisis this week. We have said that often before, but now I do not see how it can be postponed.

However, the President's aides in Paris all felt that before taking any such abrupt step as withdrawing the American Delegation there must be vigorous clarification by the President of the failure of the Allies to make the Treaty along the lines to which they had agreed on November 4, 1918. The White House Secretary, Joseph P. Tumulty, in Washington, had the same reaction, and on April 9 cabled the President through Admiral Grayson:

The ordering of the *George Washington* to return to France looked upon here as an act of impatience and petulance on the

President's part and not accepted here in good grace by either friends or foes. It is considered as an evidence that the President intends to leave the Conference if his views are not accepted. I think this method of withdrawal most unwise and fraught with the most dangerous possibilities here and abroad, because it puts upon the President the responsibility of withdrawing when the President should by his own act place the responsibility for a break of the Conference where it properly belongs. The President should not put himself in the position of being the first to withdraw if his 14 points are not accepted. Rather he should put himself in the position of being the one who remained at the Conference until the very last, demanding the acceptance of his 14 principles. Nothing should be said about his leaving France, but he ought when the time and occasion arrive to re-state his views in terms of the deepest solemnity and yet without any ultimatum attached and then await a response from his associates. In other words, let him by his acts and words place his associates in the position of those who refuse to continue the Conference because of their unwillingness to live up to the terms of the Armistice. Then the President can return to this country and justify his withdrawal. He cannot justify his withdrawal any other way. Up to this time the world has been living on stories coming out of Paris that there was to be an agreement on the League of Nations. Suddenly out of a clear sky comes an order for the *George Washington,* an unofficial statement of the President's withdrawal. A withdrawal at this time would be a desertion.

TUMULTY

Ray Stannard Baker had the same idea:

That evening [April 7] I went up to see the President — the first time since he had fallen ill — and had a long talk. . . . In regard to the calling of the *George Washington,* he said:

'Well, the time has come to bring this thing to a head . . .'

I then urged, as I had done before, that a statement be issued at once setting forth the specific applications of his principles. This we discussed, he being doubtful about too detailed a statement upon the specific issues. All that was necessary to say, he thought, was that he proposed to stand upon his principles. . . .

He said that a League of Nations founded upon an unjust peace could have no future. He was going to fight to the end. He had reached the point where he could give no further. . . .

I, too, made a suggestion for bringing his colleagues to their senses. In a note of mine to the President on April 11 in connection with other subjects, I said:

> It grows upon me daily that the United States is the one great moral reserve in the world today and that we cannot maintain the independence of action through which this reserve is to be sustained if we allow ourselves to be dragged into detailed European entanglements over a period of years.
>
> In my view, if the Allies cannot be brought to adopt peace on the basis of the Fourteen Points, we should retire from Europe lock, stock and barrel, and we should lend to the whole world our economic and moral strength, or the world will swim in a sea of misery and disaster worse than the Dark Ages. If they cannot be brought to accept peace on this basis, our national honor is at stake and we should have to make peace independently and retire.

My belief was that the Allies were in the end bound to accept the League or lose American financial support; that the independence of most of the new nations in Europe had already been established by their own revolutions; and that if the Allies would not accept the President's "basis of peace" with the enemy states, it would be better for them to take the responsibility of making their own agreements with them.

Henry White, a member of the American Delegation, also had something to say in a letter of April 12 to the President:

> DEAR MR. PRESIDENT:
>
> I have been thinking about your reply to my inquiry yesterday afternoon as to the progress which you are making towards a settlement of the important questions still at issue in the Council of Four; and, in the event of a continuation of the tendency to prolong the discussion with a view to further delay....

After suggesting that the President abandon secret sessions and conduct negotiations before plenary sessions of the Conference, White continued:

> Believe me, the secrecy of the proceedings of the Council of Ten and still more of the Four, is being used in this country and in England as well as at home, to discredit you.... The position you occupy will be materially, if not irreparably, compromised....

...I would offer the following suggestion:

That you make known to the Council of Four as soon as possible that not one American soldier, dollar or pound of supplies for military purposes will be furnished until Peace is made....

I am enclosing for your information a telegram from the Daily News' correspondent at New York, showing how generally public opinion is supporting you in the maintenance of the fourteen points and what a favorable impression has been produced by the "George Washington's" having been sent for.

Believe me, dear Mr. President,

Very sincerely yours,

HENRY WHITE

However, the President decided to try it again with the Big Four. As to this, Ray Stannard Baker writes:

But the days from April 9 onward were not happy days for any of the negotiators, least of all for Wilson. . . .

Today, when I went into his study, he looked old and worn. Things are not going well. He had two conferences of the Big Four today, and the League of Nations Commission last evening until midnight. . . .

I discuss later what took place during the ensuing weeks, but I may recount here a development which began the day after the President resumed his Big Four conferences, for it provides light on the attitudes of his Allied colleagues and on subsequent events.

In the sessions of the Big Four, on April 10 the Italians contended that the territories allotted to them for annexation in the secret Pact of London were not sufficient recognition of their needs. They set up a demand for Fiume and a larger part of Dalmatia.

The President had never agreed to the secret Treaty of London and this expansion was a blatant violation of his principles. His efforts to persuade Prime Minister Orlando had no effect and, at a session of the Big Four on April 19, Lloyd George and Clemenceau agreed with the President and promised that if he brought the matter into the open by denouncing the Italian claims they would publicly support him. He did so on April 23 with an elaborate and eloquent statement denying the Italian demands. The President's statement was over 2,500 words and space here permits only a condensation. He said:

When Italy entered the war she entered upon the basis of a definite ... understanding with Great Britain and France, now known as the Pact of London. Since that time the whole face of circumstances has been altered. Many other powers, great and small, have entered the struggle, with no knowledge of that private understanding.

The Austro-Hungarian Empire ... no longer exists. ... Parts of that Empire ... it is agreed now by Italy and ... her associates, are to be erected into independent States. ... They are ... among the smaller States whose interests are henceforth to be safeguarded as scrupulously as ... the most powerful States.

The war was ended, moreover, by proposing to Germany an armistice and peace which should be founded on certain clearly-defined principles which set up a new order of right and justice. ...

If those principles are to be adhered to, Fiume must serve as the outlet of the commerce, not of Italy, but of the land to the north and northeast. ... To assign Fiume to Italy would be to create the feeling that we have deliberately put the port ... in the hands of a power of which it did not form integral part ... not ... identified with the commercial and industrial life of the regions which the port must serve. It is for that reason, no doubt, that Fiume was not included in the Pact of London, but there definitely assigned to the Croatians [later part of Yugoslavia].

He then recounted the great benefits the Italians had already received.

... on the north and northeast her natural frontiers are completely restored, along the whole sweep of the Alps from northwest to southeast to the very end of the Istrian Peninsula, including all the great watershed within which Trieste and Pola lie, and all the fair regions whose face nature has turned toward the great peninsula upon which the historic life of the Latin people has been worked out through centuries of famous story ever since Rome was first set upon her seven hills.

Her ancient unity is restored. Her lines are extended to the great walls which are her natural defense.

The President then added an expression of the deep affection of the American people for the Italian people.

Two entries in Vance McCormick's Diary throw some light on Mr. Wilson's difficulties over this episode. On April 24 he writes:

Whole town excited over President Wilson's statement published this morning on Italian situation. French Press inclined to blame President Wilson. Never mentioned that statement had full approval of Lloyd George and Clemenceau. Always trying to make the U.S. the goat. Many think, however, statement made most favorable impression and will call the bluff of Italians who have overplayed their game.

On April 29 he records:

During the discussion the President mentioned to Davis on the side that both Lloyd George and Clemenceau had promised him to make a public statement on the Italian question but so far they had failed him. It has been unfair the way they have pushed him out into the light to bear the brunt of all unpopular moves. Loucheur, French Minister of Reclamation, told me today that the propaganda of the Italians in French papers cost the Italians eight million francs.

Mrs. Wilson, in her *Memoir*, gives the best account of this incident under date of April 19, 1919:

Italy's great grievance was Fiume. Mr. Wilson had steadfastly refused to give this port to Italy, on the ground that, by right of nationality, it belonged to the new Jugo-Slav State. France and England concurred, but let Wilson do most of the fighting. On a Saturday Orlando, Clemenceau, Balfour and my husband met at our house for a final discussion. Orlando remained obdurate in his opposition to the other three. The meeting adjourned with the understanding that Clemenceau, Balfour and my husband were each to give to the press a statement of his country's view of the question.

All Sunday forenoon the President worked on his statement, for, realizing the seriousness of the matter, he wished to make things clear not only at home but in Italy as well.... About lunchtime, when the draft was ready to be typed, a messenger arrived from Mr. Balfour saying, as he had not had time to write his statement, would President Wilson kindly permit him to have a copy of what he had written to use as an outline. This my husband did, and on the Wednesday following gave a copy to the press as agreed.

Next morning the President's statement was on the front page of every paper at home and abroad, but not one word from either Balfour or Clemenceau. A deluge of adverse comment came from the Italian Commission—all directed against my husband. He was white with anger. When an explanation was asked for, the smug answer was that, after seeing President Wilson's paper, Mr. Balfour had conferred with M. Clemenceau, whereupon both felt that Wilson had made such a fine exposition of the situation nothing they could add would strengthen the case against Italy: so they had agreed to make no statement. In other words, knowing it would be an unpopular decision in Italy, they decided to hide behind the President and shirk responsibility.

The Italian Delegation withdrew from the Conference on April 25 and on its return to Italy there were many fiery speeches denouncing the President. The Italian people tore down their tributes to Mr. Wilson and burned him in effigy. However, Prime Minister Orlando did not engage in criticism of the President.[6]

Tumulty had sent a message of approval to the President. In Mr. Wilson's reply is this sentence: "The difficulties here would have been incredible to me before I got here."

But the President was to meet with an ordeal even more serious.

---

[6]Vittorio Emanuele Orlando, *Discorsi per la guerra e per la pace*, F. Campitelli, Foligno: 1923.

14

THE PRESIDENT'S ORDEAL OF COMPROMISE

Within two weeks after recovery from his illness, President Wilson found himself in deep troubles besides those with the Italians. By their withdrawal from the Conference it was presumed they would neither sign the Treaty nor join the League.

The Japanese were quick to see the President's difficulties and demanded immediate agreement to their assumption of the German rights in Shantung Province in China, which had been arranged in their secret treaty with the British and French. They implied that they, too, would withdraw from the Conference if their claims were not met.

The Germans had been invited by the Big Four to be in Paris on April 28—presumably to receive the peace terms. The whole world was expecting the signing of the peace.

In the latter part of April, the President, being faced with pressures from every quarter, began to compromise all along the line for the best terms he could obtain in order to rescue the League.

Having made up his mind, he acted quickly. The compromises to which he yielded rather than lose the League sowed the whole earth with dragon's teeth. But he held the faith that the League could redeem the world from these evils.

The Japanese Compromise

As background for the Japanese pressures I may recall that the Germans, some years previously, had established territorial and economic "rights" for themselves in the province of Shantung. With the European war in motion, the Japanese had taken these "rights" from the Germans by force of arms. The British, on February 16, 1917, to induce the Japanese to join them in the war, confirmed these "rights" and agreed upon a division of the German Pacific islands between themselves and the Japanese. The American Delegation became aware of this secret treaty two years later in February 1919 —three months after the President arrived in Paris.

The President resisted the Japanese claims as a violation of his "basis of peace." Paul Mantoux, the official interpreter in the secret sessions of the Big Four, in his book records that in these discussions the President made a bitter attack on the proposed provisions in the Treaty confirming these rights.

His press secretary, Ray Stannard Baker, summed up the situation of what Mr. Wilson did at Paris as follows:

> In this crisis Mr. Wilson was face to face with difficult alternatives. If he stood stiffly for immediate justice to China, he would have to force Great Britain and France to break their pledged word with Japan. Even if he succeeded in doing this, he still would have had to face the probability, practically the certainty, that Japan would withdraw from the Conference and go home. This would not only keep Japan out of the League, but it would go far toward eventually disrupting the Peace Conference, already shaken by the withdrawal of Italy....

Even the ever-devoted Tumulty could not wholly swallow such a compromise with Japan, and wrote to the President from Washington on April 24, 1919:

> As we see it from this distance, the selfish designs of Japan are as indefensible as are those of Italy. The two situations appear to parallel each other in their bearing upon the fate of weak and helpless nations. Would it not be an opportune time to cast another die, this one in the direction of Japan, that the whole world may know once and for all where America stands upon this, the greatest issue of the peace we are now trying to make? Now is the time to use your heavy artillery and emphasize the danger of secret treaties and selfish designs of certain big nations.

On April 25 Secretary Lansing made the following memorandum:

> Apparently the President is going to do this to avoid Japan's

declining to enter the League of Nations. It is a surrender of the principle of self-determination, a transfer of millions of Chinese from one foreign master to another. This is another of those secret arrangements which have riddled the "Fourteen Points" and are wrecking a just peace.

In my opinion it would be better to let Japan stay out of the League than to abandon China and surrender our prestige in the Far East for "a mess of 'pottage'"—and a mess it is. I fear that it is too late to do anything to save the situation.

Mr. White, General Bliss, and I, at our meeting that morning before the plenary session, and later when we conferred as to what had taken place at the session, were unanimous in our opinions that China's rights should be sustained even if Japan withdrew from the Peace Conference. We were all indignant at the idea of submitting to the Japanese demands and agreed that the President should be told of our attitude, because we were unwilling to have it appear that we in any way approved of acceding to Japan's claims or even of compromising them. General Bliss volunteered to write the President a letter on the subject, a course which Mr. White and I heartily endorsed.

The next morning the General read the following letter to us and with our entire approval sent it to Mr. Wilson.

April 29

My Dear Mr. President:

Last Saturday morning you told the American Delegation that you desired suggestions, although not at that moment, in regard to the pending matter of certain conflicting claims between Japan and China centering about the alleged German rights. My principal interest in the matter is with sole reference to the question of the moral right or wrong involved. From this point of view I discussed the matter this morning with Mr. Lansing and Mr. White. They concurred with me and requested me to draft a hasty note to you on the subject.

Since your conference with us last Saturday, I have asked myself three or four Socratic questions the answers to which make me, personally, quite sure on which side the moral right lies.

... If it be right for a policeman, who recovers your purse, to keep the contents and claim that he has fulfilled his duty in returning the empty purse, then Japan's conduct may be tolerated.

If it be right for Japan to annex the territory of an Ally, then it cannot be wrong for Italy to retain Fiume taken from the enemy. . . .

Frederick Palmer quotes a letter General Bliss had written to Mrs. Bliss on April 28:

> The next thing to find out is Japan's attitude. Their head delegate, Chinda, says that if we do not recognize all her rights of conquest in China, she will refuse to sign the treaty and decline to enter the League of Nations. This makes some of us afraid that some concession will be made to Japan that will be irreconcilable with our attitude towards the Italian claims. My advice is to let them both go, if they want to go. It is time to clear the air—to draw a line on one side of which will stand the robbers and on the other side will stand the honest men.

Ray Stannard Baker in his *American Chronicle* confirmed the attitude of Lansing and Bliss, noting on May 1:

> I found that no one of our Commissioners had known about it [the Japanese dilemma] until I told them. . . . Williams, Hornbeck, and others of our experts were openly sympathizing with and helping the Chinese. I had a long talk with Secretary Lansing, . . . and found him quite inconsolable. He said he would not, under any circumstances, defend the decision. He would not attack it. He would remain silent. He was for the right of the matter, he said, regardless of consequences.
> "And break up the Peace Conference?" I asked.
> "Even that, if necessary."
> Both General Bliss and Henry White sided with Lansing.

Colonel House states that, in a verbal understanding with Mr. Balfour, the Japanese said that they would surrender the territorial "rights" in China at some future time but that they would hold the economic "rights." How far the President believed these Japanese assurances given to Balfour, I do not know. On April 30 he instructed Tumulty how to explain the matter to the American people, but the instructions did not mention the verbal understanding. Baker says that on May 3 the Chinese delegates, informed of this promise, made a public protest that even with this agreement the Japanese economic "rights" amounted practically to annexation. Lansing says this oral undertaking "failed of confirmation in writing or by formal public declaration."

Nevertheless, the President yielded to Japan as part of his compromise to save the League.

Swem states that the President, on June 20, instructed Lansing to secure a written confirmation of this verbal promise. He did not secure it and the Japanese rights were confirmed in the Treaty.[1]

No Compromise with the Italians

Paul Mantoux, in his book records that on April 19 the Treaty of London, by which Italy entered the war, came up for discussion and that the President said:

> ... I do not know whether my French and English colleagues think that the Treaty of London can be reconciled with the peace that we want to establish. But, as for me, who am free from any treaty obligation, I say that it is not. The Treaty of London is one of those secret treaties which we have declared ourselves to be against. ...
>
> I have already said that I do not see how we can make peace with Germany according to one principle while we invoke others to deal with Austria and with the other powers. I am not criticizing the Treaty of London; I know in what circumstances it was signed. But to say that you are going to carry out this treaty would be to put the Government of the United States in an impossible situation.

Baron Sonnino said:

> We are not asking you to subscribe to this treaty.

The President remarked:

> No, but you are asking me to accept what it contains.

Colonel House writes in his Diary on May 8:

> ... Clemenceau and George, particularly George, say if the Italians come back and demand the Treaty of London, they will have to live up to their obligations. The President told them that we would not sign a treaty which recognized the Treaty of London, and that France and England would have to choose between Italy and the United States. George and Clemenceau hoped that no such choice would have to be made, but if it came to that, they would have to recognize their obligation to the Treaty of London no matter what the consequences.

---

[1]As a matter of fact, the Chinese rights to Shantung were restored only three years later at the insistence of the United States Secretary of State Charles E. Hughes.

The President was disturbed and came immediately to the Crillon and had a conference with Bliss, White and myself, Lansing being absent. I tried to stir him from his inflexible position and made several suggestions regarding a settlement which might be satisfactory to both sides....

The other members of the delegation also thought there should be some compromise with Italy. On May 26 they addressed a letter to the President as follows:

DEAR MR. PRESIDENT:

We have just been confidentially informed by Colonel House that the Italians propose demanding, in the Council of Four this morning, the fulfillment of the Treaty of London in its entirety.

In view of the fact that when we discussed with you a fortnight ago, or thereabouts, the possibility of such a demand, and of the further fact that you seemed inclined at that time to inform the British and French Prime Ministers that the American Delegation would withdraw from the Conference rather than assent to the recognition of the Treaty of London, we venture to express the hope that you will not take any final step in the matter without a further conference with us.

We feel that circumstances, which we shall be glad to explain to you in conversation, have occurred during the last few weeks which would not justify our breaking up the Conference now on account of the Adriatic situation, and that we should not have the support of our own people in doing so.

Yours very sincerely,

ROBERT LANSING
HENRY WHITE
TASKER H. BLISS

The President never did agree to recognize the Treaty of London nor was it confirmed in the Treaty with Germany.

However, immediately after the Armistice, the Italians had acquired most of what they wanted, except Fiume, by *fait accompli*.

The Orlando Ministry resigned on June 19, and Francesco Nitti became Prime Minister and arranged for the same delegation under Orlando to return to Paris and sign the Treaty, including the League Covenant, on June 28.

THE COMPROMISE WITH FRENCH DEMANDS

Clemenceau, after recovery in early March from the attempted assassination, began making demands for specific concessions, most of which negated the November 4, 1918, agreement on the basis of peace.

He sought to reduce the military strength of Germany to impotence by dismembering it in both the east and the west. He sought the annexation of the Rhineland and the Saar to France and to stifle Germany with reparations.

Tardieu states that President Wilson and Lloyd George, on March 25, offered him a military guarantee against German aggression in lieu of these annexations to France. Clemenceau, however, refused.

CLEMENCEAU'S DISMEMBERMENT OF GERMANY

A preliminary step to the dismemberment of Germany began with the insistence that the Treaty prohibit Austria and Germany from joining together. To this the President agreed. To weaken Old Austria, France had been chiefly instrumental in transferring 2,000,-000 Sudeten Germans from Austria to Czechoslovakia. About 1,500,000 Austro-Germans went to Italy under the secret Pact of London. Thus, Austria was left a truncated state with only 6,000,-000 people, of whom 2,000,000 were in Vienna without adequate resources to support such a city.

Actual dismemberment of Germany was accomplished in the east under the Treaty by establishing the Polish Corridor to the Baltic, making Danzig a free city, and the annexation of a part of Upper Silesia to Poland, by which about 1,500,000 Germans in effect went to Poland. To the west, two small areas were annexed to Belgium and Denmark. The President agreed to these settlements. He had advocated in his "Fourteen Points" the justice of the return of Alsace-Lorraine to France.

At one time, the French hoped that the dismemberment of their ancient foe would be extended to include the separation of Bavaria from the Reich. On March 27, I was called to a meeting of the Council of Ten since my Relief operations were involved. The following are the pertinent paragraphs of the minutes:

> M. PICHON explained the political importance of allowing Bavaria to get supplies from other directions than the north. At present all the supplies for Bavaria were sent by the... [Ebert Government], and this tended to increase the political influence of Prussia.

The best way to obviate this was to enable Bavaria to receive supplies from the south. . . .

M. SEYDOX thought that the revictualling of Bavaria from the south could be carried on outside of the decisions taken at Brussels. He proposed to import into France from Bavaria certain goods which the French needed and to ship the food into Germany via France.

MR. LANSING said that the real question involved was one of policy. Did we want to separate Bavaria from Germany?

MR. HOOVER said that the Allied and Associated . . . [Governments] had entered into a series of contracts with the German Central Government, under which the latter had undertaken the fair distribution of supplies throughout the whole of Germany, including Bavaria. There was a financial problem involved. The people with whom the Allied and Associated Powers were dealing drew on the resources of the whole of Germany for payments. To make a separate financial arrangement would involve separate means of payment being found for Bavaria. If . . . [their] goods came to France from Bavaria, it was doubtful if France had food supplies to furnish in return. To replace them, therefore, food supplies would have to be imported from elsewhere, and dollars or credits would have to be found. . . .

MR. HOOVER, continuing, said that in any event the supplies would have to receive access to Bavaria by the Rhine. Otherwise, they would have to be brought from Bordeaux right across France, whereas, by using the Rhine, an immediate and easy transport was available.

MR. LANSING said that if our object was to get rid of Bolshevism the best way was to . . . [sustain] the Berlin Government which was certainly not Bolshevist. He doubted the expediency of interfering with the internal affairs of any country.

Paul Mantoux, in his book, records that, when this subject came up in a meeting of the Big Four, the President agreed to inform me of the political reasons which had been stated by Clemenceau for helping the independence movement led by a Dr. Muehlon. While the President told me the purpose, he certainly did not urge any separation of food supplies from the Central Government.

However, Clemenceau was not satisfied and again raised this idea in a letter to President Wilson. The President requested that I give him a note of my opinion on the whole business, which I did:

April 3, 1919

DEAR MR. PRESIDENT:

With respect to feeding Bavaria [separately] through Switzerland or France, this is totally infeasible in any volume worth considering, both from a transportation, food and financial point of view.

For your confidential information, the whole of this question has been repeatedly agitated by the French Minister at Berne, who is constantly endeavoring to create a Separatist spirit in Bavaria and who wishes to send a few carloads into Bavaria under the French flag. The pressure from this quarter became so great in this particular about ten days ago that it was raised before the Council of [Ten]....

As quickly as the first German ... [merchant] ship left the German harbors, and before any of the financial arrangements were completed, I diverted several cargoes intended for other quarters into German harbors. ... I may add, however, that the situation in Germany is extremely dangerous (Bavaria is leaning to Communism) and ... I am not at all sure that our food supplies have not arrived sixty days too late. In any event, it is a neck and neck race as to whether food will maintain stability as against the other forces that have grown out of hunger in the meantime.

Yours faithfully,

HERBERT HOOVER

Clemenceau pursued the matter no further and the French plan for detachment of Bavaria as an independent state fell through.

President Wilson especially and my organization in support of him certainly saved this much of the dismemberment of Germany.

But now Clemenceau made two further demands for dismemberment.

SEPARATION OF THE RHINELAND

A major goal of Clemenceau's was in some fashion to separate the Rhineland from the Reich. In February, my Relief staff reported that the French were conspiring with Rhenish industrialists to declare the Rhineland an independent state and thus not subject to reparations.

Colonel House in his Diary confirms these activities, saying in an entry on March 12, 1919:

... In the afternoon I went to the Quai d'Orsay, where the air terms were taken up. Lloyd George asked to see me in the anteroom.... He said he was seriously troubled concerning the French. In the first place, he could not agree with them upon the question of the boundary of the Rhine and the creation of a Rhenish Republic upon the terms they had in mind....

Colonel House also records that Dr. Isaiah Bowman, a member of the American Delegation, reported a meeting with the President on this matter on March 28. He said:

Three of us were asked to call at the President's house, and on the following morning at eleven o'clock we arrived.... He remarked:

"Gentlemen, I am in trouble and I have sent for you to help me out. The matter is this: the French want the whole left bank of the Rhine. I told M. Clemenceau that I could not consent to such a solution of the problem. He became very much excited and then demanded ownership of the Saar Basin. I told him I could not agree to that either because it would mean giving 300,000 Germans to France.... I do not know whether I shall see M. Clemenceau again. I do not know whether he will return to the meeting this afternoon. In fact, I do not know whether the Peace Conference will continue. M. Clemenceau called me a pro-German and abruptly left the room."

On April 22 the President agreed to a compromise by which German sovereignty would be maintained over the Rhineland but Allied Armies would occupy the area and the bridgeheads for fifteen years, with a neutral zone to be established beyond the bridgeheads.

The French still had lingering hopes of creating an independent Rhenish state, as shown by a letter from President Poincaré addressed to Mr. Wilson on April 28, urging greater French authority over the Rhineland. The President replied on May 7:

I do not think it wise to go further than we have gone in the treaty in respect to the occupation of the Rhine territory.

That they still did not give up hope is shown in a letter from Mr. Wilson to Clemenceau on May 23, which is recorded in Clemenceau's book:

MY DEAR PRIME MINISTER:

I have just received a message from the General commanding our army of occupation, which causes me serious anxiety. It is as follows:

This morning General Mangin, the general commanding the

French Army in Mainz, sent a colonel on his Staff to General Liggett's headquarters at Coblenz, to ask what our attitude would be with regard to a political revolution on the left bank of the Rhine with a view to establishing a free Rhineland republic, independent of Germany. He asked what the American attitude would be toward such a new republic.

"The staff officer assures us that they had fifty deputies ready to come into the American zone to help to put the revolution in motion. The meaning of the word deputies in this connection was not clearly understood, but it was manifest that Frenchmen were referred to."

General Liggett very properly refused to consider this proposal, and his attitude has my entire approval. He has been given instructions to prohibit political agitators from entering our zone, whatever orders they may invoke to justify their action, and I feel persuaded that these instructions will meet with your own approval.

Cordially and sincerely yours,

WOODROW WILSON

A pertinent paragraph in the Treaty (Article 429) provided:

If at the end of fifteen years the guarantees against unprovoked aggression by Germany are not considered sufficient by the Allied and Associated Governments, the evacuation by the occupying troops may be delayed to the extent regarded as necessary for the purpose of obtaining the required guarantees.

THE SAAR COMPROMISE

The French also claimed the Saar, a rich but small German coal district. They rightly urged compensation for the willful destruction of their coal mines in Northern France. House describes a bitter exchange between Clemenceau and the President over this question, saying:

. . . The President told Clemenceau that the French were bringing up territorial questions that had nothing to do with the war aims of anybody, and that no one had heard of their intention to annex the Saar Valley until after the Armistice had been signed. Clemenceau grew angry at this and said that the President favored the Germans. The President replied that such a statement was untrue and that Clemenceau knew that it was.

Clemenceau then stated that if they did not receive the Saar Valley, he would not sign the Treaty of Peace. To this the President replied, "Then if France does not get what she wishes, she will refuse to act with us. In that event do you wish me to return home?" Clemenceau answered, "I do not wish you to go home, but I intend to do so myself," and in a moment he left the house.

When the President's opposition to the Saar annexation became apparent, various alternatives were discussed and in the end the President accepted a compromise whereby the coal mines would be operated by a commission under the League for fifteen years; the French would receive the whole coal output; but the sovereignty of Germany would be preserved and a plebiscite taken at the end of fifteen years.[2]

THE COMPROMISES ON THE MILITARY ALLIANCE

Neither the ban on German union with Austria, nor the separation from Germany of its eastern border areas, nor the Rhineland and Saar settlements, nor Germany's economic exhaustion by reparations satisfied the Old Tiger that France was safe from further aggression. With his unfailing recollection of two hideous invasions and the fact that 60,000,000 Germans still faced 45,000,000 Frenchmen, he did not forget the Lloyd George–Wilson proposal of a joint military guarantee for France against German aggression in lieu of his demands as to the Rhineland. Having obtained as much as he could get on the Rhineland, he now pressed for the military alliance. This, of course, was a violation of the President's "basis of peace," which stipulated there would be no more military alliances except as implied in the League itself.

This French proposal was described in a note dated March 20 in Secretary Lansing's records:

> An instance of the lengths to which these compromises and makeshifts are going, occurred this morning when [the Delegation was asked] . . . for our opinion [on] the following proposal: That the United States, Great Britain, and France enter into a formal alliance to resist any aggressive action by Germany against France or Belgium, and to employ their military, financial, and economic resources for this purpose in addition to exerting their moral influence to prevent such aggression.
>
> We three agreed that, if that agreement was made, the chief reason for a League of Nations, as now planned, disappeared. So far

---

[2]The plebiscite was overwhelmingly for the Saar's return to Germany.

as France and Belgium were concerned the alliance was all they needed for their future safety. They might or might not accept the League. Of course they would if the alliance depended upon their acceptance. They would do most anything to get such an alliance. . . .

What impressed me most was that to gain French support for the League the proposer of the alliance was willing to destroy the chief feature of the League. . . .

Secretary Lansing expands on this subject in his book:

. . . M. Clemenceau, who naturally favored the idea, continued to press the President to agree to the plan [the alliance]. What arguments were employed to persuade him I cannot say. . . . It should be remembered that at the time both the Italians and Japanese were threatening to make trouble unless their territorial ambitions were satisfied. With these two Powers disaffected and showing a disposition to refuse to accept membership in the proposed League of Nations the opposition of France to the Covenant would have been fatal. It would have been the end of the President's dream of a world organized to maintain peace by an international guaranty of national boundaries and sovereignties. Whether France would in the end have insisted on the additional guaranty of protection I doubt, but it is evident that Mr. Wilson believed that she would and decided to prevent a disaster to his dreams by acceding to the wishes of his French colleague.

According to Frederick Palmer, General Bliss penciled a memorandum of comment on March 20:

This draft [of the alliance] is a modification of one proposed by Mr. House, and which he suggested to meet the French threat that they could not accept the League of Nations unless this promise was made by the United States. Neither Mr. Lansing nor Mr. White nor I approve of this draft or anything like it. It will surely kill the League of Nations Covenant.

However, Clemenceau won on May 6. Ray Stannard Baker, in his Papers, summarizes it as follows:

. . . In addition to the securities afforded in the Treaty of Peace, the President of the United States has pledged himself to propose to the Senate of the United States, and the Prime Minister of Great Britain has pledged himself to propose to the Parliament of Great Britain an engagement, subject to the approval of the

Council of the League of Nations, to come immediately to the assistance of France in case of unprovoked attack by Germany.

On the morning of June 28, the same day on which the Treaty of Versailles was signed, the military treaty with France was executed at the President's residence by Premier Clemenceau and Foreign Minister Pichon for the French Republic, by President Wilson and Secretary Lansing for the United States, and by Prime Minister Lloyd George and Foreign Minister Balfour for Great Britain.

THE REPARATIONS COMPROMISE

The Armistice Agreement of November 11, 1918, provided that the enemy should pay all war damages to the Allied and Associated Governments. A Committee was appointed from the Conference delegates to report on the amount to be paid by Germany, and the method of payment.

On February 21, 1919, the American members of the Reparations Committee reported on the progress of the Committee; House records as to the Allied demands:

> The British now put in a tentative total demand on Germany of one hundred and twenty billion of dollars, and the French think Germany should pay a total of two hundred billion of dollars. In other words, the French want Germany to pay two hundred times as much as the French paid the Germans in '71 and which the French then claimed to be excessive. They wish the payments to run for fifty-five years. . . .
>
> Our people think the maximum cannot be over twenty-two billions of dollars and are inclined to believe that it should be under that amount.

There was no doubt in the minds of the Americans at Paris that Germany must pay to the utmost. But realistically, she could not in the long run pay in cash more than she could earn by the surplus of exports over imports. In addition, she could pay something more "in kind" by exporting goods to the Allies if they could absorb them.

Above all, we Americans contended that to induce Germany to pay, a moderate fixed sum should be set, payable over a term of years, so that she might have freedom in sight. The President advocated this course.

But overhanging the Conference were the campaign promises

of Lloyd George, Clemenceau and Orlando to get back every penny of damages. The Prime Ministers argued that any fixed sum would fall short of the expectations of their peoples. In April the President agreed to their formula of unstated totals.[3]

There was one definite sum upon which the Allies did agree. That was that Germany should pay five billion dollars in cash and in kind of "liquid" character prior to May 1, 1921, or within two years. This would take more than all Germany's working capital in cash, credit or goods and if carried out would destroy her ability to get production going again. I later discuss my protests, which were amply justified by subsequent experience.[4]

---

[3]While the initial "claims" totaled over three hundred and twenty billion dollars, the Reparations Commission subsequently fixed the total at sixty-six billions.

[4]On May 1, 1921, the Germans claimed that they had delivered over five billion dollars in cash or in kind, but the Reparations Commission refused to credit them with more than one billion two hundred million dollars of deliveries.

At an Allied meeting in London in May, 1921, the total debt was reduced to forty-four billion dollars. This having proved impossible to meet, Germany's currency crashed in 1922. On October 17 of that year, Secretary of State Charles Evans Hughes suggested a committee of American businessmen to study the situation. On November 30, 1923, the Reparations Commission agreed to such a study. General Charles G. Dawes, as Chairman, conducted the study. The "Dawes Plan" was evolved, which provided for a new currency and fixed annuities for reparations of about six hundred million dollars with supposed elaborate securities for payments under economic control by an Agent General of reparations.

The Dawes Plan having proved unequal to restoring economic stability, on December 22, 1928, at a meeting of Allied representatives, another group of experts was appointed under the chairmanship of an American, Owen D. Young. This committee began work in February 1929 and reported on June 7, 1929. It reduced the annuities, abolished the securities and controls of the Dawes Committee, abolished the Agent General of Reparations and called for the creation of the Bank of International Settlements to handle international payments. The plan was finally adopted on January 20, 1930. It had no effect on the restoration of the European economy.

In June 1931, with the whole world in a gigantic depression resulting from the economic crash of all Central and Eastern Europe, I (then in the White House) proposed a world moratorium on all intergovernmental debts until June 30, 1932. Even this did not stay the depression, and I proposed a further measure in July 1931 by which a standstill agreement was created for all German foreign bank obligations.

Without going into further details, I may point out that Germany, up to March 31, 1937, had paid a total of about five billion three hundred million dollars of reparations in one form or another, and that was the end.

See United States Department of State, *Papers Relating to the Foreign Relations of the United States* [The Paris Peace Conference, 1919], vol. XIII, United States Government Printing Office, Washington: 1947, pt. VIII. pp. 383–439 *passim*.

I might add that Hitler's rise to power in 1933 was based upon his promises—and considerable successes—in the reunification of Germany, all of which had to do with the origins of the Second World War.

GERMAN WAR CRIMES COMPROMISE

Paul Mantoux records in his book a long debate in the Big Four over a proposed Treaty provision for punishment of German crimes. President Wilson stood staunchly for determination of individual crimes on an individual basis and by judicial processes. The President's proposals were adopted as shown by the following provisions (Article 227) in the Treaty:

> A special tribunal will be constituted to try the accused, thereby assuring him the guarantees essential to the right of defence. It will be composed of five judges, one appointed by each of the following Powers: namely, the United States of America, Great Britain, France, Italy and Japan.
>
> . . . It will be its duty to fix the punishment which it considers should be imposed.
>
> The Allied and Associated Powers will address a request to the Government of the Netherlands for the surrender to them of the ex-Emperor in order that he may be put on trial.

Further articles provided for trial of persons accused of having committed acts in violation of the laws and customs of war and of criminal action against any national of the enemy powers. They required the Germans to furnish documents and information of every kind in relation to such acts.[5]

However, Lloyd George and Clemenceau insisted upon a Treaty provision for guilt confession by the German people as a whole. In spite of the President's dissent, it was placed in the Treaty.

THE MANDATES COMPROMISE

Another highly important compromise of much earlier date should be included here. This one involved the designation of the mandatories.

Before arriving in Paris the President recognized that the so-called "backward peoples" which formerly made up part of the old empires of Germany, Russia and Turkey must have a transitional period of guardianship. He proposed that they be placed in trust with the League of Nations and that mandates for administration of the trusteeships be given to the small neutral states to prevent them

---

[5]The Government of Holland refused to surrender the former Emperor and as war emotions cooled off, these provisions tapered down to trials by German courts which produced small results.

from becoming the basis of further imperial expansion. He made this proposal to the members of his staff accompanying him on the *George Washington* on his first journey to the Peace Conference. Among these men were Professor Isaiah Bowman of Johns Hopkins University and Professor Charles Seymour of Yale University.

Professor Bowman states:[6]

He [Wilson] thought that the German colonies should be declared the common property of the League of Nations and administered by small nations.

Bowman also says:[7]

. . . The idea of a trusteeship for backward peoples was not new. It had been advocated by various writers on colonial problems, and a year previous it was incorporated in a memorandum on Mesopotamia written for Colonel House's Inquiry by George Louis Beer and turned in on January 1, 1918. . . . This memorandum, according to J. T. Shotwell, "happens to contain the first project for a 'mandate' in the sense in which that term ultimately was used in the Treaty."

Seymour reports the President's views:

He argued [at that time] that those territories should be administered not by the Great Powers but by smaller States.[8]
. . . Such States as Holland or one of the Scandinavian nations.[9]

This idea of mandates to small nations fitted neither with the imperial ambitions of the Allied Governments nor with their secret treaties, wherein annexations had already been agreed upon. On January 24, 1919, the leaders of Britain, Australia, South Africa, France and Italy, meeting in Paris, demanded that such annexations be divided among them.

Various writers have assumed that the President adopted the idea of mandates from a pamphlet written by General Smuts. But this pamphlet was not issued until after the President's arrival in Europe with the mandate idea already in his mind.

There was an inherent conflict between Smuts' proposals and

---

[6]Charles Seymour, *The Intimate Papers of Colonel House,* vol. IV, Houghton Mifflin Co., Boston: 1926, pp. 281–282.
[7]*Ibid.,* pp. 283–284.
[8]*Ibid.,* p. 285.
[9]Charles Seymour,*Woodrow Wilson and the World War,* Yale University Press, New Haven, Conn.: 1921, p. 288.

those of the President. However, General Smuts secured a compromise from the President that the trusteeships of the League should be administered by mandates to the Allied nations on the grounds of their past experience.

The President's agreement to this compromise came sometime during the drafting of the League Covenant. The text of the article introduced in the Covenant for this purpose was drafted, not by the subcommittee entrusted with that job, but by the Council of Ten, which included the Prime Ministers, on January 30.

The provision in Article XIX was:

> To those Colonies and territories which as a consequence of the late war have ceased to be under the sovereignty of the States which formerly governed them and which are inhabited by peoples not yet able to stand by themselves under the strenuous conditions of the modern world, there should be applied the principle that the well being and development of such peoples form a sacred trust of civilization and that securities for the performance of this trust should be embodied in the constitution of the League.
>
> The best method of giving practical effect to this principle is that the tutelage of such peoples *should be entrusted to advanced nations who by reason of their resources, their experience or their geographical position,* can best undertake this responsibility, and that this tutelage should be exercised by them as mandatories on behalf of the League. . . .

Whether the President resisted this compromise with Smuts I do not know. But by this device for all practical purposes the "backward peoples" were annexed to the Allied empires. Also, it extinguished in several important areas the aspirations of peoples for self-government and independence. It was all neatly managed so as to comply with many of the secret treaties which had divided these areas prior to the President's arrival in Paris (see Chapter 8).

General Smuts' formula, thus introduced in the Covenant, was one of the most monumental attainments in the history of Old World diplomacy. And by this device Smuts was to annex huge areas in Africa to the Union of South Africa.

No one since has been able to find any practical difference between these mandated areas and the other British, French, Italian or Japanese colonies or imperial possessions. Moreover, the people of Syria, Iraq, Jordan, Palestine, and Lebanon were demanding self-government and independence. These aspirations were bottled up for many years by these peoples being placed under mandates.

I am convinced that the judgment and attitude of the President in these matters were due to his unfamiliarity with Old World diplomacy and too much confidence in General Smuts when that statesman's own imperial interests were at stake.

It is my belief that the President, to put it bluntly, was just fooled. He was certainly under an illusion as to the ultimate effect of the mandates.

The Swem Papers show that during his visit to Washington two weeks after the adoption of this provision in the Covenant he made an off-the-record address to the Democratic National Committee on February 28, 1919, in which he obviously had not understood its full effect:

> ... I was one of the first advocates of the mandatory. *I do not at all believe in handing over any more territory than has already been handed over to any sovereign.* I do not believe in putting the *people of the German territories at the disposition, unsubordinated disposition, of any great power, and therefore I was a warm advocate of the idea of General Smuts* ... who propounded the theory that the pieces of the Austro-Hungarian Empires and the pieces of the Turkish Empire and the German colonies were all political units or territorial units which ought to be accepted in trust by the family of nations, *and not turned over to any member of the family,* and that therefore the League of Nations would have as one of its chief functions to act as Trustee for these great areas of dismembered empires. . . .

Yet the embarrassing moment came when they asked if the United States would be willing to accept a mandatory. The President admitted that the Allies had proposed that the United States take the mandate for Armenia, as to which he said:

> I had to say offhand that it would not be willing. . . . [I want to avoid] what I may call without offence Pharisaical cleanliness and not take anything out of the pile. . . . They said that . . . it would greatly advance the peace of the world and the peace of mind of Europe if the United States would accept mandatories. I said, I am perfectly willing to go home and stump the country and see if they will do it, but I could not truthfully say offhand that they would, because I did not know.

The President in the same speech proposed that the United States accept a mandate over Armenia, Constantinople and the Dardanelles, saying:

> Now what I wanted to suggest is this: Personally, and just within the limits of this room, I can say very frankly that I think we ought to. I think there is a very promising beginning in regard to countries like Armenia. . . .

He then described the many bonds between the American people and the Armenians and continued:

> But the place where they all want us to accept a mandate most is at Constantinople. I may say that it seems to be rather the consensus of opinion there that Constantinople ought to be internationalized, so that the present idea apparently is to delimit the territory around Constantinople to include the straits and set up a mandate of the territory which will make those straits open to the nations of the world without any conditions and make Constantinople truly international — an internationalized free city and a free port — and America is the only nation in the world that can undertake that mandate and have the rest of the world believe that it is undertaken in good faith and that we do not mean to stay there and set up our own sovereignty. So that it would be a very serious matter for the confidence of the world in this treaty if the United States did not accept a mandate for Constantinople.

He urged the members of the National Committee to advocate that the United States accept this mandate.

The President's participation in the assignment of some of the mandates is confirmed in a communiqué to the public from the Big Four on May 7, 1919, which read:

> The Council . . . [including President Wilson], yesterday decided as to the disposition of the ex-German colonies as follows: —
>
> TOGOLAND AND CAMEROONS   France and Great Britain shall make a joint recommendation as to the League of Nations as to their future.
>
> GERMAN EAST AFRICA   The mandate shall be held by Great Britain.
>
> GERMAN SOUTH WEST AFRICA   The mandate shall be held by the Union of South Africa.
>
> THE GERMAN SAMOAN ISLANDS   The mandate shall be held by New Zealand.

THE OTHER GERMAN PACIFIC POSSESSIONS SOUTH OF THE EQUATOR excluding the German Samoan Islands and Naura, the mandate shall be held by Australia.

NAURA   The mandate shall be given to the British Empire.

THE GERMAN PACIFIC ISLANDS NORTH OF THE EQUATOR   The mandate shall be held by Japan.

Later rules were established for the government and protection of the mandated peoples and the mandates were divided into three classes: the former Turkish possessions, the backward areas of Africa, and some minor areas to be administered under the laws of the mandatory.[10]

The total territory annexed under the mandate system was about 1,132,000 square miles, or one-third the size of continental United States.

The mandates were divided as follows:

Mandate	Mandatory	Population (1931)	Area, square miles
A MANDATES			
Palestine	United Kingdom	1,035,154	9,010
Trans-Jordan	United Kingdom	305,584	15,444
Syria and Lebanon	France	2,656,596	62,163
B MANDATES			
Cameroons	France	2,186,015	165,928
Cameroons	United Kingdom	774,585	34,236
Ruanda-Urundi	Belgium	3,450,000	20,541
Tanganyika	United Kingdom	5,063,660	374,085
Togoland	France	725,580	20,077
Togoland	United Kingdom	293,671	13,240
C MANDATES			
Islands, North Pacific	Japan	73,027	830
Nauru	British Empire (Australia acting)	2,692	8.
New Guinea and islands	Australia	392,816	93,000
South-West Africa	South Africa	242,290	322,393
Western Samoa	New Zealand	46,023	1,133[11]

---

[10]Whether these peoples were "trusteeships" or "annexations" is indicated by their destiny in the Second World War. All that remained of them were then annexed for good.

[11]United States Department of State, *Papers Relating to the Foreign Relations of the United States* [Paris Peace Conference, 1919], vol. XIII, United States Government Printing Office, Washington: 1943, p. 102.

Thus, in the name of mandates the sum total of peoples and territories annexed by the Colonial powers were:

	Population	Square miles
British Empire	8,156,475	862,549
French Empire	5,568,191	248,168
Belgian Empire	3,450,000	20,541
Japanese Empire	73,027	830

While on this subject, I may point out the further imperial acquisitions which resulted from the treaty making. Japan got special rights in the Chinese province of Shantung, consisting of 80,000 square miles with 20,000,000 inhabitants, and Italy acquired 23,726 square miles and 1,672,000 inhabitants from the old Austrian Empire.

Closely related to imperialism were the "spheres of influence" set up in the secret treaties. Thus, by the secret treaty with Russia, the British held a sphere of influence over Southern Persia, Mesopotamia and Egypt.

At the moment the Treaty of Versailles was signed, the British, through mandates and "spheres," controlled all the huge oil resources along the Persian Gulf.

Colonel House, in mid-May, informed me that the President had the United States in mind to be mandatory of Armenia and Constantinople and that I would be appointed Governor. I was directing the relief of Armenia and Constantinople at this time and knew from hard experience much about this part of the world. I was sure the President knew little of the conditions which had to be met in undertaking such a mandate.

I told the Colonel that the Armenian state was made up only of those Armenians who had declared their independence from old Russia; that while there were probably 1,500,000 original inhabitants, over 400,000 Armenian refugees had now swarmed into Armenia to escape Turkish persecution; and that there were probably 400,000 more still in Turkey. I advised him that Armenia could never protect herself from her fierce neighbors—Turkey and Azerbaijan—without a foreign garrison of at least 150,000 troops. Further, I said that she could never become self-supporting without including all of old Turkish Armenia and another piece of Turkey or Kurdistan to give her agricultural strength. Also, she must have a piece of Georgia for an outlet to the Black Sea. I suggested that, if these conditions were complied with, any one of the Allied Governments would be glad to take the mandate. With all of this in mind, I proposed to the Colonel (and later to the President) that a competent mission be sent to Armenia to investigate the problem and suggested General James G. Harbord as chairman. The matter was still unsettled when the President left Europe in June.

On July 3, 1919, Mr. John Foster Dulles of the State Department, then in Paris, joined with me in a cable to the President urging General Harbord's appointment. He was appointed and I secured for him as members of his mission William B. Poland, James McKnight, and Harold W. Clark of my staff. The mission arrived August 15 and reported its findings late in September. As I had ended my official job in Europe and had left for the United States, I did not see the report.[12]

THE COMPROMISE ON REIMPOSING THE BLOCKADE
TO FORCE GERMAN SIGNATURE ON THE DOTTED LINE

Another compromise was made over the measures to be taken if Germany refused to "sign on the dotted line."

General Foch had insisted at all times that a threat to reimpose the blockade was the way to make the Germans sign the Treaty. On May 5 the French members of the Superior Blockade Council submitted plans to the Council to reimpose the blockade if the Germans showed any hesitation. On May 8 the Big Four asked the representatives of the Economic Council to discuss with them reimposing the blockade.

---

[12]The Allies continued to press the United States to undertake this mandate. On May 24, 1920, at the Allied Conference at San Remo, they specifically requested the United States to undertake it. The President sent a long message to the Congress, recommending that the United States take the mandate, but made no mention of the requirements for assuring a stable state other than the inclusion of some minor districts (vilayets) from Turkey.

The President at this time was without experienced advice. Colonel House and Secretary Lansing had both ceased to advise him. I was not consulted, although I was still conducting the relief of Armenia through our American Relief Administration. The Senate rejected the President's recommendations on June 1, 1920.

In any event, the whole question was taken out of the hands of the Allies or the United States a year later in April 1921, when the Russian Communists took over their old province of Armenia and made it a Communist satellite.

The outcome was particularly sad to me, for no real effort had been made to reconstruct a stable and defensible Armenia which could protect all Armenians and in so doing create a state for which some European government would have been glad to take the mandate. In addition to urging these measures for Armenia I had, against great odds, for two years after the Treaty found the finance for, and directed the relief and reconstruction of, Russian Armenia and its refugees, a more ample statement of which will be found in Chapter 10.

McCormick's Diary on May 9 reflects his reaction:

> Went to special committee of the Supreme Blockade Council at the Commerce Department to discuss plans for blockade in the event of Germany refusing to sign Treaty. We came to agreement. I notified Council, while approving the plan, that I hoped the Allies would not use it as it would make more chaos. In my opinion, the only solution of the question would be military occupation.

However, the Big Four requested a detailed plan for reimposing the blockade from the Economic Council. As a member of this Council I objected to the whole idea, stating that a peace signed under such pressure would not survive the revulsion of world opinion. It was proposed that the Economic Council make public its plan. Both McCormick and I objected in the Council meeting because neither of us approved.

As I did not like any aspect of reimposing the blockade, I addressed a protest to the President:

Paris, 14 May 1919

Dear Mr. President:

    . . . [First I wish to express] . . . my strong view that we should not be led into joining with the Allies in a food blockade against Germany as a method of forcing peace. The margins on which the German people must live from now until next harvest are so small that any cessation of the stream of food, even for a short time, will bring the most wholesale loss of life. It might be that the imposition of a blockade would be effectual in securing the German signature to the peace. *I seriously doubt whether when the world has recovered its moral equilibrium that it would consider a peace obtained upon such a device as the starving of women and children as being binding upon the German people.* If the Germans did resist, it is my impression that it would throw Germany into complete chaos and military occupation would need to follow in order to save Europe.

    My second point is that I am placed in a serious embarrassment by the threat of a blockade, because we have a constant stream of nearly one hundred million dollars worth of food in motion towards Germany. With all the effort they make, they are scarcely able to keep pace with their gold and security payments with the actual arrivals in Germany, so that the total risk of this vast current of foodstuffs is now falling on my shoulders. If the current were stopped, it would mean we would have to pile up large amounts of foodstuffs in Europe, a large part of which is not of the type at present salable to the Allied countries. For instance, we are shipping rye, which the Allies do not eat, and types of fats of which the Allies have ample supply. We would have to face very great loss and seriously jeopardize the financial stability of the Food Administration. I have been willing to take the risk, in the feeling that without it peace and stability will not be secured, but I seriously doubt whether I have any right to involve you in the ensuing difficulties if I were to continue without your approval after I knew the gate to Germany would probably be closed. . . .

Faithfully yours,

HERBERT HOOVER

McCormick's Diary contains this entry for the same day:

Was called to the President's house at 11:00 to submit to Big Four our plan for blockade in the event of Germany refusing to sign. . . . When we started meeting I handed the President a letter I had just written him strongly recommending the use of military occupations instead of blockade in the event of Germany not signing. . . . I told the President this could not be and that the alternative was starvation and revolution in Germany. Everything would be lost to the Allies while occupation would save something out of the wreck. President made this statement to the Big Four and urged occupation.

McCormick's Diary the next day contains this entry:

At 2:00 went to President's house with Hoover, Davis, and Baruch to discuss with the President the blockade policy as to food if Germany refused to sign. Hoover urging food should go to Germany in any event. . . . President told him of our conversation with Big Four yesterday and that he advocated military occupation rather than starvation methods. President discussed freely his difficulties with his colleagues in Council — called them mad men, particularly Clemenceau. . . . He spoke feelingly of his struggles with Clemenceau and Lloyd George to hold them down to justice and reason and could not vouch for his being able to convince them that military occupation was better than the starvation method because the military occupation would cost more in money. . . .

As shown by his Papers, I discussed the matter with Colonel House and gave him an account of the suffering which existed due to the world shortage of food. He agreed with me on the evils of reimposing the blockade. Later, in describing a discussion of the subject with General Smuts, House records:

> We agreed that while public opinion did sustain the Entente in its blockade of Germany when they were fighting for their lives, it would not sustain them when they were starving women and children for the purpose of trying to force the signing of a treaty.
>
> . . . I sincerely trust that this ordeal will not have to be faced. I shall not be in favor of starving the people of Germany. At one time I thought perhaps this would be the only way out in the event Germany did not sign, but at that stage I did not know the real conditions in Germany and how much suffering there was. . . .

On June 13 the Supreme Council communicated its decision to the Economic Council:

> The Council of the Principal Allied and Associated Powers have . . . decided that the Blockade Council should make every preparation for the re-imposition of the Blockade but that its actual enforcement should not be undertaken, even in the event of the refusal by the Germans to sign the Treaty of Peace, without a decision from the Council of the Principal Allied and Associated Powers. No actual threat should be made public that the Blockade is to be reimposed but, short of this, steps should be taken to give the public impression that preparations are in hand. If practicable, these steps should include the despatch of destroyers to show themselves in the Baltic.
>
>   *(Initld)*
>   W. W.
>   G. C.
>   D. L. G.
>   S. S.
>   N. M.

McCormick's Diary on June 14 contains this item:

> Lunched with [the President's Committee of Economic] advisers in my room — General Bliss, Admiral Knapp, Hoover, Baruch, Davis, B. Palmer present. Hot discussion on treaty and blockade. Hoover and Bliss think it too hard; Baruch and I think it just and workable. *Hoover says if* blockade imposed he will resign. . . .

He might have added that my reason was a refusal to starve millions of innocent human beings. Also he could have added that Norman Davis agreed with Bliss and me.

15

THE DOTTED LINE

From the European point of view the focal point of the Conference was not the Covenant of the League but the Treaty with Germany. I have already dealt with President Wilson's triumph in winning agreement to the Covenant, although at the cost of serious compromises. Through the Treaty the entire structure of Europe was to be rebuilt.

The Treaty was formulated by various subcommittees made up from the different delegations, subject to higher authority—originally the Council of Ten, and later the Big Four. Each subcommittee cut a piece of the mosaic, but it was not assembled and printed as a whole until the day before the Germans were to receive it. The final document comprised about 75,000 words, 4,000 of which were devoted to the League Covenant.

The German Delegation of more than 100 members headed by Foreign Minister Count Brockdorff-Rantzau had been waiting in Versailles since April 29, but the Treaty was not ready until May 7. After it had been given to them, they were to be allowed a period in which to propose amendments. After Allied acceptance of any of the proposed changes, they were to be shown the dotted line.

At four o'clock on the morning of May 7 I was awakened by a troubled servant, who explained that there was a messenger waiting with an important document which he would put into no hands other than mine. It was the printed draft of the Treaty, which was to be handed to the Germans that day. At once I scanned its important parts. Although I had known the gist of many of the segments, I had not before had opportunity to envision it as a whole. Aside from the League Covenant, many provisions had been settled without considering their effect on others.

I certainly had no admiration for the conduct of the German militarists. But if the world was to have peace, it had, in my mind, to choose one of two alternatives: to reduce Germany to such poverty and political degradation that initiative and genius would be extinguished; or to give her terms that would permit the new representative government under President Ebert to live with the hope that free government might develop the nation as a peaceful member of the family of mankind. If this were not done, there would come either a return of the sullen militarists or the already infectious Communists—both with aggression in their souls.

I was convinced that the terms set up in this draft of the Treaty would degrade all Europe and that peace for the long run could not be built on these foundations. I believed the Treaty contained the seeds of another war. It seemed to me that the economic provisions alone would pull down the whole Continent and, in the end, injure the United States.

I arose at early daylight and went for a walk in the deserted streets. Within a few blocks I met General Smuts and John Maynard Keynes of the British Delegation. We seemed to have come together by some sort of telepathy. It flashed into all our minds why each was walking about at that time of morning. Each was greatly disturbed. We agreed that the consequences of many parts of the proposed Treaty would ultimately bring destruction. We also agreed that we would do what we could among our own nationals to point out the dangers.

General Smuts had full knowledge of Old World diplomacy, an independent mind and often real statesmanship. Keynes was the economist for the British Delegation. Lloyd George apparently did not like him and referred to him as the "Puck of Economics." He had a brilliant mind, powerful in analysis, and the gift of expression. Like most intellectuals, he was usually groping for new shapes and forms for the world, rather than for wisdom in what to do next. That sort of mind has a high place in the world, although it sometimes gets on the nerves of the fellow who must keep the machinery of civilization operating in the meantime. However, Keynes and I agreed fully on the economic consequences of the Treaty.[1]

Later that morning, I called together the thinking members of my own organization who were in Paris. These men knew every economic and political back alley of Europe better than any one group of the peacemakers. They could appraise the hard problems of the political and economic consequences of the proposed Peace Treaty with objective minds, free from hate and violence.

We sat for hours poring over the document. A summary of our views is worthy of record. The first question was: "How can the feeble German Republic endure if the Allies reimpose the food blockade to force its signature?" At this time our organization was struggling desperately against the world's shortage of food to prevent acute starvation in Germany. The delay in getting food to the Germans, by continuing the blockade for four months despite the promise made at the time of the Armistice, had drained almost the last remnants of breadstuffs and fats from their farms. The supplies which we could command with the shipping available were already below the need, and there was much suffering among the German workers. The situation was so bad that, in order to save the children of Germany, we had to channel a considerable part of the food supplies to this pitifully undernourished multitude, which added to the privation of their elders.

We were in a daily race against the spread of Communism (the Spartacists), which was steadily weakening the new German Republic under Ebert and Scheidemann, who, while they had no hesitation in using machine guns, were in fact using the food we supplied as their major weapon in maintaining order. The Communists had periodically seized various cities and provinces after the Armistice and had been suppressed in a sea of blood. Only a month before, the Spartacist Government of the Ruhr had been overthrown by bloody action. Twice Bavaria had gone Spartacist, and the last

[1] I at least won his commendation, for in a book published later he remarks:

Mr. Hoover was the only man who emerged from the ordeal of Paris with an enhanced reputation. This complex personality, with his habitual air of weary Titan (or, as others might put it, of exhausted prize fighter), his eyes steadily fixed on the true and essential facts of the European situation, imported into the Councils of Paris, when he took part in them, precisely that atmosphere of reality, knowledge, magnanimity and disinterestedness which, if they had been found in the other quarters, also would have given us the Good Peace.

time had been only seven days before. Despite all this, the Big Four had overridden the President and decided to reimpose the blockade until the Germans signed on the dotted line. My staff and I asked ourselves how many days of starvation the German Government could endure before it went over to Communism or to military dictatorship.

Even if the German Republic did not succumb to Communism or militarism, we feared that the separation of segments of the German people on her east and west borders would make Germany a poisonous breeding ground for unification movements. The Treaty would reduce the population from about 90,000,000 to about 60,000,000 under the Reich. We recalled that, in the past, European statesmen had periodically dismembered Germany and had lived to see it unified in the explosion of war.[2]

We canvassed the consequences of the transfer of segments of other races to Poland, Czechoslovakia and Rumania. Some of these nations were already virtually at war over their boundaries.

Along with these doubts, we were completely agreed that the provisions for monetary and commodity reparations required from Germany would bring quick disaster. We were certain that the claims for damages without some fixed sum within her capacity to pay would stifle her ability and incentive to maintain production. We believed the initial reparations payment of five billion dollars in cash, coal, machinery, tools and ships would strip Germany of working capital. This alone would prevent her from regaining industrial productivity from which reparations could be paid. Our calculations, for instance, showed that Germany's possible coal supply would be cut nearly in half by her loss of Alsace-Lorraine, the Saar and parts of Silesia. The Germans would have no fuel for household use if they were to keep their industries going.

We examined the question of mandates and the elements of positive empire building among the mandatories. We believed the repression of freedom movements in the Arab States would yield only trouble. The great injury to China, by assigning the German titles in the Shantung Province to Japan, would keep Asia in a turmoil.

---

[2] Hitler's rise with the German people fourteen years after Versailles was largely due to his crusade for unification, his strength increasing with every step he took in recreating political unity, until 80,000,000 Germans were incorporated within the Reich. He became strong enough to repudiate the whole Treaty; then attacked Poland, France and their Allies.

We were all staunchly for the Covenant of the League but had fears of the outcome of Article X and the coercion provisions.

My colleagues and I were of the opinion that the Germans, when they had their say, would no doubt point out with truth that the Treaty was far removed from the President's "basis of peace," upon which they had surrendered. They would probably indicate every pinhole in the Treaty with vigor and would no doubt ask for more than they deserved. Those of my group who knew the members of the German Ministry were convinced that the Germans could not sign the Treaty as it stood and survive politically at home.

We believed that, if the Germans did sign without substantial relaxation in terms, there could be no real recovery in Germany and the Treaty would sooner or later need to be revised. On the other hand, we believed that, if they signed on the proposed terms, the economic degeneration in the rest of the world would be checked. Its signing should end the killing of men; it would end the blockade and the black lists; it would restore many technical treaties upon which international commerce revolved; it would tend to reduce the vast unemployment over the world; it would bring new hope to the rest of the world.

However, my colleagues and I concluded that the first thing to do was to use our influence, however minor, in order to improve the Treaty.

When the Treaty was presented to the Germans on May 7, Clemenceau made a short and pointed speech, part of which was as follows:

> ... It is neither the time nor the place for superfluous words. You have before you the accredited plenipotentiaries of all the Small and Great Powers united to fight together in the war that has been so cruelly imposed upon them. The time has come when we must settle our accounts. You have asked for peace. We are ready to give you peace.
>
> We shall present to you now a book which contains our conditions. You will be given every facility to examine those conditions, and the time necessary for it. Everything will be done with the courtesy that is the privilege of civilized nations.
>
> To give you my thought completely, you will find us ready to give you any explanation you want, but we must say at the same time that this Second Treaty of Versailles has cost us too much not to take on our side all the necessary precautions and guarantees that this peace shall be a lasting one.

German Foreign Minister Count von Brockdorff-Rantzau read a prepared address from which I concluded that his delegation expected the worst.

The Germans began their replies to Allied demands in a series of notes beginning on May 10, the first of which read in part:

> The German Peace Delegation has finished the first perusal of the Peace Conditions which have been handed over to them. They have had to realize that on essential points the basis of the Peace of Right, agreed upon between the belligerents, has been abandoned. They were not prepared to find that the promise, explicitly given to the German People and the whole of mankind, is in this way to be rendered illusory.
>
> The draft of the Treaty contains demands which no nation could endure; moreover, our experts hold that many of them could not possibly be carried out.
>
> The German Peace Delegation will substantiate these statements in detail and transmit to the Allied and Associated Governments their observations and their material continuously.

On May 29 the Germans had completed their analysis in the form of dispatches or protests. They repeatedly pointed out the entire failure to adhere to the "Fourteen Points and the subsequent addresses" which they insisted were the basis of their surrender. They claimed that they were unnecessarily humiliated by the requirements that they admit complete guilt for the war and surrender the Kaiser and his warmakers for trial by the Allies. They asked for more amendments than were warranted. But some of their criticism was sound from the viewpoint of common world interests and was in accord with the objectives for which Woodrow Wilson had contended.

Smuts and Keynes at once became active among the British, urging amendments. They and others on the British Delegation communicated their views to the British Cabinet in London. Some of the leaders of their Government came to Paris to discuss Lloyd George's handiwork in shocked terms.[3] Lloyd George was easily adaptable.

---

[3]Gordon Auchincloss (Colonel House's secretary) on June 2, 1919, records in his Diary:

> ...The British Cabinet came to Paris on Sunday and told Lloyd George very plainly that British people were not behind him and would not support the peace that he had proposed to have Germany sign. Accordingly as soon as the Germans made their answer, Lloyd George started to run and now wants to

As time went on, the British shifted sensibly.

I brought about a meeting of Smuts and Keynes with McCormick and myself in order that McCormick might learn our joint views. Now that Colonel House had faded into the background, McCormick and Baruch had more personal influence with the President at this time than any other Americans in Paris. But we found that McCormick was in favor of the Treaty except that he wanted a forty billion dollar limit on reparations. He told me and the others repeatedly that I was wrong; that I exaggerated the consequences. My only reply could be, "Just wait about five years and see."

The views of my colleagues and myself in the Relief Organization as to the dynamite planted in the Treaty were shared by other responsible men in Paris.

Secretary Lansing, in his book, vows his disbelief that the Treaty would bring peace. He cites a memorandum which he had prepared on May 8, the day after the Germans had first been presented with the Treaty:

> . . . for the first time in these days of feverish rush of preparation there is time to consider the Treaty as a complete document.
>
> The impression made by it is one of disappointment, of regret, and of depression. The terms of peace appear immeasurably harsh and humiliating, while many of them seem to me impossible of performance.
>
> The League of Nations created by the Treaty is relied upon to preserve the artificial structure which has been erected by compromise of the conflicting interests of the Great Powers and to prevent the germination of the seeds of war which are sown in so many articles and which under normal conditions would soon bear fruit. The League might as well attempt to prevent the growth of plant life in a tropical jungle. Wars will come sooner or later. . . .

He further states:

> We have a treaty of peace, but it will not bring permanent peace because it is founded on the shifting sands of self-interest.
>
> The day following my return from London on May 17, I

---

make all kinds of concessions. I have very little sympathy for him for he has got himself into the mess that he is in. The President tried to oppose the peace terms as finally put up particularly the economic ones but whenever he raised objections Lloyd George flattened him out or cajoled him into accepting the British proposals. . . .

received...letters from five of our principal experts protesting against the terms of peace and stating that they considered them to be an abandonment of the principles for which Americans had fought. One of the officials, whose relations with the President were of a most intimate nature, said that he was in a quandary about resigning; that he did not think that the conditions in the Treaty would make for peace because they were too oppressive. ...This official was evidently deeply incensed, but in the end he did not resign, nor did the five experts who sent letters, because they were told that it would seriously cripple the American Commission in the preparation of the Austrian Treaty if they did not continue to serve.

Professor Joseph V. Fuller, an important member of the American Delegation, resigned, writing in part to Undersecretary of State Grew on May 15:

MY DEAR MR. GREW:

...We have bartered away our principles in a series of compromises with interests of imperialism and revenge, until hardly a shadow of them remains. Instead of assuring the peace of the world by a just reconstitution, this treaty seeks guarantees for a settlement in favor of the victors which reduces the vanquished to a powerless and indefinite servitude. Such a settlement assures neither permanence nor tranquility. My earnest conviction is that our country dishonors itself in adding its signature and guarantee.

If, in view of these opinions, my services should be no longer desired, I shall be glad to be relieved from my duty with the Commission.

General Bliss, in Palmer's account, wrote to Mrs. Bliss:

Tuesday [May 6] we had a secret plenary seance to listen to a stupid exposition of the Peace terms for the benefit of the smaller Powers. None of us had seen the treaty. I have never seen such a glaring case of secret diplomacy, notwithstanding all our protestations. The outrageous yielding to Japan on the Shantung question could never have happened if it had not been done secretly. The protests of the world would have prevented it. Thank God, my skirts are clear (or at least my conscience is) of any of the wrong doing.

Yesterday the Treaty was handed to the Germans.

A month later, on June 6, he wrote to Mrs. Bliss:

... The Council of the Powers is still discussing whether it will listen to the counter proposals of the Germans. Five years from now the world will condemn the Conference if it does not listen to them. The Treaty as it stands is unworkable. . . .

On June 16 he again wrote:

... What a wretched mess it all is! If the rest of the world will let us alone, I think we had better stay on our own side of the water and keep alive the spark of civilization to relight the torch after it is extinguished over here. If I ever had any illusions, they are all dispelled. The child-nations that we are creating have fangs and claws in their very cradles and before they can walk are screaming for knives to cut the throats of those in the neighboring cradles.

General Bliss informed me that he was asked to sign a statement with other Americans that he "heartily and unreservedly" approved of all the "provisions of this important document." He said that his conscience would not permit him to sign, as he had written a letter to the President against the Shantung concession and because there were other provisions which he did not approve.

House records in his Diary for May 16:

General Smuts called in the morning to tell me that he and Botha had almost decided not to sign the Treaty if the Entente refused to make such changes in it as the Germans suggested, and which the liberal world would approve. He thought the Germans would win a decided diplomatic victory by pointing out the many injustices which the Treaty contained. He also thought in the event the Entente refused these just demands, and should then undertake to blockade Germany and starve her people into submission, it would cause world-wide revulsion.

Ray Stannard Baker, who was in charge of the President's Press Bureau, records in his *American Chronicle*:

When I read the first proofs of the Treaty as it was originally drawn, it seemed to me a terrible document; a dispensation of retribution with scarcely a parallel in history. I thought the German delegation, which had then arrived at Versailles, would fall in a swoon when they saw it. I questioned whether they would sign it. "If they do," I wrote, "it will be with crossed fingers. I can see no real peace in it. They have tempered justice with no mercy."

Even the President said to me, "If I were a German, I think I should never sign it."

Baker also writes:

This Treaty seems to me, in many particulars, abominable. How can I go home and support it, support the League of Nations founded upon it, support Wilson? Yet I cannot commit the folly of mere empty criticism, harking back to what might have been done. I know too well the impossible atmosphere of greed, fear, hatred, he has had to work in. I have felt it myself, every day, every hour.

Baker, at another point recalled:

The mercurial Lloyd George, especially, was seriously alarmed. He had Colonel House to lunch with him and told him in so many words that the liberal and labor criticism in England was reaching great strength and that he favored making changes, even considerable changes, in the Treaty. The next morning Clemenceau told the Colonel that he was against any changes whatever in the Treaty. He was for forcing it straight through.

On May 30, General Smuts wrote the President, the gist, according to the Baker Papers, being:

DEAR PRESIDENT WILSON:

Even at the risk of wearying you I venture to address you once more.

The German answer to our draft Peace Terms seems to me to strike the fundamental note which is most dangerous to us, and which we are bound to consider most carefully. They say in effect that we are under solemn obligation to them to make a Wilson Peace a peace in accordance with your Fourteen Points and other Principles enunciated in 1918. To my mind there is absolutely no doubt that this is so....

...it has been one of our most important war aims to vindicate international law and the sanctity of international engagements. If the Allies end the war by following the example of Germany at the beginning, and also confront the world with a "scrap of paper," the discredit on us will be so great that I shudder to think of its ultimate effect on public opinion....

I think the Germans make out a good case in regard to a number of provisions....

There will be a terrible disillusion if the people come to

think that we are not concluding a Wilson Peace, that we are
not keeping our promises to the world or faith with the public. . . .
Yours very sincerely,

J. C. SMUTS

I could have given more credence to this stand of the General
had it not been for his record on the mandates.

Baker records, in his *American Chronicle*:

When I went up to see the President on the evening of May
31, I raised the urgent problem of possible changes. . . . He asked
me what my own opinion was; I could not help saying exactly
what I thought: that it was an unworkable treaty.

"If the economic clauses are enforced, there is no hope of
collecting the reparations. The two clauses are mutually destructive."

"I told Lloyd George and Clemenceau as much when we had
it under discussion," he said, "but there was no changing them."

I observed that Lloyd George seemed now inclined to make
modifications.

He asked if I thought our people were interested in the details.

"Not now," I said, "but they will be later. When your enemies
in the Senate, Mr. President, begin to discuss the League of
Nations they will want to examine the basis upon which it rests
and what it is they are guaranteeing — and that will mean a close
scrutiny of the Treaty."

I am afraid I pushed the argument too far, for the President
arose abruptly and made an end of the conversation. But I had
at least cleared by own mind and expressed my own doubts.

Norman Davis and I called upon the President and urged that
we take advantage of the British recantation. We pointed out many
provisions in the Treaty which he had opposed.

According to the Baker Papers, Norman Davis wrote to the
President on June 1:

We strongly recommend that a definite amount be fixed,
[apparently 20 billion dollars], that Germany be permitted to retain
her present required working capital, that some arrangement be
made whereby Germany may retain enough of her own mercantile
marine for her own requirements, and that the Repatriation Commission be given more constructive and fewer destructive powers.

NORMAN H. DAVIS

General Bliss urged the President to call the leading Americans on his staff into conference and seek their views. This he agreed to do. The meeting took place on June 3 with thirty-nine present. There are fragmented accounts but no complete minutes of what was said.

Although many present had previously expressed their misgivings to me, the only persons who really spoke out were Norman Davis, General Bliss and myself. Davis urged the necessity of a moderate, fixed sum of reparations spread over a period of time in such a way as to inspire German incentive to meet it. General Bliss protested the Rhineland and other military proposals. I expressed the belief that there was great danger that the Ebert Republic might not survive the Treaty. I mentioned various dangerous provisions and cited the effect on German coal supplies as an example.

The discussion rambled over many immaterial questions, such as when the Germans might join the League and what the respective Polish and German populations were in Silesia and which of them were the first owners of that area hundreds of years ago.

At one point I stated that certain things proposed were not expedient if we expected the Germans to carry out the Treaty in good faith.

Vance McCormick in his Diary under the date of June 3 gives this version of the President's reply:

> . . . It was not a question of expediency but one of being satisfied in our own consciences that we were doing the just thing and then stick to our demands whatever the result. . . . The Treaty is a hard one, but a hard one was needed. . . .

The minutes of the meeting recorded in the Baker Papers state that I replied:

> . . . But we look at expediency in many lights. It may be necessary to change the terms of the reparation in view of getting something, rather than to lose all. And it is not a question of justice; justice would require, as I see it, that they pay everything they have got or hope to get. But in order to obtain something, it may be expedient to do this, that and the other. . . .

The President concluded, according to Baker's book, *Woodrow Wilson and World Settlement:*

Personally I think the thing will solve itself upon the admission of Germany to the League of Nations. . . . But we cannot arrange that in the treaty because you cannot fix the date at which Germany is to be admitted into the League.

Since the debate at this meeting was mostly desultory, I did not feel that my statement at the time fully expressed my views. Therefore, on June 4, I followed up with this note to Mr. Wilson:

MY DEAR MR. PRESIDENT:

In this most critical moment, I know you will not take it amiss if I express my views somewhat more fully than is possible at such a conference as that of Tuesday morning. I, of course, have had no part in the Treaty making, and for this reason and the independent sources of information which I have enjoyed, I have had perhaps a useful opportunity in objective observation. I do wish you to feel that what ever the course you may choose I am, for what I am worth, prepared to stand by.

I am convinced the Germans will not sign the Treaty without considerable modification. I do not feel that strict justice is now in question, for no adequate punishment of German crimes is possible or is even dealt out in the present draft treaty, although some points relate to this issue. From an American point of view, we have been fighting autocracy and militarism and I feel that the paramount issues now are to secure stability of government in Europe, to secure the establishment of democracy in Germany and of a League of Nations, which may be able to further correct the international wrongs which have accumulated over centuries; deter them in the future, and give security to the many nations that have been re-created.

I feel that even if Germany signed the present terms, we would not secure stability and that if she refuses we will have extinguished the possibility of democracy in favor of either Communism or reaction, and that we will have wrecked the very foundation of the League of Nations.

To secure the signature of the Treaty by blockade or the bombing of German towns would itself guarantee a later revision of the Treaty by the moral shock to the world. Military occupation, I am convinced, will be welcomed by the Germans as an alternative to the Treaty in its present form, for occupation would be a guaranty of the survival of the German people at the expense of the Allies.

I feel that many issues in the Treaty which prevent its acceptance have been pressed into the draft in shapes against what you and your American colleagues have consistently contended with farsighted statesmanship. There has been a tendency [of the Americans] to yield on these points because of the belief that the very survival of 200 million people revolved around early conclusion of these negotiations; their return of these populations to production, and that time and economic forces would remedy the worst phases. I see in the present British change of heart a tendency to recognition of the wisdom of your original positions and this fact offers an opportunity not only to remind them of your original proposals and to state to them that we are glad that they have come to a realization and are ready to support important modifications which affect themselves as well as others. If such modifications do not secure signature, it will have at least demonstrated our faithfulness to your high objectives.

Faithfully yours,

HERBERT HOOVER

The next day Secretary Lansing, who was, as I have indicated earlier, opposed to parts of the Treaty, and who had seen my letter to the President, requested that I amplify the subject in a memorandum for him. He sent a copy to the President. The important parts of the memorandum were as follows:

DEAR MR. SECRETARY:

In any discussion of the draft treaty, I think it must be accepted as a premise that real justice can never be meted out, for no adequate punishment of German crimes is conceivable or even compassed in the present draft treaty. Therefore, if we strip the subject of questions of punishment and also of all humanitarian views toward the Germans the impression I get from a study of the situation is as follows:

A

The objectives [in the Treaty] desired appear to me to be:

I. To take all the economic surplus of Germany for a generation. This premise necessarily assumes that it is not desired to claim more than the surplus, for in such case the population will either (a) die, (b) migrate, or (c) plunge into economic chaos that will engulf Europe, and in either case yield no surplus.

II. To effect such regime and control as will strip Germany of the power of political and military offensive. This premise assumes that it is desired to establish stable democracy in Germany, for otherwise she will turn either to Communism or to reaction, and will thereby become either militarily or politically on the offensive.

III. To secure signature to and acquiescence in the treaty by the German people. This premise necessitates that the signature should be obtained without either (a) blockade, (b) bombing of towns, or (c) military occupation. I assume that a treaty signed under either blockade or bombing would be revised within twelve months under the recoil of the moral shock to the world, and I also assume that military occupation means not only further enormous sacrifices to the Allies but also developing political entanglements amongst themselves. Furthermore, it is not at all certain that it would be unwelcomed by a very large part of Germany as a guarantee of food, industrial recuperation and protection of private property; under any occupation the population must be fed and put to production, and this will be at least at the initial expense of the Allies.

B

As I weigh the draft treaty on these premises and alternatives, I am convinced that: (a) the demands made are greater than the economic surplus; (b) that the regime and controls are such as endanger stable democracy in Germany; and (c) that the Germans will never sign the treaty in its present form. The present Government in Germany is the only alternative to either Reactionary or Communistic Government, and if it fails we have political debacle....

C

I am not unaware that criticism is easy, nor am I unaware that the problem involved is the most difficult that statesmen have been confronted with, because it resolves itself into the degree with which all the objectives above can be imposed and still not create the adverse currents to which I have referred. Nor am I unaware of the fact that every statesman will have a different view as to the degree with which these demands can be imposed with success.

The point I would like to make is, however, that many of the demands in the draft treaty are impossible either of acceptance or, if accepted, will not obtain the results expected. They have been included against the protest of the President and his colleagues, but yielded by them because of their belief that the very survival of 200 million people revolved around the immediate conclusion of these negotiations and the return of these populations to production.

D

I see in the present British change of heart a tendency to the recognition of the President's original "propositions," and it appears to me that it offers an opportunity for the President now to definitely insist from an American point of view that these modifications should be carried out.

E

I am not sure how far we ought to sacrifice the United States to the objectives of the European Allies. To me, from an American point of view, we have been fighting autocracy and militarism and it has been destroyed. I feel that the paramount issues are now to secure stability of government in Europe; to secure the establishment of democracy in Germany; to secure a League of Nations that may be able to further correct the international wrongs which have been accumulated over centuries and deter the repetition of such wrongs in the future; to give security to the many nations that have been re-created and to secure to the Allies any practicable reparation.

If tested by this touchstone alone, modifications in the proposed treaty will not involve or jeopardize these points, whereas the failure to make immediate stable peace does jeopardize them. These are the high objectives which the President has held constantly before him as in the interest of the world as a whole, and I feel that the opportunity is arriving for the President to absolutely insist on his original contentions, even at the risk of disruption of the Conference. I believe this disruption is the least of evils; I do not believe it will happen. . . .

HERBERT HOOVER

A few days after the President had received this memorandum, he requested me to call on him to discuss the Treaty situation. I was, perhaps, overemphatic that we join with Lloyd George although I intended no personal criticism of Mr. Wilson. The President appeared to be a very tired man. He interrupted me sharply with the startling information that "Lloyd George will not stand up against Clemenceau despite what he says." I agreed that if this were the case, and the Germans signed the Treaty, then he must sign or there would be chaos over the whole earth.

Bernard Baruch later informed me that to satisfy the urgings of the Americans, the President (accompanied by Baruch) called upon Lloyd George and stated flatly that the Americans would go to any length to accept German amendments which the British would also accept. But inasmuch as he had in the first place opposed these very inclusions in the Treaty, which Lloyd George now proposed to amend, and as the British Prime Minister had sided with Clemenceau, he (the President) insisted that Lloyd George first obtain Clemenceau's agreement.

Mr. Wilson has been blamed because he did not get more revisions in the Peace Treaty when the British recantation gave him the opportunity. This is obviously unjust.

The Old Tiger refused to budge. On June 10, Tardieu states in his book, *The Truth about the Treaty*, that he wrote Colonel House a letter which constituted a formal notice from Clemenceau that the French would agree to no substantial changes whatever. He said:

> . . . These public discussions between Allies over the Treaty drawn up between Allies weaken us more every day in the eyes of an adversary who respects only firmness. . . .
>
> . . . a week ago, we ought to have answered the Germans, "We will change nothing." If we had only made this answer, the Treaty would be signed to-day. . . .
>
> No one has a right to ask France to accept such terms. . . .

The President concluded that the men and forces which dominated Europe could not be surmounted at this time, that the world must be saved from chaos by signing the Treaty and that there was hope that its wrongs could be cured in time by the League.

Ray Stannard Baker, in his *American Chronicle,* gives an interesting sidelight on the final draft of the Treaty:

> When the Treaty was being finally revised — that crowded Sunday and Monday — the French and British experts were there on the job watching every turn; our own, with the exception of the conscientious Haskins of Harvard and one other, were not there. "Jokers" were the result. For example, the French and British wanted us committed absolutely to permanent membership in the Reparations Commission; we, however, demanded and got a provision that any nation might withdraw from the Reparations Commission on twelve months' notice. . . . When, however, the Treaty itself appeared, this particular clause was missing. Who left it out? How was it left out? When the omission was discovered,

Lamont, Davis, and others rushed over to the President and the whole thing was brought before the Big Four and the earlier reading restored.

Another "joker" was discovered by the President himself. The words "for the mother country" had been added to the clause of the Covenant which provided for raising troops in colonies under mandatory, making it possible, for example, if France and Britain should go to war, for each to raise, say Arab troops, for fighting the other. Thus Arabs would be fighting Arabs for no cause of their own. When traced down it was found that Clemenceau himself had added the words — though he was not on the League of Nations Commission and had nothing to do with the Covenant, which had already been adopted at a plenary session. It took all the influence of both Lord [Robert] Cecil and Colonel House to get the French secretariat to make a change in the original text.

Baker also notes:

I made an opportunity in one of my talks with him [the President], to suggest again that the Treaty itself be released in America, so that our people could be promptly informed. No one over there had yet seen anything but our summary. This he objected to, saying that it would hamper them (the Council of Four) in making changes. I did not quite see how, for Herbert Hoover brought me two copies of a German translation of the Treaty that he bought at Rotterdam for two francs each.

On June 16, the German Delegation was given the Allied reply to their demands with an ultimatum to sign within five days.

In the Allied reply, a quotation was given from a speech by Lloyd George on December 14, 1917:[4]

There is no security in any land without the certainty of punishment. There is no protection to life, property or money in a state where the criminal is more powerful than the law. . . . There have been, many times in the history of the world, criminal states. We are dealing with one of them now . . . and the punishment of international crime becomes too sure to make it attractive.

Certain concessions were made to the Germans, principally as

---

[4] United States Department of State, *Papers Relating to the Foreign Relations of the United States* [The Paris Peace Conference, 1919], vol. VI, United States Government Printing Office, Washington: 1946, p. 928.

to plebiscites, in the areas designated for transfer to Denmark, Belgium, and Upper Silesia.

The other modifications were minor, and an assurance was given that with good conduct Germany could become a member of the League.

On June 16 Premier Clemenceau sent the following note to Count Brockdorff-Rantzau: [5]

> SIR:
>
> The Allied and Associated Powers have considered the Note of the German Delegation of even date, and in view of the shortness of the time remaining feel it their duty to reply at once.
>
> Of the time within which the German Government must make their final decision as to the signature of the Treaty, less than twenty-four hours remain. The Allied and Associated Governments have given the fullest consideration to all of the representations hitherto made by the German Government with regard to the Treaty, have replied with complete frankness, and have made such concessions as they thought it right to make, and the present Note of the German Delegation presents no arguments or considerations not already examined.
>
> The Allied and Associated Powers therefore feel constrained to say that the time for discussion has passed. They can accept or acknowledge no qualification or reservation, and must require of the German representatives an unequivocal decision as to their purpose to sign and accept as a whole or not to sign and accept the Treaty as finally formulated.
>
> After the signature the Allied and Associated Powers must hold Germany responsible for the execution of every stipulation of the Treaty.
>
> CLEMENCEAU

The German Delegation at Versailles refused to sign and took the train for Weimar to inform the German Ministry. They arrived in Weimar on June 19. Count Brockdorff-Rantzau recommended that the Treaty not be signed, saying: [6]

> If we can "hold out" for two or three months, our enemies will be at loggerheads over the division of the spoils, and then we shall

---

[5] Karl Friedrich Nowak, *Versailles*, Payson and Clarke Ltd., New York: 1929, pp. 279–280.

[6] *Ibid.*, pp. 264–265.

get better terms. If we sign now, no one will trouble to ask later on whether we signed under duress or not; our signature will have provided them with a formal legal authorization for all their demands.

If we refuse to sign, we shall be in purgatory for a time, for two or at most three months. If we sign, it means a lingering disease, of which the nation will perish.

Chancellor Scheidemann and six members of the Ministry resigned on June 20, refusing to be a party to the Treaty. A new and weak ministry sent two obscure persons to sign. But history has proved that with the threat of starvation and Foch's army pointed at them, the Germans signed with the belief that the Treaty would fall of its own weight, especially if they gave it systematic pushes.

On Saturday, June 28, we all went to the Hall of Mirrors at Versailles to witness the signing by thirty-two nations. General Smuts signed the Treaty as a British delegate and at the same time issued a press statement denouncing it and demanding revision.

I took satisfaction in the great spiritual lift the ceremony gave to the French people, as it was in this same Hall nearly fifty years before where they had been ruthlessly humiliated by the Germans. But I had difficulty in keeping my mind on the ceremony. It was constantly traveling over the fearful consequences of many of the paragraphs which these men were signing with such pomp, and then going back to the high hopes with which I had landed in Europe eight months before. I did not come away exultant.

16

WOODROW WILSON'S ORDEAL
OF SMOLDERING ENMITY

Before we leave the European scene I should record the unfriendly and cynical attitudes of the European leaders toward Mr. Wilson, his ideals and principles. There can be no doubt that, despite his efforts to ignore them, these emotions contributed greatly to his many ordeals and to his final tragedy. The reader must never lose sight of the fact that Prime Ministers Lloyd George, Clemenceau, and Orlando had accepted the President's proposals on November 4, 1918, which established the "Fourteen Points and the subsequent addresses" as the "basis of peace."

The minutes of the Allied meetings and the statements made by the Allied leaders, published years later, reveal clearly the smoldering enmity toward the President and his "basis of peace."

PRIME MINISTER LLOYD GEORGE

Lloyd George writes in his *War Memoirs:*

A few days later President Wilson gave utterance to his famous Fourteen Points. This declaration, which subsequently played such an important part at the Armistice and the Peace Conference, was not regarded by any of the Allies as being at variance on vital matters, except in respect of Freedom of the Seas, with their own declarations—*although we never formally accepted them, and they constituted no part of the official policy of the Alliance.*[1]

---

[1]This is a considerable variation, not only from the Agreement of November 4, 1918, but also from a speech made by Lloyd George himself at a review of the American troops near Paris, on July 5, 1918, when he said:

Lloyd George refers again to the "points":

> ...they were in places phrased in the language of vague idealism which, in the absence of practical application, made them capable of more than one interpretation.[1] It was not sufficient for Germany to express readiness to negotiate on the basis of the Fourteen Points, unless we were in a position to insist on her accepting our exegesis of the sacred text.

In his book, *The Truth about the Peace Treaties*, Lloyd George expresses his personal attitude toward Mr. Wilson, and at the same time reveals some of Clemenceau's attitudes:

> Clemenceau followed his movements [Wilson's] like an old watchdog keeping an eye on a strange and unwelcome dog who has visited the farmyard and of whose intentions he is more than doubtful....
>
> I really think that at first the idealistic President regarded himself as a missionary whose function it was to rescue the poor European heathen from their age-long worship of false and fiery gods. He was apt to address us in that vein, beginning with a few simple and elementary truths about right being more important than might, and justice being more eternal than force.... They [the Allies] were therefore impatient at having little sermonettes delivered to them, full of rudimentary sentences about things which they had fought for years to vindicate when the President was proclaiming that he was too proud to fight for them....
>
> ... He was the most extraordinary compound I have ever encountered of the noble visionary, the implacable and unscrupulous partisan, the exalted idealist and the man of rather petty personal rancours.

Other British leaders who were skeptical or downright opposed

---

> ...What are we here for? Not because we covet a single yard of German soil. Not because we desire to dispossess Germany of her inheritance. Not because we desire to deprive the German people of their legitimate rights. *We are fighting for the great principles laid down by President Wilson.*

For full text see *The New York Times*, July 7, 1918. The "great principles" referred to by Lloyd George would include the President's addresses of January 8, 1918, February 11, 1918, and July 4, 1918, which altogether would include 30 of his "points."

Discussing the peace terms in an address at Manchester on September 12, 1918, Lloyd George said, "President Wilson has stated them [the terms] from time to time and we stand by them."

to the President included Mr. Balfour, the Minister of Foreign Affairs, Lord Curzon, Walter Long and Winston Churchill—all members of the British Cabinet.

Churchill provides an account of a meeting at the Quai d'Orsay on the afternoon of October 29, 1918, four days prior to the British acceptance of the President's "basis of peace" (except for the point on the freedom of the seas). Present at this meeting were Lloyd George, Clemenceau, Mr. Balfour, Baron Sonnino and Colonel House. The question was how the Allies should reply to President Wilson's note asking them formally to confirm his proposals for the "basis of peace" with Germany. Churchill relates:[2]

> Mr. Lloyd George said that there were two closely connected questions. First there were the actual terms of an armistice. With this was closely related the question of terms of peace. If the notes which had passed between President Wilson and Germany were closely studied, it would be found that an armistice was proposed on the assumption that the peace would be based on the terms in President Wilson's speeches. The Germans had actually demanded an armistice on these conditions; consequently, unless something definite was said to the contrary, the Allies would be committed to President Wilson's peace terms. Hence, the first thing to consider was whether these terms were acceptable. He asked Colonel House directly whether the German Government were counting on peace being concluded on the basis of President Wilson's Fourteen Points and his other speeches. Colonel House said this was undoubtedly so. Mr. Lloyd George said that unless the Allies made their attitude clear, they would in accepting the armistice be bound to these terms.
>
> M. Clemenceau asked whether the British Government had ever been consulted about President Wilson's terms. France had not been. If he had never been consulted, he did not see how he could be committed. He asked if the British Government considered themselves committed. Mr. Lloyd George replied that they were not committed yet, but if he accepted an armistice without saying anything to the contrary, he would undoubtedly regard the British Government as committed to President Wilson's terms. Mr. Balfour confirmed this. Then said Clemenceau, "I want to hear the Four-

---

[2]See also dispatches from Colonel House to President Wilson on October 30, 1918, in United States Department of State, *Papers Relating to the Foreign Relations of the United States, 1918* (The World War supplement 1), vol. I, United States Government Printing Office, Washington: 1933, pp. 421–426.

teen Points." [The President had submitted the terms which he had settled with the Germans six days before the meeting on October 23.]

Lloyd George in his book, *The Truth about the Peace Treaties,* gives an account of a meeting of the British Cabinet and the Dominion Premiers to consider President Wilson's terms of peace about January 2, 1919—two months after they had already agreed to the President's "basis of peace." Lloyd George's report includes the interesting opinions of Winston Churchill:

> Mr. Churchill considered that the only point of substance was to induce the United States to let us off the debt we had contracted with them, and return us the bullion and scrip we had paid over, on the understanding that we should do the same to the Allies to whom we had made advances. If President Wilson were prepared to do that, we might go some way towards meeting his views.... For the rest, we should be civil and insist on our essential points.

Lloyd George continues his account of this meeting:

> Mr. Hughes [Prime Minister to Australia and a delegate to the Peace Conference] said that if we were not very careful, we should find ourselves dragged quite unnecessarily behind the wheels of President Wilson's chariot. He readily acknowledged the part which America had played in the war. But it was not such as to entitle President Wilson to be the god in the machine at the peace settlement, and to lay down the terms on which the world would have to live in the future. The United States had made no money sacrifice at all. They had not even exhausted the profits which they had made in the first two and a half years of the war. In men, their sacrifices were not even equal to those of Australia.... America had neither given the material nor the moral help which entitled her to come before France.... He hoped that Great Britain and France, which had both sacrificed so much, would defend their own interests, and not let their future be decided for them *by one who had no claim to speak even for his own country.* Mr. Lloyd George had received an overwhelming vote from his fellow-countrymen.... He and M. Clemenceau could settle the peace of the world as they liked. They could give America the respect due to a great nation which had entered the war somewhat late, but had rendered great service. It was intolerable, however, for President Wilson to dictate to us how the world was to be governed. If the saving of civilization had depended on the United States, it would have been in tears

and chains to-day. As regards the League of Nations, Mr. Hughes considered that a League of Nations which was to endure and weather the storms of time would have to be a thing like the British Empire, framed in accordance with historical associations and practical needs. President Wilson, however, had no practical scheme at all, and no proposals that would bear the test of experience. The League of Nations was to him what a toy was to a child—he would not be happy till he got it. His one idea was to go back to America and say that he had achieved it, and that everything else could then be left for the League of Nations to complete.... Speaking for Australia, he [Mr. Hughes] wanted to know what Australia was to get for the sacrifices she had made. When he had secured what he wanted... and reparation and indemnities, then he would have no objection to handing over other matters to a League of Nations.... He insisted that in any case we should not commit ourselves to the League of Nations until the Conference had completed its labours....

Lloyd George continues:

Lord Curzon considered that Mr. Hughes' views were shared by many members of the Imperial War Cabinet....

Mr. Long agreed cordially with the views expressed by Lord Curzon....

Curzon and Long were members of the British Cabinet.

Mr. Churchill, in his book, *The Aftermath,* is most bitter toward Mr. Wilson, saying:

The American peace argosy wended on across the waters bearing a man who had not only to encounter the moral obliquity of Europe, but to produce world salvation in a form acceptable to political enemies whom he had deeply and newly offended. Upon him centered the hopes of the world. Before him lay the naughty entanglements of Paris; and behind him, the sullen veto of the Senate.

If Mr. Wilson had been either simply an idealist or a caucus politician, he might have succeeded. His attempt to run the two in double harness was the cause of his undoing. The spacious philanthropy which he exhaled upon Europe stopped quite sharply at the coasts of his own country.

He did not wish to come to speedy terms with the European Allies; he did not wish to meet their leading men around a table; he saw himself for a prolonged period at the summit of the world, chastening the Allies, chastising the Germans and generally giving laws to mankind. He believed himself capable of appealing to peoples and parliaments over the heads of their own governments.... In the Peace Conference—to European eyes—President Wilson sought to play a part out of all proportion to any stake which his country had contributed or intended to contribute to European affairs.... He sought to bend the world—no doubt for its own good—to his personal views.... If President Wilson had set himself from the beginning to make common cause with Lloyd George and Clemenceau, the whole force of these three great men, the heads of the dominant nations, might have played with plenary and beneficent power over the wide scene of European tragedy. He consumed his own strength and theirs in conflicts in which he was always worsted.

MINISTER OF FOREIGN AFFAIRS BALFOUR

Lloyd George in his book, *The Truth about the Peace Treaties*, quotes British Foreign Minister Balfour's explanation at a meeting of the British Delegation on June 1 and 2, 1919, of how they came to agree to the "Fourteen Points":

> ... The Prime Minister and he suddenly found themselves faced with the Fourteen Points and the time was too short to discuss them [11 months had elapsed since Wilson's enunciation]. There was really no question whether there should be an Armistice or not. There had to be an Armistice. Time was the essence of the matter. They had no option but to take the Fourteen Points. They made some corrections in them, and they were supplemented by some perorations. He agreed that if the Fourteen Points were pressed from a legal point of view, it was possible to make out an awkward case, but it was only necessary to read the Fourteen Points to see that they were incapable of being treated in that strictly legal manner. For example, one point dealt with Russia, and by it all the Allies pledged themselves to welcome her into the League of Free Nations and to give her assistance of any kind which she might need or desire. It was impossible to interpret these words literally and to make a contract out of them. The point dealing with Italy afforded another example. It provided that a readjustment of the frontiers of Italy should be effected along recognisable lines of nationality.

PREMIER CLEMENCEAU'S VIEWS

Clemenceau in his book, *Grandeur and Misery of Victory,* makes a large variety of disparaging statements:

Mr. Wilson, when he sent us the American Army, had put to us the famous Fourteen Points. Were we prepared to cease fighting on the day when the Germans accepted these various points? If I had refused to reply in the affirmative it would have been nothing less than a breach of faith, and the country would have denounced me with one voice, while our soldiers would have disowned me, and with good reason....

Later there comes on the scene President Woodrow Wilson, armoured in his Fourteen Points, symbolized in as many pointed wisdom teeth that never let themselves be turned aside from their duty.

Doubtless he [President Wilson] had too much confidence in all the talky-talk and super-talky-talk of his "League of Nations."

... England in various guises has gone back to her old policy of strife on the Continent, and America, *prodigiously enriched by the war,* is presenting us with a tradesman's account that does more honour to her greed than to her self-respect.

President Wilson, the inspired prophet of a noble ideological venture, ... had insufficient knowledge of ... Europe.... It became incumbent on him to settle the destiny of nations by mixtures of empiricism and idealism.... He acted to the very best of his abilities in circumstances the origins of which had escaped him and whose ulterior developments lay beyond his ken.

Mr. Wilson had produced a marvellous effort of ideology when he proposed, systematically, and in accordance with their interdependence, to solve a mass of European problems which had long been the source of disturbance in the civilized world. At the word of the President saviour the old injustices were to be redressed.

... [The League of Nations] ... was nothing more than an epitome of the Parliaments of all nations, to which all historic disagreements, all diplomatic intrigues, all coalitions of national, or even private, egoisms were to come and concentrate, multiply, intensify, and perhaps sometimes even find some momentary mitigation.

Six months after the proclamation of the Fourteen Points Mr. Wilson, following up his idea without worrying about ways and means, submitted to American public opinion, in a speech at the

Independence Day celebrations at Mount Vernon (July [4,] 1918) the notions for a general peace on which his mind was centered. This time it was a question of four new points forming a sort of mystical creed defining the objects to be attained through the League of Nations. And to realize this work of pure ideology, in which the orator imperturbably entrenches himself, he concludes confidently that a simple "organization of peace" will "make this result certain."

There are probably few examples of such a misreading and disregarding of political experience in the maelstrom of abstract thought.

In his book, Lloyd George writes of the French Premier:

... he [Clemenceau] did not believe in the principle of self-determination, which allowed a man to clutch at your throat the first time it was convenient to him, and he would not consent to any limitation of time being placed upon the enforced separation of the Rhenish Republic from the rest of Germany....

The Prime Minister of Italy, Vittorio Orlando, although deeply hurt by Mr. Wilson's statement on Fiume, which caused his withdrawal from the Conference, did not in any of his writings attack Mr. Wilson. In fact, he was a most loyal supporter of the President's ideals and purposes among the European statesmen at the Conference—except as to Fiume.

But Francesco Nitti, who succeeded Orlando as Prime Minister of Italy before the Treaty was signed, had this to say:

... President Wilson, by his League of Nations, has been the most responsible factor in setting up barriers between nations.

Christopher Columbus sailed from Europe hoping to land in India, whereas he discovered America. President Wilson sailed from America thinking that he would bring peace to Europe, but he succeeded in bringing her only confusion and war.

On the other hand, the President on his return to the United States was most generous about his colleagues at Paris. He may have been under illusions about the feelings of some of them toward him.

Vance McCormick, in his Diary under date of July 5, 1919, says:

The President sent for Lamont, Davis, Baruch and me with Dr. Taussig to come to his room [on the *George Washington* returning to the United States] after lunch to read us his message to Congress to get our suggestions and criticisms.

We had few changes to suggest as it was an excellent general statement of the situation at Paris and the problems that confronted him. *We raised the question as to the praise given his colleagues and developed from him a real feeling of friendship for his colleagues whom he said privately were in accord with the principles we were fighting for* but were hampered and restricted by their own political conditions at home, due to the temper of their people. He said he was surprised *to find they had accepted the Fourteen Points not for expediency only but because they believed in them.*

He had probably mistaken politeness for friendship or failed to realize that "Truth is the first fatality of war."

17

WHAT WOODROW WILSON SAVED AT PARIS

In spite of failure and tragedy which was to come, it should be recorded here that Woodrow Wilson made great gains for mankind, and the influence of his ideals has extended over these many years.

Through his leadership and his sacrifices, he established for the first time in history a systematic and powerful organization of nations to maintain peace. Furthermore, he contributed a major part to the establishment of the Permanent Court of International Justice at The Hague and he established the International Labor Organization at Geneva.

Beyond these accomplishments he contributed greatly to establishing the rights of peoples to political independence and self-determination. This basis of freedom was not new but had seen little expression since early Greek and Roman times until it was reborn in the New World. Truly the great principles of personal liberty were pioneered in England before the American Revolution, but the American people expressed, and in some degree expanded, them in written constitutional law.

Prior to the First World War the fundamental beliefs and condition of free men had spread to only about 400,000,000 people —80 per cent of the human race was still oppressed.

Woodrow Wilson's expression of his ideals and his eloquent statements on the "basis of peace" brought a renewed thrust for freedom to mankind.

The press of every nation in the world carried his demands that:

There shall be no annexations.

National aspirations must be respected; peoples may now be dominated, and...[may now] be governed only by their own consent. "Self-determination" is not a mere phrase. It is an imperative principle of action....

Peoples and provinces are not to be bartered about from sovereignty to sovereignty as if they were mere chattels and pawns in a game....

Every territorial settlement involved in this war must be made in the interest and for the benefit of the populations concerned.

Its peace must be planted upon the tested foundations of political liberty.

After America entered the war in April 1917, under Mr. Wilson's banner of freedom, twenty-one races of men threw off their oppression by revolution.[1]

Woodrow Wilson never claimed the credit for this great upheaval. But there can be no doubt that his prior declaration of New World ideals had been a vital stimulant to these peoples to declare their freedom from oppression. History should record the role of his great proclamations in the quest for freedom, and the many acknowledgments from people who attained it.

It should not be forgotten that it was Woodrow Wilson who, at the time of the Armistice, nurtured and supported the organization of the greatest battle against famine and pestilence in the history of the world. Included in this work was the rehabilitation of millions of children, who otherwise would have brought inexpressible ills upon the world through their stunted minds and bodies. And it was under Wilson's leadership that America furnished 95 per cent of the materials and money for this battle to save Europe. Not only did his idealism save hundreds of millions of human beings, but he himself

---

[1] Estonia declared its independence on November 28, 1917; Finland on December 6, 1917; Latvia on January 12, 1918; Lithuania on February 26, 1918; Georgia, Azerbaijan and Russian Armenia on May 26, 1918; Czechoslovakia had given freedom to three races on October 25, 1918; four Southern Slav races, Croatia, Slovenia, Montenegro and the Banat, joined with Serbia on October 29, 1918, under a constitutional monarchy; Poland declared its independence on November 5, 1918; and the Hejaz (Saudi Arabia) on May 20, 1927. Of the enemy states, Germany established a republic on November 9, 1918; Hungary on November 16, 1918; Austria on September 10, 1919; Turkey on October 29, 1923.

refused to stoop to use the powers which American resources offered him in carrying out his terms of peace.

In my constant relations with the President on these matters, I learned of his forceful and clear mind, his administrative strength and his courage. He gave me unfailing support and encouragement in every position that I served under him and on every problem that I placed before him.

It is true that the President's compromises with the Allied demands for territorial spoils under the mandates and some of the secret treaties temporarily extinguished the aspirations to freedom in parts of Germany, the Middle East and parts of China.

But an enumeration of the "points" which the President lost at Paris is of little importance to history except as a demonstration of the hostility of Old World concepts to New World ideals. What needs to be recorded are the lasting upsurging toward freedom and the world organization for enduring peace which Woodrow Wilson brought to a distraught world.

18

THE PRESIDENT'S CRUSADE FOR
RATIFICATION OF THE TREATY

President Wilson finally left France for the United States on June 28, 1919, and arrived in New York on July 8. I bade him good-by at the station in Paris and had no opportunity to talk with him again at any length for over two years.

Upon the President's return home, he launched his crusade for Senate ratification of the Treaty. With an accompanying statement of great eloquence, he submitted the Treaty to the Senate on July 10 and the French-British-American military alliance on July 29. On August 19 he conferred with the members of the Senate Foreign Relations Committee.

By this time, Senators were in a sharp debate over the Treaty that was fully reflected in the press.

My own return home was delayed for over two months after the President's departure. The Relief and Reconstruction had to settle accounts amounting to billions of dollars with about thirty governments. We had undertaken to replace ourselves with a new volunteer organization to carry on the rehabilitation of millions of children and other great relief operations. We were still battling the gigantic typhus epidemic in Eastern Europe. In addition, the Governments in that part of the Continent had decided to maintain, at their own expense, some of the economic missions of our organization. This required us to install them in their new posts of railway, coal, and other economic agencies.

At the President's request I made a journey through Eastern Europe which involved meetings with the Austrian, Czechoslovakian and Polish Governments. Mr. Wilson thought that public appearances by me for purposes of "morale building" would be desirable.

The Supreme Council, on which Frank Polk, Undersecretary of State, was now substituting for the President, also gave my organization many missions. These stemmed from the invasion by Hungary of Czechoslovakia, of Hungary by Rumania, the settlement of little wars between Poland and Germany and between Poland and the Russian Communists, the uprisings of the Balts in Latvia and other such problems.

My staff and I in Paris were naturally interested in the events in Washington. We received cabled texts of the President's statements from the American Embassy and daily columns of news and comments on the discussions going on back in the States from the European press.

Although it was a busy time, in our spare moments our chief topic of conversation was the strategy being used by the President to obtain ratification. We realized that tactically, with the opposition the President had to meet in the Senate and from racial groups of enemy-state origin, he could not admit to his enemies that there was anything very seriously wrong with the Treaty or the Covenant if he were to secure ratification.

It was obvious that the opposition in the Senate and the country to ratification of the Treaty was concentrating mainly on Article X of the Covenant, which read:

> The Members of the League undertake to respect and preserve as against external aggression the territorial integrity and existing political independence of all Members of the League. In case of any such aggression or in case of any threat or danger of such aggression the Council shall advise upon the means by which this obligation shall be fulfilled.

The President's statements greatly stressed the inviolability of this article. To the Senate Foreign Relations Committee on August 19, he said:[1]

> Article X seems to me to constitute the very backbone of the whole Covenant. Without it the League would be hardly more than an influential debating society.

---

[1] *The New York Times*, August 20, 1919.

However, it was the view of my staff and myself that the Covenant would be more effective without Article X. We felt that the Covenant provided a powerful organization; that its provisions for determining aggressors, and its authority to use economic and military sanctions, were ample weapons against aggression. We felt that the major purpose of the League was to serve as a medium of pacific settlement of controversies among free nations. We had grave doubts about guaranteeing the boundaries of all the thirty-two signatories to the League, as some of them were already at war over boundary disputes.

Whatever our anxiety over these secondary questions, we were united on one overriding issue—the economic and social degeneration of Europe in the war, intensified in the eight months since the Armistice, was so appalling that Europe had to have peace, and at once.

In the midst of the discussions at home I was bombarded by the American press to make a statement on the Treaty. I did so on July 28, not only out of a sense of loyalty to the President but because I considered the Treaty an absolute necessity if *this* war were to be ended. Moreover, I believed that the League was our one hope of correcting the dangers in the Treaty.

My statement gives a picture of the situation in Europe at this time:

> There are one or two points in connection with the present treaty that need careful consideration by the American public. We need to digest the fact that we have for a century and a half been advocating democracy not only as a remedy for the internal ills of all society, but also as the only real safeguard against war. We have believed and proclaimed, in season and out, that a world in which there was a free expression and government based on the will of the majority was essential for the advance of civilization, and that we have proved its enormous human benefits in our own country.
>
> We went into the war to destroy autocracy as a menace to our own and all other democracies. If we had not come into the war every inch of European soil today would be under autocratic government. We have imposed our will on the world. Out of this victory has come the destruction of the four great autocracies in Germany, Russia, Turkey and Austria and the little autocracy in Greece. New democracies have sprung into being. . . .

We have been the living ... [force] for this last century and a half from which these ideas have sprung, and we have triumphed. The world today, except for a comparatively few reactionary and communistic autocracies, is democratic and we did it. ...

These infant democracies all have political, social and economic problems involving their neighbors that are fraught with the most intense friction. There are no natural boundaries in Europe. Races are not compact; they blend at every border. They need railway communication and sea outlets through their neighbor's territory.

Many of these States must for the next few years struggle almost for bare bones of existence. Every one of them is going to do its best to protect its own interests, even to the prejudice of its neighbors.

We in America should realize that democracy, as a stable form of government as we know it, is possible only with highly educated ... [peoples] and a large force of men who are capable of government. Few of the men who compose these governments have had any actual experience at governing and their populations are woefully illiterate.

They will require a generation of actual national life in peace to develop free education and skill in government.

Unless these countries have a guiding hand and referees in their quarrels, a court of appeals for their wrongs, this Europe will go back to chaos. If there is such an institution, representing the public opinion of the world, and able to exert its authority, they will grow into stability. We cannot turn back now. ...

Outside of the League of Nations the treaty itself has many deficiencies. It represents compromises between many men and between many selfish interests, and these very compromises and deficiencies are multiplied by the many new nations that have entered upon its signature and the very safety of the treaty itself lies in a court of appeal for the remedy of wrongs in the treaty.

One thing is certain. There is no body of human beings so wise that a treaty could be made that would not develop injustice and prove to have been wrong in some particulars. As the Covenant stands to-day there is a place at which redress can be found and through which the good will of the world can be enforced. The very machinery by which the treaty is to be executed, and scores of points yet to be solved, which have been referred to the League of Nations as a method of securing more mature judgment in a less heated atmosphere, justifies the creation of the League. ...

It would take the exposure of but a few documents at my hand to prove that I have been the most reluctant of Americans to become involved in this situation in Europe. But having gone in with our eyes open and with a determination to free ourselves and the rest of the world from the dangers that surrounded us, we cannot now pull back from the job. It is no use to hold a great revival and then go away....

We wound up our official Relief and Reconstruction organization in Europe early in September and installed in its place the American Relief Administration based upon charity.

I called on Premier Clemenceau on September 3 to express my appreciation for his undeviating support of my work. In another memoir, I have recalled:

... He was in a gloomy mood, saying, "There will be another world war in your time and you will be needed back in Europe."[2] We would not have agreed on the methods of preventing it, so I did not pursue the subject. But to lighten the parting, I said, "Do you remember Captain Gregory's report on the decline and fall of the Hapsburgs?" He laughed, pulled out a drawer in his desk and produced the original telegram, saying, "I keep it close by, for that episode was one of the few flashes of humor that came into our attempts to make over the world." He was still chuckling when we parted.

Upon leaving Europe I received generous messages of appreciation from him and thirty other Presidents or Prime Ministers together with all the great religious prelates in Europe. I arrived home on September 13, 1919.

THE PRESIDENT'S CRUSADE

While the President actually began his crusade for Senate ratification in his statement accompanying submission of the Treaty to the Senate on July 10, his major effort began on September 4, when he started west to carry the fight for Treaty ratification to the country. On this journey he made forty addresses (often two in a single city), in twenty-seven cities, stretching from Washington to the Pacific coast.

---

[2]The Premier was fairly accurate on both counts. The Second World War began twenty-one years after the end of the first one. I was back in Europe in 1946 to coordinate world food supplies to meet the second terrible famine, which was inevitable from that war.

He discussed the League at length in almost every address. His speeches were moving and impressive. He often referred to the vital relationship of Article X to the entire settlement. He was adamant against accepting any reservations to the Treaty. He devoted much time to explaining the compromise by which Japan was assigned the German rights in Shantung; he vigorously defended the mandates; he expounded on the changes made in the original draft of the Covenant to meet Senatorial concern for the Monroe Doctrine, to provide the right of withdrawal from the League and to safeguard our internal affairs. He explained the necessity for compromises on reparations and other features of the Treaty.

Mostly, the President spoke extemporaneously, and was often on his feet several hours during a day. This strain, together with the attendant travel and the necessity for constant contact with individuals, was greater than any human being should have risked— let alone a man physically weakened by the stresses of the war and seven months of negotiation in Paris.

The President collapsed after his speech at Pueblo, Colorado, on September 25. Through no fault of his own Woodrow Wilson's crusade was over.[3]

---

[3]When the President collapsed, I felt it my duty, out of loyalty to him and to my beliefs, to give him public support for Treaty ratification. I spent a week preparing a speech which I delivered at Stanford University on October 2.

I made addresses to various public meetings and made press statements frequently —about twenty in all—on the League and the Treaty from that time until the Presidential election of 1920.

19

WOODROW WILSON'S ORDEAL OF
STROKE AND PARALYSIS

There was so much mystery, misunderstanding and misrepresentation about Mr. Wilson's physical collapse that it is possible only in retrospect to appraise the facts, some of which were initially suppressed.

The amount of confusion among the public and even in the Cabinet as to the character or the degree of the President's illness was evidenced from many quarters. Colonel House was probably the best collector of Washington gossip. He writes in his Diary, under date of October 21, 1919, a month after Pueblo:

> The President's condition is such that no one is seeing him outside of his physician and Mrs. Wilson. Both Burleson and Lansing have been here to see me. Burleson came at the request of Secretary Baker. The entire Cabinet are greatly exercised over the President's inability to transact executive business....
>
> There is much discussion in Washington and elsewhere as to whether the President has suffered a stroke. McAdoo, who has seen him, declares Grayson says he has not had one. On the other hand, when the President became so much worse after he returned to Washington, Tumulty told Lansing the President had had a stroke which affected his left side. . . .

On December 27, three months after the stroke, another entry in the Colonel's Diary records a conversation with Lansing:

> He [Lansing] believes the President is much sicker than the public is led to believe. He does not think the President is writing

any of the papers purporting to come from him. Lansing himself wrote the Thanksgiving Proclamation, and it came back unchanged with the President's signature, I understood him to say, on the top instead of at the end. The signature was almost illegible.

David Lawrence has said that the President extracted a promise from his intimates that his condition would not be made known while he was President.[1]

In any event, the seriousness of the President's illness did not become generally known to the public until long afterward. The most important sources of accurate information are the books written two years after the President's collapse by Joseph P. Tumulty, the White House Secretary, and the much more ample disclosures of Mrs. Wilson in her *Memoir*, published two decades afterwards. Both Mrs. Wilson and Mr. Tumulty were at the President's side at all times during this period.

Mrs. Wilson says that Admiral Grayson, the President's doctor, had advised against the undertaking of his crusade in September, that severe headaches began early on the journey and that he became physically exhausted with his address at Pueblo on September 25. Under Doctor Grayson's orders the remaining speeches were canceled and the train was directed to return at once to Washington.

As to whether there was evidence of paralysis on the journey there is difference of opinion. In any event, on October 2, on arriving at the White House, the President's left side was completely paralyzed. Mrs. Wilson's record of what followed is:

> Nurses came and the house was organized as a hospital. Dr. Francis X. Dercum, the great nerve specialist of Philadelphia, Dr. Sterling Ruffin and Admiral E. R. Stitt of the Naval Medical Corps, were summoned.

Mrs. Wilson's account reflects both her devotion and her intelligence. She was an effective guardian over him.

> ...For days life hung in the balance. Then the will to live, to recover and fight on for his League of Nations, almost imperceptibly at first, began to gain ascendency over the forces of disease, and the President got a little better.
>
> A workable system of handling matters of State had scarcely

---

[1]David Lawrence, *The True Story of Woodrow Wilson*, Doubleday & Company, Inc., New York: 1924, p. 290.

been evolved when a terrible complication interrupted the progress of our patient. A stricture occurred, blocking elimination from the bladder. Its continuance meant death. A consultation of specialists was called—Dr. Hugh Young of Johns Hopkins, Dr. H. A. Fowler of Washington, Dr. Dercum, Dr. Ruffin, Dr. Stitt and Dr. Grayson. It was the seventeenth day of October. After an unsuccessful attempt to relieve the patient by means of local applications, the doctors retired to come to a final decision....

... Finally the nurse came to say that the President was asking for me. When I rose to go Dr. Young called after me: "You understand, Mrs. Wilson, the whole body will become poisoned if this condition lasts an hour, or at the most two hours, longer. . . ."

The two hours had gone by and we were well into the third when, suddenly, the tense condition relaxed and Nature again asserted her power over disease. The temperature receded, and the weary patient slept. The doctors went home to rest, and again peace descended upon my spirit.

This crisis proved a serious setback, however, taking much of my husband's vitality. Patiently we went to work to build him up again.

Once my husband was out of immediate danger, the burning question was how Mr. Wilson might best serve the country, preserve his own life and if possible recover. Many people, among them some I had counted as friends, have written of my overwhelming ambition to act as President; of my exclusion of all advice, and so forth. I am trying here to write as though I had taken the oath to tell the truth, the whole truth, and nothing but the truth—so help me God.

I asked the doctors to be frank with me; that I must know what the outcome would probably be, so as to be honest with the people. They all said that as the brain was as clear as ever, with the progress made in the past few days, there was every reason to think recovery possible....

But recovery could not be hoped for, they said, unless the President were released from every disturbing problem during these days of Nature's effort to repair the damage done.

"How can that be," I asked the doctors, "when everything that comes to an Executive is a problem? How can I protect him from problems when the country looks to the President as the leader?"

Dr. Dercum leaned towards me and said: "Madam, it is a grave situation, but I think you can solve it. Have everything come to you; weigh the importance of each matter, and see if it is possible by consultations with the respective heads of the Departments to solve them without the guidance of your husband. In this way you can save him a great deal. But always keep in mind that every time you take him a new anxiety or problem to excite him, you are turning a knife in an open wound. His nerves are crying out for rest, and any excitement is torture to him."

"Then," I said, "had he better not resign, let Mr. Marshall succeed to the Presidency and he himself get that complete rest that is so vital to his life?"

"No," the Doctor said, "not if you feel equal to what I suggested. For Mr. Wilson to resign would have a bad effect on the country, and a serious effect on our patient. He has staked his life and made his promise to the world to do all in his power to get the Treaty ratified and make the League of Nations complete. If he resigns, the greatest incentive to recovery is gone; and as his mind is clear as crystal he can still do more with even a maimed body than any one else. He has the utmost confidence in you. Dr. Grayson tells me he has always discussed public affairs with you; so you will not come to them uninformed."

So began my stewardship. I studied every paper, sent from the different Secretaries or Senators, and tried to digest and present in tabloid form the things that, despite my vigilance, had to go to the President. I, myself, never made a single decision regarding the disposition of public affairs. The only decision that was mine was what was important and what was not, and the very important decision of when to present matters to my husband.

He asked thousands of questions, and insisted upon knowing everything, particularly about the Treaty. He would dictate notes to me to send to Senator Hitchcock who was leading the fight for the Treaty in the Senate. Or he would tell me what Senators to send for, and what suggestions he had to make to them. These directions I made notes of, so, in transmitting his views, I should make no mistake; and I would read them to him before going to the interviews. This method of handling interviews was another suggestion of the doctors. It is always an excitement for one who is ill to see people. The physicians said that if I could convey the messages of Cabinet members and others to the President, he would escape the nervous drain audiences with these officials would entail. Even the necessary little courteous personal conversations that go with an official interview would consume the President's strength.

As an indication of the strains of the period, Tumulty describes a call by Secretary Lansing at the White House:

> A few days after the President returned from the West and lay seriously ill at the White House, with physicians and nurses gathered about his bed, Mr. Lansing sought a private audience with me in the Cabinet Room. He informed me that he had called diplomatically to suggest that in view of the incapacity of the President we should arrange to call in the Vice-President to act in his stead as soon as possible, reading to me... the following clause of the United States Constitution:
>
>> In case of the removal of the President from office, or his death, resignation, or inability to discharge the powers and duties of the said office, the same shall devolve upon the Vice-President.

Tumulty records his indignation at the proposal but it was freely discussed in the press. The President probably never saw these comments.

However, according to Secretary of the Treasury David Houston, the Cabinet met regularly to transact interdepartmental business but had little contact with the President except through Tumulty. The President was so ill that he was unable to meet with the Cabinet until April 13, 1920, an interval of more than seven months.

During this time the accounts of Secretary Tumulty and Mrs. Wilson record a formal call of the King and Queen of the Belgians on October 30 and of the Prince of Wales on November 15. On December 4 the Senate appointed Senator Fall and Senator Hitchcock as a committee to inquire about the President's condition. They reported that his mind was clear and that he was getting better.

Mrs. Wilson also recorded a visit by Bernard Baruch and Senator Hitchcock. But the President's old friends, including Colonel House and Ray Stannard Baker, were not allowed to see him.

In the midst of this period, on February 11, 1920, a political explosion was touched off by the President in a letter to Secretary Lansing, which read in part:

> While we were still in Paris, I felt, and have felt increasingly ever since, that you accepted my guidance and direction on questions with regard to which I had to instruct you only with increasing reluctance....

...I must say that it would relieve me of embarrassment, Mr. Secretary, the embarrassment of feeling your reluctance and divergence of judgment, if you would give your present office up and afford me an opportunity to select some one whose mind would more willingly go along with mine.

On the following day, February 12, Lansing resigned as Secretary of State and Bainbridge Colby was appointed to replace him on February 25.

I held Secretary Lansing in high esteem for his outstanding capabilities as an international lawyer and a man of keen intellectual attainments. He had been a great help to me in the Belgian Relief as early as 1915. He ably supported my operations in every Allied meeting in Paris where they were under discussion and always used his position to help.

The Secretary felt it his duty to advise the President at times of his disapproval of Presidential policies. His opposition to the President's going to Europe, his opposition to including the Covenant of the League in the Treaty and his criticism of parts of the Treaty gradually built up Mr. Wilson's distrust of him. Lansing did not publicly oppose the President. He signed the Treaty and supported its ratification by the Senate. I greatly regretted his break with the President and felt the President's action was that of a very sick man.[2]

In his book, Secretary Houston describes the first meeting of the Cabinet as follows:

> A Cabinet meeting was held in the President's study in the old Cabinet room in the White House proper on April 13th. This was the first meeting with the President since August, 1919, the first meeting since he went on his Western trip. I arrived several minutes late. The President was already seated behind a desk at the far end of the room.... The President looked old, worn, and haggard. It was enough to make one weep to look at him. One of his arms was useless. In repose, his face looked very much as usual, but, when he tried to speak, there were marked evidences of his trouble. His jaw tended to drop on one side, or seemed to

---

[2]In the years after the Secretary left the Cabinet he published a book and deposited his Diary in the Library of Congress, giving an account of all of his frictions with the President in detail.

do so. His voice was very weak and strained. I shook hands with him and sat down. He greeted me as of old. He put up a brave front and spent several minutes cracking jokes. Then there was a brief silence. It appeared that he would not take the initiative. Someone brought up the railroad situation for discussion. The President seemed at first to have some difficulty in fixing his mind on what we were discussing. Doctor Grayson looked in the door several times, as if to warn us not to prolong the discussion unduly for fear of wearying the President. The discussion dragged on for more than an hour. Finally Mrs. Wilson came in, looking rather disturbed, and suggested that we had better go.

While this first meeting after his stroke indicated some recovery, it is also clear from Houston's statement that the President had not recovered his full mental and physical vigor. There were some occasional Cabinet meetings thereafter, but with Mrs. Wilson always on guard to terminate discussions if it were necessary. He gained some strength after this, but was not able to take a substantial part in the Presidential campaign. David Lawrence, an eyewitness, records in his book the continued impairment of the President's health as indicated by an incident in December 1920, after the election. At that time the committee of the Congress came to notify the President, as was the custom that it was ready for business.

Mr. Lawrence says in his book:

They were received in the Blue Room where they waited for the door of the Red Room to be opened. An attendant stood beside the President as the door swung open. . . . The President entered the Blue Room, leaning on his cane; the attendant stood aside.

. . . As the President spoke, his head was bowed. He did not stand with the same erectness which had so often characterized his meetings with people in the White House. His eyes were turned downward. His voice was not strong, but it was clear. . . .

It is obvious that at least during the seven months from the time of his stroke to his first Cabinet meeting there was a filter through which all public business functioned. The President, under this guardianship to prevent "every disturbing problem," certainly did not have the advantage of personal contacts and information upon which to form judgments. His mind may have been clear but in his seclusion his judgment must have been uncertain as to the course of action in public affairs.

Tragically the seven vital months of his acute illness covered the entire time when the battles in the Senate over the ratification of the Treaty were being waged.

20

WOODROW WILSON'S BATTLE FOR RATIFICATION
BY THE SENATE

Twice during the seven months of President Wilson's most acute period of his illness, and his isolation from public participation in the battle, ratification of the Treaty was voted upon in the Senate.

The First Battle

The Senate first brought the ratification of the Treaty to a vote on November 19, 1919. In the preceding months it had voted a number of amendments into and out of the Treaty. However, on October 23, the majority report of the Foreign Relations Committee, under the chairmanship of Senator Lodge, settled on fourteen amendments, of which ten related to the League Covenant and four to the Treaty as distinguished from the League.

Shorn of legal verbiage these reservations were:

1. That the United States could withdraw from the League by resolution of Congress and was to be the sole judge as to whether all its obligations had been fulfilled.

2. That the United States assumed no obligation to interfere in controversies between nations as set forth under Article X or to employ military or naval forces without authority of the Congress.

3. That the United States should accept no mandate for overseas territory except by authority of the Congress.

4. That the United States reserved the right to decide what questions are within its domestic jurisdiction.

5. That the United States would not submit to arbitration or inquiry by the League into matters which the United States considered covered by the Monroe Doctrine.

6. That the United States withheld approval of Japanese control of the province of Shantung and reserved full liberty of action regarding any controversy between China and Japan.

7. That the Congress would provide by law for the appointment of United States representatives to the League and to commissions or committees under the Treaty and that no person should be selected or appointed without Senate approval.

8. That the Reparations Commission could not regulate import-export trade between the United States and Germany without the approval of Congress.

9. That the United States was not to be obligated to contribute to the expenses of the League or any agencies under the League or the Treaty unless an appropriation of funds were made by the Congress.

10. That the United States, if it should join in the limitation of armaments, reserved the right to increase armaments in the event or threat of war.

11. That the United States reserved the right to permit nationals of Covenant-breaking states who resided in the United States to continue business relations within the United States.

12. That no part of the Treaty should contravene the rights of citizens of the United States.

13. That the United States should not be represented on the Reparations Commission without the approval of Congress.

14. That the United States should not, in case of a dispute affecting the United States, be bound by any decision where any nation cast more than one vote (directed at the six votes of the British Empire).

Ratification of the Treaty without some of these reservations raised important Constitutional questions. The particular provision in the Constitution involved was:

> This Constitution and the laws of the United States which shall be made in pursuance thereof and *all treaties* made, or which shall

be made, under the authority of the United States, *shall be the supreme law of the land. . . .*

It was widely contended that reservations 2, 7, 8, 9, and 13 were necessary to safeguard the authority of the Congress to declare war; to confirm the appointments of important officials; to control exports and imports; to appropriate all expenditures; and to approve the creation of high official positions. Altogether the Treaty provisions appeared in some minds to invade the responsibilities and independence of the legislative branch of the Government.

Whatever the reservations implied, they did not in my mind destroy the great major functions of the League and except for Article X they could possibly be modified. And I was convinced that the European League members were so anxious for American cooperation in world problems that they would accept the reservations —if their acceptance were necessary.

The President's reaction to the Committee report is clear from Mrs. Wilson's account in her book:

> . . . Friends, including such a valued and persuasive friend as Mr. Bernard M. Baruch, begged Mr. Wilson to accept a compromise, saying "half a loaf is better than no bread." . . .
> . . . Senator Hitchcock came to tell me that unless the Administration forces accepted them the Treaty would be beaten. . . . In desperation I went to my husband. "For my sake," I said, "won't you accept these reservations and get this awful thing settled?"
> He turned his head on the pillow and stretching out his hand to take mine answered in a voice I shall never forget: "Little girl, don't you desert me; that I cannot stand. Can't you see that I have no moral right to accept any change in a paper I have signed without giving to every other signatory, even the Germans, the right to do the same thing? It is not I that will not accept; it is the Nation's honour that is at stake.
> "Better a thousand times to go down fighting than to dip your colors to dishonourable compromise."
> . . . When I went back to the President's room he dictated a letter to Senator Hitchcock. . . .

The letter was:[1]

---

[1]Henry Cabot Lodge, *The Senate and the League of Nations,* Charles Scribner's Sons, New York: 1925, p. 215.

THE WHITE HOUSE,
18 November, 1919

MY DEAR SENATOR:

You were good enough to bring me word that the Democratic Senators supporting the treaty expected to hold a conference before the final votes on the Lodge resolution of ratification and that they would be glad to receive a word of counsel from me.

I should hesitate to offer it in any detail but I assume that the Senators only desire it upon the all-important question of the final vote on the resolution containing the many reservations of Senator Lodge. On that I cannot hesitate, for in my opinion the resolution in that form does not provide for ratification, but rather for the nullification of the treaty.

I sincerely hope that the friends and supporters of the treaty will vote against the Lodge resolution of ratification.

I understand that the door will then probably be open for a genuine resolution of ratification.

I trust that all true friends of the Treaty will refuse to support the Lodge resolution.

Cordially and sincerely yours,
WOODROW WILSON

Not being allowed to see the President, I wrote him a letter on November 19, 1919, prior to the Senate vote, urging the acceptance of a compromise. However, I do not believe he was well enough to read this letter. Certainly I received no acknowledgment of it. I wrote:

DEAR MR. PRESIDENT:

I take the liberty of urging upon you the desirability of accepting the reservations now passed, except for the removal of objectionable provisions in the preamble and in addition with such other changes in their text as can be obtained by compromise without running the great dangers of voting the treaty out.

Some of the reservations are constructive particularly in rendering it clear that the war power must be invoked by Congress. Others are interpretive in line with the original intent of the Covenant. One arouses the amour propre of a great many American people, the raising of which should not have been inflicted on us by the British Government, . . . others of the voted reservations are in part . . . undesirable, but taken as a whole they do not seem to me to imperil the great principle of the League of Nations to prevent war.

I have the belief that with the League once in motion it can within itself and from experience and public education develop such measures as will make it effective. I am impressed with the desperate necessity of early ratification.

The delays have already seriously imperiled the economic recuperation of Europe. In this we are vitally interested from every point of view. I believe that the Covenant will steadily lose ground in popular support if it is not put into constructive operation at once because the American public will not appreciate the saving values of the Covenant as distinguished from the wrongs imposed in the Treaty. These wrongs will day by day become more evident to the entire world and will be confused with the Covenant itself. For instance, it can only be days until actual starvation begins in Vienna for which the insistence by England, France and Italy upon the political isolation of Austria from Germany must bear the fundamental responsibility.

We must recognize that if Europe is to survive it must import an enormous quantity of supplies from the United States, that these supplies can only be found on credit, that already the existing supplies show exhaustion in many parts of Europe, that no credit facilities or commercial machinery for meeting this situation can be erected until ratification is over. . . .

If we have the great misfortune of the Treaty becoming a political issue in the Presidential election it will become confused with our own domestic issues, our own racial prejudices, the constant blame of every difficulty in Europe upon the Treaty. It will be impossible to secure the clear voice of the American people on the Covenant itself. Moreover the shades of difference between Democratic and Republican reservations are too fine for alignment of public opinion.

My own feeling is therefore that this great constructive effort is mainly accomplished as it stands and its operation can repair mistakes in its building and that the world issues are so great as not to warrant the risks involved in delay of getting it into service in the hope of securing a few per cent more ideal structures.

Yours sincerely,

HERBERT HOOVER

There were other friends of the President's besides Mr. Baruch and myself who favored accepting a compromise on the reservations.

David Hunter Miller, who had a large part in drafting the Covenant, agreed with me that the President was attaching too much importance to the reservations. He confirmed this in a later publication, saying:

> . . . So far as the Lodge reservations made changes in the League, they were of a wholly minor character, they left its structure intact, and they would have interfered with its workings not at all.

THE SENATE VOTE ON NOVEMBER 19, 1919

In the voting on November 19 the Senators quickly rejected the reservations which related to the Treaty as distinguished from the Covenant. This was effected by a combination of Republican and Democratic Senators who favored the League. The voting thus largely concerned the reservations on the Covenant. The first vote was upon ratification of the Treaty with the reservations and was defeated by fifty-five votes. Of those voting against ratification with reservations, forty-two were Democrats and thirteen were Republicans. A motion for unconditional ratification, offered by Senator Oscar W. Underwood of Alabama, failed by seven votes of the necessary two-thirds of the Senators present.

Somewhat belatedly after the defeat of the Treaty on this occasion, Colonel House, according to his Diary, wrote to the President:

NEW YORK, November 24, 1919

DEAR GOVERNOR:

I hesitate to intrude my views upon you at such a time, but I feel that I would be doing less than my duty if I did not do so, since so much depends upon your decision in regard to the Treaty. Its failure would be a disaster not less to civilization than to you.

My suggestion is this: Do not mention the Treaty in your message to Congress, but return it to the Senate as soon as it convenes. In the meantime, send for Senator Hitchcock and tell him that you feel that you have done your duty and have fulfilled your every obligation to your colleagues in Paris by rejecting all offers to alter the document which was formulated there, and you now turn the Treaty over to the Senate for such action as it may deem wise to take.

I would advise him to ask the Democratic Senators to vote for the Treaty with such reservations as the majority may formulate, and let the matter then rest with the other signatories of the Treaty. I would say to Senator Hitchcock that if the Allied and Associated Powers are willing to accept the reservations which the Senate see fit to make, you will abide by the result being conscious of having done your full duty.

The Allies may not take the Treaty with the Lodge Reservations as they now stand, and this will be your vindication. But even if they should take them with slight modification, your conscience will be clear. After agreement is reached, it can easily be shown that the Covenant in its practical workings in the future will not be seriously hampered and that time will give us a workable machine.

A great many people, Democrats, Progressives, and Republicans, have talked with me about ratification of the Treaty and they are all pretty much of one mind regarding the necessity for its passage with or without reservations. To the ordinary man, the distance between the Treaty and the reservations is slight.

Of course, the arguments are all with the position you have taken and against that of the Senate, but, unfortunately, no amount of logic can alter the situation; therefore my advice would be to make no further argument, but return the Treaty to the Senate without comment and let Senator Hitchcock know that you expect it to be ratified in some form, and then let the other signatories decide for themselves whether they will accept it.

The supreme place which history will give you will be largely because you personify in yourself the great idealistic conception of a league of nations. If this conception fails, it will be your failure. To-day there are millions of helpless people throughout the world who look to you and you only to make this conception a realization.

Affectionately yours
E. M. House

Three days later the Colonel wrote another letter to the President:

New York, November 27, 1919

Dear Governor:

I am wondering if I made myself clear to you in my letter of the other day.

I wish to emphasize the fact that I do not counsel surrender. The action advised will in my opinion make your position consistent and impregnable. Any other way out that now seems possible of success would be something of a surrender.

Practically every one who is in close touch with the situation admits that the Treaty cannot be ratified without substantial reservations. You must not be a party to those reservations. You stood for the Treaty as it was made in Paris, but if the Senate refuses to ratify without reservations, under the circumstances, I would let the Allies determine whether or not they will accept them.

This does not mean that no effort will be made by those Senators and others who favor the Treaty as it is to make the reservations as innocuous as possible. Neither does it mean that the Allies will accept the Treaty as the Senate majority have desired it.

If you take the stand indicated, it will aid rather than hinder those working for mild reservations. It will absolutely ensure the passage of the Treaty and probably in a form acceptable to both you and the Allies.

I did not make the suggestion until I had checked it up with some of your friends in whom I felt you had confidence, for the matter is of such incalculable importance that I did not dare rely solely upon my own judgment.

In conclusion, let me suggest that Senator Hitchcock be warned not to make any public statement regarding your views. When the Treaty is ratified, then I hope you will make a statement letting your position become known.

I feel as certain as I ever did of anything that your attitude would receive universal approval. On the one hand your loyalty to our Allies will be commended, and, on the other, your willingness to accept reservations rather than have the Treaty killed will be regarded as the act of a great man.

Affectionately yours

E. M. House

It is unlikely that the Colonel's letters ever reached the President, because of his illness and since House had been out of favor with both the President and Mrs. Wilson for some months.[2]

---

[2]To round out this sad event, reference should be made to the President's dropping his old pilot, Colonel House. The beginnings of this may be found at the time the President returned to Paris on March 15, 1919. Mrs. Wilson's memoir gives ample evidence. It was at this time the President created the Supreme Council consisting of himself and the three Prime Ministers—the Big Four. House was not allowed to attend the meetings except during the few days when the President fell ill in early April 1919. The Colonel, however, as "handy man," performed many secondary negotiations. Prior to the signing of the Treaty in Paris, the President had appointed the Colonel to an inter-Allied committee to formulate rules for the assignment and management of the mandates. House remained in Europe on this mission for a period of about three months.

Ray Stannard Baker, although one of the President's oldest and most loyal friends, favored reservations. He was not allowed to see the President but did see Mrs. Wilson. According to his *American Chronicle*, he summarized his views in a letter to her on January 25, 1920 as follows:

MY DEAR MRS. WILSON:

Since our talk on Thursday, I have had the present situation very deeply upon my mind. I have the feeling that all the President went to France to fight for—for which he fought so nobly—is being swept away: that the chance for world reorganization, which is the President's high purpose, is more and more threatened. And I feel so strongly that if the President were not ill — if he were himself — he could and would save the situation. I believe the people of the country are just in the mood to respond to the kind of moral appeal which the President, beyond any other living man, is best able to

---

Many stories were circulated in the press that the President had broken with the Colonel. According to the Colonel's Diary, House took note of this and issued a denial on August 28, 1919. Again on September 4, he expressed his disbelief that his relations with the President had changed.

On September 21 he takes note of this again and in his Diary, says:

. . . It looks as if I may have a serious controversy with the President over my return home. I am so certain that I am right in going home that unless the President declares his belief that my return may defeat the Treaty, I shall go.

The Colonel arrived in the United States on October 19, 1919. He was not allowed to see the President. An entry in his Diary on January 31, 1920, contains the following:

There is so much mystery surrounding the President and his condition that I am wholly at a loss to form an opinion as to the truth. I wish I knew. I am not writing to him or to Mrs. Wilson for the very good reason that I have had no replies to my letters of November 24th and 27th. . . .

He recorded that Tumulty had publicly denied there was any "break" but that Mrs. Wilson refused to deny it.

A good account of what really had happened is given by the Colonel in his Diary on October 14, 1921 — a year after returning home. This he received from Irving Hoover, who was the chief usher at the White House and had accompanied the President to Paris as his major servant. In giving this entry in the House Diary, I have eliminated the secondhand gossip, as it is only Irving Hoover's direct statement that is of importance. The Colonel records:

The most interesting happening of my visit [to Washington] was a call from Irving Hoover. . . . He remained for more than an hour and told something of what had occurred during the last two years. He said the President's change of feeling toward me began at Paris just after his return from the United States in March. Somewhat to my surprise and much to my regret Hoover laid it chiefly upon the President himself saying that those around him fanned the flame. . . . What he told agrees almost wholly with the conclusions I had already reached without having all the facts upon the subject, that is, there was no particular incident which caused the cooling of his friendship for me. . . . From that time it was easy for others to increase this feeling.

make. The people want the League: they are for the reality — the spirit — which lives in the idea: but they are bitterly confused over the present minor disagreements. Their thoughts go straight to the heart of the matter — which is to get something started quickly, some going organization to meet the problems of the world, some group of men sitting in common council. They know that no document is or can be final, and that a real League will grow as it begins to function. . . .

People in the future will forget about the minor disagreements, if the thing itself comes into being. . . .

Baker later added:

I knew well enough that this letter implied a criticism of the President's course, especially the references I made to the disagreements as being "minor."

It is also improbable that this letter ever reached the President because it would have been very disturbing.

THE SECOND BATTLE IN THE SENATE FOR RATIFICATION

During the debate before and after the November 19 vote, the Senators had gradually aligned themselves into three different groups. About a dozen Democratic and Republican Senators opposed the Treaty in any form — the so-called "irreconcilables." Many of the Democratic Senators would follow only the President's wishes. Then there were many Republican and Democratic Senators who earnestly wanted the Treaty ratified but felt that some reservations were necessary. This group favored some moderate reservations except as to Article X which they, too, entirely opposed.

But the President's attitude showed little softening. In a statement he sent to the Jackson Day dinner in Washington on January 8, 1920, there were two paragraphs of small comfort to those who were seeking to find a basis of ratification. They were:[3]

I have endeavored to make it plain that if the Senate wishes to say what the undoubted meaning of the League is I shall have no objection. There can be no reasonable objection to interpretations accompanying the act of ratification itself. But when the treaty is acted upon, I must know whether it means that we have ratified or rejected it.

We cannot rewrite this treaty. *We must take it without changes*

---

[3]*The New York Times,* January 9, 1920.

which alter its meaning, or leave it, and then after the rest of the world has signed it, we must face the unthinkable task of making another and separate treaty with Germany. . . .

Under the Treaty, the President was to call the first meeting of the League. This call was issued on January 12, 1920, and the League Assembly met on February 11, 1920, without an American member. Ultimately sixty-three nations joined.

According to Secretary Houston's book, Senator Hitchcock made a strong effort to obtain a relaxation of the President's attitude and finally received the following letter from him:

THE WHITE HOUSE,
January 26, 1920

MY DEAR SENATOR HITCHCOCK:

I have greatly appreciated your thoughtful kindness in keeping me informed concerning the conferences you and some of your colleagues have had with spokesmen of the Republican party concerning the possibility of ratification of the Treaty of Peace, and send this line in special appreciative acknowledgment of your letter of the twenty-second. I return the clipping you were kind enough to inclose.

To the substance of it I, of course, adhere. I am bound to. Like yourself, I am solemnly sworn to obey and maintain the Constitution of the United States. But I think the form of it very unfortunate. Any reservation or resolution stating that "the United States assumes no obligation under such and such an article unless or except" would, I am sure, chill our relationship with the nations with which we expect to be associated in the great enterprise of maintaining the world's peace.

That association must in any case, my dear Senator, involve very serious and far-reaching implications of honour and duty which I am sure we shall never in fact be desirous of ignoring. It is the more important not to create the impression that we are trying to escape obligations.

But I realize that negative criticism is not all that is called for in so serious a matter. I am happy to be able to add, therefore, that I have once more gone over the reservations proposed by yourself, the copy of which I return herewith, and am glad to say that I can accept them as they stand.

I have never seen the slightest reason to doubt the good faith of our associates in the war, nor ever had the slightest reason to fear that any nation would seek to enlarge our obligations under the Covenant of the League of Nations, or seek to commit us to lines of action which, under our Constitution, only the Congress of the United States can in the last analysis decide.

May I suggest that with regard to the possible withdrawal of the United States it would be wise to give to the President the right to act upon a resolution of Congress in the matter of withdrawal? In other words, it would seem to be permissible and advisable that any resolution giving notice of withdrawal should be a joint rather than a concurrent resolution.

I doubt whether the President can be deprived of his veto power under the Constitution, even with his own consent. The use of a joint resolution would permit the President, who is, of course, charged by the Constitution with the conduct of foreign policy, to merely exercise a voice in saying whether so important a step as withdrawal from the League of Nations should be accomplished by a majority or by a two thirds vote.

The Constitution itself providing that the legislative body was to be consulted in treaty making, and having prescribed a two thirds vote in such cases, it seems to me that there should be no unnecessary departure from the method there indicated.

I see no objection to a frank statement that the United States can accept a mandate with regard to any territory under Article XIII, Part I, or any other provision of the Treaty of Peace, only by the direct authority and action of the Congress of the United States.

I hope, my dear Senator, that you will never hesitate to call upon me for any assistance that I can render in this or any other public matter.

Cordially and sincerely, yours,
WOODROW WILSON

There was considerable confusion in this letter as to how far it went. Subsequently, Senator Hitchcock introduced into the Senate a new draft of reservations in accordance with his understanding of the President's letter.

So far as the fourteen Lodge reservations were concerned, Senator Hitchcock's proposals and the President's letter might have solved the questions of the Monroe Doctrine (No. 5), one vote for the British (No. 14), and no commitment to assume mandates (No. 3).

As I was in Washington by appointment of President Wilson as Vice-Chairman of the Second Industrial Conference I had many opportunities to discuss the Treaty with Senators of both parties. A large number of Republican Senators informed me that they would accept some reservations except on Article X of "milder" character than the Lodge reservation. With the support of Senator Frank B. Kellogg and Senator Porter J. McCumber, this group became known as the "mild reservationists." The old League to Enforce Peace, headed by former President Taft, former Secretary of State Root, former Attorney General Wickhersham and Charles Evans Hughes, urged ratification with the "mild" reservations.

On the Democratic side there were also many Senators who would agree to these "mild" reservations. I was convinced that among them was Senator Hitchcock, the ranking member and leader of the Democratic side, who would go along with such a compromise if the President would consent. My understanding was that the "mild reservationists" would accept the wording of the three Hitchcock reservations.

On February 7, 1920, the Senate by a combination of Democrats and the Republicans who genuinely wanted ratification on some terms voted to reconsider the Treaty.

On February 23, 1920 I made an address at Johns Hopkins University, presenting the point of view of the Taft-Root Committee:

> The Treaty, as distinguished from the Covenant, was born in a fire of suffering, a sense of wrong, the passions of revenge and fear that grew from them. To some of us many of the features of the Treaty itself were the result of compromises with these forces. Already many of its signatories are acknowledging it must be revised. Its settlements did not sufficiently recognize the necessity of economic solidarity between different parts of Europe. . . .
>
> . . . The conflicting groups [in the Senate] over the character of the reservations have gradually abandoned their extreme ground and have come closer and closer to a common mind. . . . In the meantime, the world is held in suspense. Infinite misery goes on accumulating. Forces are set in motion that may yield new conflicts. . . .
>
> It appears to many of us that the most practical hope of immediate ratification lies in . . . accepting the proposals of the "mild reservationists." The two [groups] combined [Democrats and mild Reservationists] can pass the Treaty. It also appears to us that, even from the point of view of the "lesser reservationists," they will have secured all of the major functions and values of the League.

If it be put into being and if it prove its living value in the world, no one can doubt that any necessary changes will be granted to it by common consent as years go on. The League is not a principle; it is an organization. Its greatest function is to organize moral forces. Its major authority will be moral force. For my part, if the League cannot prove its value under the . . . proposals of the "mild reservationists" it will never prove them. . . .

. . . The war has brought us many new relationships which we cannot escape. Our old relations will be expanded, . . . by our vitally enlarged economic and social interest abroad, by the calls of humanity in the alleviation of misery. We have two extreme views among our people. . . . Many of us want neither extreme. . . .

On March 18, 1920 I gave an interview to the press which said in part:

Regardless of what any of us may think should have been the provisions of either the League or the Treaty, we and the world should not be kept waiting longer for a settlement. The whole process of peace has been necessarily one of compromises and so long as the final form gives us freedom of action and room for constructive development of peace, I believe it should be accepted. The [mild] reservations should satisfy the most timid as to entanglements. . . .

. . . The League is not a document. It is an organization of the moral sense of the civilized states. . . .

Two years ago . . . [with almost] the entire world aligned against Germany, our prayer was that we were fighting the last great war — that something better should come to the world in return for the sacrifice. Today the world is drifting back. . . .

THE VOTE ON MARCH 19, 1920

On March 19, 1920, the Treaty came to a vote in the Senate again. The only important change made in the Lodge reservations was in respect to the Japanese-Shantung question and in the inclusion of a cheap political maneuver, the substance of which was:

That in ratifying the treaty, the United States adheres to the principle of self-determination and declares that when Ireland attains a government of its own choice, it should be admitted to the League.

The vote was forty-nine in favor of ratification with the Lodge reservations and thirty-five against. Those for ratification with the reservations included twenty-eight Republicans and twenty-one Democrats; those against included twelve Republicans and twenty-three Democrats.

Of the total of eighty-four votes cast — twelve Senators either abstained or were absent — only seven votes more in favor of ratification would have provided the necessary two-thirds for approval of the Treaty.

The President had accepted far more of "the lesser evils" at Paris than were implied in the reservations. But Mr. Wilson was completely isolated from the political currents in motion and from those personal contacts essential for evolving successful cooperation with the Senate. He was a very ill man. While his mind may have been clear in the opinion of those around him, his lack of contact with the people and their leaders separated him from the reality of which sound compromises are made.

In any event, the Senate's vote on March 19 left the only hope of ratification to the Presidential election still nearly eight months distant. And that was still the hope of Woodrow Wilson.

21

WOODROW WILSON'S BATTLE FOR RATIFICATION
IN THE PRESIDENTIAL CAMPAIGN OF 1920

The League and the Treaty were inevitably a major issue in the Presidential campaign of 1920. It was part of the tragedy of Woodrow Wilson that he was physically unable to take part in the great national debate.

THE DEMOCRATIC CONVENTION AND CAMPAIGN

The Democratic Convention met on July 5, at San Francisco. The speakers and the platform gave full support to President Wilson, the League and the Treaty. Also, they expressed their repugnance for Republicans generally.

The Convention witnessed a bitter contest by the President's son-in-law, William G. McAdoo, for the Presidential nomination. Finally Governor James M. Cox of Ohio was nominated, with Franklin D. Roosevelt as the candidate for Vice-President.

The Democratic organization and the candidates made a continuous and valiant fight for the League and the Treaty without reservations.

The President received Governor Cox and Mr. Roosevelt on July 19 and expressed to them his confidence that the people would support the League.

Mr. Wilson was unable to take an active part in the campaign, but two vigorous statements were issued from the White House, one on October 3, the other on October 27. They were good campaign documents.

On October 23, a strong group of thirty-one advocates of the League, including several Republicans, joined in support of the Democratic candidates under the leadership of President Charles W. Eliot of Harvard University.

To protect the President from worry, he apparently was not informed as to the drift of the public mind during the campaign, for Tumulty records in his book:

> It was really touching when one conferred with him to find him so hopeful of the results. Time and time again he would turn to me and say, "I do not care what Republican propaganda may seek to do. I am sure that the hearts of the people are right on this great issue and that we can confidently look forward to triumph."
>
> I did not share his enthusiasm, and yet I did not feel like sending reports to him that were in the least touched with pessimism because of the effect they might have upon his feelings.

THE REPUBLICAN CONVENTION AND CAMPAIGN

The Republican Convention met on June 8, at Chicago. Senator Lodge was named temporary chairman and delivered the keynote speech of nearly 10,000 words — seldom equaled in bitterness. The platform attacked the League but contained words on the desirability of "an agreement among nations to preserve the peace of the world." It was a weak attempt at a straddle.

The Convention, on June 12, nominated Senator Warren G. Harding for President, as a compromise, having discarded two better men — Governor Frank O. Lowden and General Leonard E. Wood. Calvin Coolidge was nominated for Vice-President.

Despite the weak Republican platform, Republican leaders, former President Taft, former Secretary of State Elihu Root, and former Presidential candidate Charles Evans Hughes continued their committee for support of the League and Treaty with the "mild" reservations. I rejoined my lifelong Republican association after six years of rigorous nonpartisanship[1] and associated myself with the Taft Committee.

---

[1] Except for the occasion when I supported President Wilson in the Congressional campaign of 1918.

Senator Harding had voted for ratification of the Treaty with reservations in the Senate in November 1919. The Taft Committee went to work at once to get a statement from him reiterating the support implied in that vote. They obtained this statement on August 28: [2]

> There are distinctly two types of international relationship. One is an offensive and defensive alliance of great powers. . . . The other type is a society of free nations, or an association of free nations, or a league of free nations, animated by considerations of right and justice instead of might and self-interest, and not merely proclaimed an agency in pursuit of peace, but so organized and so participated in as to make the actual attainment of peace a reasonable possibility. Such an association I favor with all my heart, and I would make no fine distinction as to whom credit is due. One need not care what it is called. Let it be an association, a society or a league, or what not. Our concern is solely with the substance, not the form thereof.

On October 14, the Taft Committee issued a statement signed by thirty-seven important Republicans for ratification with "mild" reservations. They included, besides Mr. Taft, four former Cabinet officers and fourteen presidents of colleges and universities. During the campaign members of this group spoke often and persuasively; I made five addresses in various parts of the country.

As the campaign wore on, events in Europe sapped the public support of the Treaty and the League. French armies had occupied Frankfurt. At one moment came news of British and French suppression of demands of the Arab States for independence from their overlord mandatories. At another moment came news of the French expansion of military alliances and the increase in armaments of all European states except the former enemies. Small wars between Eastern European states continued, although these nations had signed the League Covenant.

Little expression of consequence came out of Europe in appreciation of the tremendous American efforts on the battlefields, our gigantic loans, charitable gifts, or our Relief and Reconstruction activities. On the other hand, there were grumblings in Europe

---

[2] *The New York Times,* August 28, 1920.

that we should cancel the war debts. We heard ourselves called "Uncle Shylock."

The weaknesses of the Treaty as distinguished from the Covenant were aired by the great groups of Americans of German, Austrian, Hungarian and Irish descent and the Covenant was violently attacked by extreme isolationist Senators and Congressmen.

Above all, the American people were tired of the war, the economic controls, the debt, and the huge taxes they paid during and after the war. They also were tired of the Peace Conference generally and its possible consequent "entanglements." They rallied to Mr. Harding's slogan, "Return to normalcy."

I encountered a token of the change of tide in an address to a large Republican meeting in Indianapolis on October 9, 1920. That part of my speech in support of the League was received almost in silence, although Mr. Wilson had received great applause from the whole city only the year before. The lady who followed me on the platform draped her oratory in the American flag and the wickedness of "entanglements." She won the crowd.

Incidentally I had, as a sacrifice hit, entered the California primaries in opposition to Senator Hiram Johnson, one of the "bitter-enders" against the Treaty. I did so for the sole purpose of giving the voters of that State, which was then considered strongly pro-League, a chance to express themselves. Johnson won.

The Election and Its Consequences to the Treaty

The Republicans won the national election by a sweeping majority.

Mr. Wilson had sufficiently recovered from his illness to maintain the tradition whereby the outgoing President accompanies the President-elect to the inaugural ceremonies at the Capitol. In his book, Tumulty describes what happened on March 4, 1921:

> . . . he was notified that the President-elect was in the Blue Room awaiting his arrival. Alone, unaided, grasping his old blackthorn stick, the faithful companion of many months, his "third leg" as he playfully called it, slowly he made his way to the elevator. . . . He was standing in the Blue Room meeting the President-elect and greeting him in the most gracious way. No evidence of the trial of pain he was undergoing in striving to play a modest part in

the ceremonies was apparent either in his bearing or attitude, as he greeted the President-elect and the members of the Congressional Inaugural Committee. . . .

. . . The ride to the Capitol was uneventful. From the physical appearance of the two men seated beside each other in the automobile, it was plain to the casual observer who was the outgoing and who the incoming President. On the right sat President Wilson, gray, haggard, broken. He interpreted the cheering from the crowds that lined the Avenue as belonging to the President-elect and looked straight ahead. It was Mr. Harding's day, not his. . . .

Mr. Wilson walked to the reception room in the Capitol, where he signed some bills. However, as it was obviously painful for him, President-elect Harding encouraged him not to attend the inaugural ceremonies. He went directly to the new residence which Mrs. Wilson had prepared.

Some sentences in Mr. Harding's inaugural address seemed to indicate support of the League but in reality they were a straddle. The attitude of the country toward ratification had so degenerated that, by the time the Senate came into session on March 5, a canvass showed that a submission of the Treaty for ratification could not have won the support of thirty Senators.

The chances for ratification continued to deteriorate even after that, and finally President Harding, upon the recommendation of Secretary of State Charles Evans Hughes, gave it the *coup de grace* in an address to the Congress on April 12, 1921, saying in part:

. . . There is no longer excuse for uncertainties respecting some phases of our foreign relationship. In the existing League of Nations, world-governing with its superpowers, this republic will have no part. There can be no misinterpretation, and there will be no betrayal of the deliberate expression of the American people in the recent election. . . . It is only fair to say to the world in general, and to our associates in war in particular, that the League covenant can have no sanction by us.

With this policy settled, Secretary of State Hughes negotiated separate peace treaties with Germany and the other enemy countries, reserving all rights agreed to in the Treaty of Versailles.

On September 21, 1921, President Harding sent these separate treaties to the Senate, and they were ratified by large majorities on November 11.

As an indication of the bitter swing of the American mind, early in 1923, Mr. Harding recommended that the United States should join the World Court. The Court was entirely independent of the League of Nations and Elihu Root had taken part in drafting its statutes. But the proposal to join was defeated by the Senate.[3]

In 1922 Secretary of State Hughes called a Conference on Naval Disarmament. It had substantial results in naval reduction. And at the same Conference he succeeded in securing the return of Shantung to China from Japan and an eleven-power guarantee of Chinese independence.

In the later Presidential campaigns ratification of the League Covenant was not an issue of importance.

---

[3] In 1929 from the White House I again submitted to the Senate a renewed proposal that we join in the World Court, but it was defeated by a combination of Republican and Democratic Senators.

However, by executive action I established systematic cooperation with the League in all its nonpolitical functions, including its military and naval conferences on disarmament. In the Japanese-Chinese conflict, I appointed representatives on the League committee to deal with the Japanese aggression.

EPILOGUE

———————————————— * * * ————————————————

Woodrow Wilson's ordeal ended on February 3, 1924. He had never fully recovered from his stroke.

Pericles' oration more than 2000 years ago over the Greeks who died for their country could well be the epilogue for Woodrow Wilson:

> So they gave their bodies to the commonwealth and received, each for his own memory, praise that will never die, and with it the grandest of all sepulchres, not that in which their mortal bones are laid, but a home in the minds of men, where their glory remains fresh to stir to speech or action as the occasion comes by. For the whole earth is the sepulchre of famous men; and their story is not graven only on stone over their native earth, but lives on far away, without visible symbol, woven into the stuff of other men's lives.

For a moment at the time of the Armistice, Mr. Wilson rose to intellectual domination of most of the civilized world. With his courage and eloquence, he carried a message of hope for the independence of nations, the freedom of men and lasting peace. Never since his time has any man risen to the political and spiritual heights that came to him. His proclaimed principles of self-government and independence aided the spread of freedom to twenty-two races at the time of the Armistice.

But he was to find that his was a struggle between the concepts of the New and Old Worlds. European statesmen were dominated by the forces of hate and revenge of their peoples for grievous wrongs; by the economic prostration of their peoples; and by the ancient system of imperial spoils. Mr. Wilson was forced to compromise with their demands in order to save the League, confident that it would in time right the wrongs that had been done.

One of his colleagues at Paris, General Jan Smuts, said of him:

> At a time of the deepest darkness and despair he had raised aloft a light to which all eyes had turned. He had spoken divine words of healing and consolation to a broken humanity. His lofty moral idealism seemed for a moment to dominate the brutal passions which had torn the Old World asunder. . . .
>
> . . . Without hesitation he plunged into that inferno of human passions. . . . There were six months of agonized waiting, during which the world situation rapidly deteriorated. And then he emerged with the Peace Treaty. It was not a Wilson peace. . . . This was a Punic peace. . . .
>
> . . . The Paris peace lost an opportunity as unique as the great war itself. In destroying the moral idealism born of the sacrifices of the war it did almost as much as the war itself in shattering the structure of Western civilization.
>
> . . . It was not Wilson who failed. . . . It was the human spirit itself that failed at Paris. . . .
>
> . . . The hope, the aspiration for a new world order of peace and right and justice—however deeply and universally felt—was still only feeble and ineffective in comparison with the dominant national passions which found their expression in the Peace Treaty. . . . And in the end not only the leaders but the peoples preferred a bit of booty here, a strategic frontier there, a coal field or an oil well, an addition to their population or their resources. . . .
>
> What was really saved at Paris was . . . the Covenant of the League of Nations. . . . The Covenant is Wilson's souvenir to the future of the world. No one will even deny him that honor.
>
> The honor is very great, indeed, for the Covenant is one of the great creative documents of human history. The Peace Treaty will fade into merciful oblivion, and its provisions will be gradually obliterated by the great human tides sweeping over the world. . . . And the leader who, in spite of apparent failure, succeeded in inscribing his name on that banner has achieved the most enviable and enduring immortality. . . .[1]

Woodrow Wilson lived to see some parts of his defeats at Paris

---

[1] For full text see *The New York Times* March 3, 1921.

become victories. He saw his ferment of freedom bring independence to Iran and Egypt. But he witnessed the Republics of Armenia, Georgia and Azerbaijan snuffed out by Communist Russia. Above all he lived to see the League of Nations come into being despite America's absence. He witnessed the settling of dangerous controversies and the making of many treaties which aided the economy, health and morals of the world. He lived to see the World Court of International Justice bring solution to many conflicts and the International Labor Organization bring benefits to men who work.

Had Mr. Wilson lived two decades longer, he would have seen the seeds planted by the Old World statesmen at Versailles bring another, and even more terrible, World War. He would have seen the freedom of a dozen nations consumed in the vortex of Communism. Yet his ferment of freedom still survives in the revolts of their people armed only with naked hands against machine guns. Also, he would have seen the Old World of Western Europe moving into a common ground of concepts of self-government and a common front against the spread of Communism.

Had he lived, he would have seen the League concept rise again from this second blood bath of mankind under the name of the United Nations. The spirit of Woodrow Wilson came to the world again.

The United Nations' organization except in one particular, follows very closely the pattern of Woodrow Wilson's League. The Council, dominated by the Great Powers, each with its veto, the Assembly, the Secretariat, the machinery for appeal in case of aggression, the processes of investigation, conciliation, arbitration, the economic and military sanctions—all these were better formulated in the League and with fewer words. But the admission of aggressive dictatorship to its membership would never have been accepted by Woodrow Wilson. He conceived the League as an association of free nations, not to include men and dictatorships conspiring for its ruin.

He stated among his principles of peace:

> ...Only free peoples can hold their purpose and their honor steady to a common end and prefer the interests of mankind to any narrow interest of their own.
>
> A steadfast concert for peace can never be maintained except by a partnership of democratic nations. No autocratic government

could be trusted to keep faith within it or observe its covenants. It must be a league of honor. . . .

With his death ended a Greek tragedy, not on the stage of imagination, but in the lives of nations. And as in the tragedies of old the inspiring words and deeds of men who failed still live.

APPENDIX

———————————— * * * ■———————————

Because of urging over a period of about twenty years by colleagues in the First World War, I have prepared some extensive memoirs relating to those times and the activities in which we were engaged. They may be published some time.

Those extensive memoirs have required the inspection of some 3,000,000 documents or items and many books. The task would have been impossible but for the devotion of old friends and my research assistants, who sifted them down to a few hundred thousand which were necessary for me to examine personally in order that I might be accurate. My own files on the First World War exceed 1,500,000 items.

From my familiarity with events and these researches I have over the years made some speeches and have written a number of articles on these subjects. In 1953 I published in my memoirs (*The Memoirs of Herbert Hoover*) a very brief description of the incidents and actions in various organizations that I directed during the First World War. In this I included a brief sketch of the peacemaking. But in these writings and speeches I made little attempt to evaluate the work of Mr. Wilson.

In the course of the work on those projects, however, I was impressed with the fact that there was a wealth of material — much of it entirely new—relating to his conduct of the war and the peace negotiations.

Therefore, with still further research into the known and several new sources made available to me, I have written this book on the ordeal of Woodrow Wilson.

In preparing this book I have condensed and included some paragraphs from my published materials, but this book is based upon a far broader foundation of documentation and records. I have included in it only the minimum of documents necessary to carry conviction. Much more could be added to confirm the conclusions I have reached.

In order not to distract the reader by a multitude of footnotes as to the origin of every document or quotation, I have given in the text the names of persons quoted. The exact page reference to these books can be obtained by inquiring at the Hoover Institution at Stanford University. The following are the major books that have been consulted:

Baker, Ray Stannard. *American Chronicle.* New York. Charles Scribner's Sons. 1945.

Baker, Ray Stannard. *What Wilson Did at Paris.* New York. Doubleday & Company, Inc. 1922.

Baker, Ray Stannard. *Woodrow Wilson: Life and Letters.* 8 vols. New York. Doubleday & Company, Inc. 1939.

Baker, Ray Stannard. *Woodrow Wilson and World Settlement.* 3 vols. New York. Doubleday & Company, Inc. 1922.

Bonsal, Stephan. *Unfinished Business.* New York. Doubleday & Company, Inc. 1944.

Churchill, Winston S. *The Aftermath.* New York. Charles Scribner's Sons. 1929.

Clemenceau, Georges. *Grandeur and Misery of Victory.* New York. Harcourt, Brace and Company, Inc. 1930.

Hoover, Herbert. *The Memoirs of Herbert Hoover.* New York. The Macmillan Company. 1953.

House, Edward, and Charles Seymour (eds.). *What Really Happened at Paris.* New York. Charles Scribner's Sons. 1921.

Houston, David F. *Eight Years with Wilson's Cabinet.* 2 vols. New York. Doubleday & Company, Inc. 1926.

Lane, Anne Wintermute, and Louise Herrick Wall (eds.). *The Letters of Franklin K. Lane.* Boston. Houghton Mifflin Company. 1922.

Lansing, Robert. *The Peace Negotiations: A Personal Narrative.* Boston. Houghton Mifflin Company. 1921.

Lawrence, David. *The True Story of Woodrow Wilson*. New York. Doubleday & Company, Inc. 1924.

Lloyd George, David. *The Truth about the Peace Treaties*. 2 vols. London. Victor Gollancz, Ltd. 1938.

Lloyd George, David. *War Memoirs*. 6 vols. Boston. Little, Brown & Co. 1933–1937.

Lodge, Henry Cabot. *The Senate and the League of Nations*. New York. Charles Scribner's Sons. 1925.

Ludendorff, Erich. *Ludendorff's Own Story*. New York. Harper & Brothers. 1920.

Mantoux, Paul. *Les Délibérations du Conseil des Quatre*. 2 vols. Paris. Editions du Centre National de la Recherche Scientifique. 1955.

Nitti, Francesco. *The Wreck of Europe*. Indianapolis. The Bobbs-Merrill Company, Inc. 1922.

Nowak, Karl Friedrich. *Versailles*. New York. Payson and Clarke Ltd. 1929.

Palmer, Frederick. *Bliss, Peacemaker*. New York. Dodd, Mead & Company, Inc. 1934.

Pershing, John J. *My Experiences in the World War*. 2 vols. Philadelphia. Frederick A. Stokes Company. 1931.

Seymour, Charles. *The Intimate Papers of Colonel House*. 4 vols. Boston. Houghton Mifflin Company. 1926.

Seymour, Charles (ed.). *Woodrow Wilson and the World War*. New Haven, Conn. Yale University Press. 1921.

Tardieu, André. *The Truth about the Treaty*. Indianapolis. The Bobbs-Merrill Company, Inc. 1921.

Tumulty, Joseph P. *Woodrow Wilson as I Knew Him*. New York. Doubleday & Company, Inc. 1921.

White, William Allen. *Woodrow Wilson*. Boston. Houghton Mifflin Company. 1924.

Wilson, Edith Bolling. *My Memoir*. Indianapolis. The Bobbs-Merrill Company, Inc. 1938.

I have used many unpublished documents and materials and give in the text the names of the authors. The unpublished materials referred to are as follows:

The Diary of Gordon Auchincloss. Yale University Library.

The unpublished papers of Ray Stannard Baker. Princeton University Library.

The Diary of Hugh Gibson. The Hoover Institution Archives. Stanford University.

The Papers of Herbert Hoover. The Hoover Institution Archives. Stanford University.

The unpublished papers of Colonel E. M. House. Yale University Library.

The Diary of Robert Lansing. The Library of Congress.

The Diary of Vance McCormick. The Hoover Institution. Stanford University.

The Papers of John J. Pershing. The Library of Congress.

The Papers of Mark Sullivan. The Hoover Institution, Stanford University.

The Papers of Charles L. Swem. Princeton University Library.

The Papers of Woodrow Wilson. The Library of Congress.

The Woodrow Wilson Collection. Princeton University Library.

Where State Department documents are quoted, they are footnoted.

Some of the personal papers and diaries above are under restricted use and permission for students to examine the originals needs to be given by the authority of the respective institutions.

INDEX

***

Allies, imperialism and colonialism of, 72–73; mandates held by, 224, 226–228; peace terms accepted by, 55–56; peace terms presented to, 42–43; relations with Baltic States, 129, 130; relations with Russia, 116, 117, 123; in Relief and Reconstruction of Europe, 89–95, 100, 107, 109; suspicion of Wilson's motives, 76; and unified military forces, 93; Wilson's dislike of word, 12–13, 93

Alsace-Lorraine, 79, 213

American Red Cross, 109

American Relief Administration, 101, 112, 113

Arab States, 192, 263n.

Armenia, 141–142, 229n.; famine in, 142–143; mandate for, 225–226, 228–229; relief for, 142–146

Armistice, Austria-Hungary requests, 29, 30; Germany requests, 28–30; military preparations for, 54–55; signed by Germany, 58; text, summary of, 58–59

Auchincloss, Gordon, 65, 86; diary quoted, 238–239n.

Austria, 108, 263n.; Communist conspiracy in, 140–141; relief for, 100, 106; Treaty provisions on, 213

Austria-Hungary, agrees to peace terms, 40; requests armistice, 29, 30; separation of, 51; Wilson's proposal on status of, 34–35

Azerbaijan, 142

Back Blocs, 115

Baker, Newton D., 10, 39n., 102, 110

Baker, Ray Stannard, 73n., 80, 189n.;

letter to Mrs. Wilson on Treaty ratification, 287–288 quoted: on alliance with France, 219–220; on compromise with Japan, 208, 210; on Treaty, 241–243, 249–250; on Wilson at Peace Conference, 201, 203

Balance of power, 27, 73–74

Balfour, Arthur James, 106, 189n.; discusses Fourteen Points, 44, 45; on secret treaties, 79, 80; in Relief and Reconstruction of Europe, 96, 97; in Peace Conference negotiations, 192, 220; attitude toward Wilson, 255, 258

Baltic States, 130–134, 174–175

Bank for International Settlements, 221

Barnes, Julius H., 12n.

Baruch, Bernard M., 11, 36, 85; opposes Wilson's attendance at Peace Conference, 61; on President's Committee of Economic Advisers, 84, 85; on Supreme Economic Council, 87, 165; in Treaty negotiations, 239, 248; as adviser to Wilson, 275, 281

Bavaria, 213–215

Belgian Relief Commission, 1–2, 4–8, 76, 156

Belgium, objections to Fourteen Points, 51–53; in Relief and Reconstruction of Europe, 89

Benes, Eduard, 54

Benson, Adm. William S., 10, 90, 113n., 124, 130, 156

Big Four (see Peace Conference, Supreme Council)

Bliss, Gen. Tasker, 54, 188; delegate to Peace Conference, 67; on President's Committee of Economic Advisers, 85; in blockade discussions, 159, 165; in Peace Conference negotiations, 211; in Treaty negotiations, 240–241, 244

LETTERS, MEMORANDA, ETC.

to American delegates against attack on Russia, 117; on French proposal for alliance, 219

to Mrs. Bliss: on compromise with Japan, 210; on Treaty, 240, 241; on Wilson at Peace Conference, 200

to Wilson on compromise with Japan, 209–210

Blockade, 5–6, 87, 89; Armistice provision for, 151; of Baltic States, 174–175; conferences on, 159–171, 174–178; end of, 178; of Finland, 124; of Hungary, 135; Norwegian attitude toward, 120; problems of, 151–178; relaxation of, 92, 101, 124, 155, 158, 162–163, 178; renewal of, 229–232, 235, 236

Bolsheviki (see Communists; Russia)

Bonsal, Stephen, 63–64

Bowman, Isaiah, 216, 223

Braun, Edler von, 171

Brest-Litovsk Treaty, 127

Bristol, Adm. Mark, 10, 15n.

Britain, alliance with France, 218–220; attitude of leaders toward Wilson, 253–258; in blockade, 155–157, 164, 166; demands at Peace Conference, 192, 194; mandates, 226–228; recognition of Finland, 126; relations with Armenia, 142, 143; relations with Baltic States, 129, 130; relations with Russia, 116; in Relief and Reconstruction of Europe, 91, 95, 104, 107, 110; secret treaties, 78–80; spheres of influence, 228

Brockdorff-Rantzau, Count von, 233, 238, 251–252

Brookings, Robert S., 12n., 15n.

Brussels, meeting with Germans at, 170–172

Budapest, 138

Bulgaria, surrender of, 29

Burleson, Albert S., 16, 271

Causey, Col. W. B., 107

Cecil, Lord Robert, 86; in blockade discussions, 164, 165; in establishment of League of Nations, 181, 183

Children, relief for, 101, 111–114

China, Japanese claims in, 79, 81, 207–211, 228

Churchill, Winston, on League of Nations, 73n.; urges attack on Russia, 116; attitude toward Wilson, 255–258

Clark, Harold W., 229

Clemenceau, Georges, 54, 74, 106, 123, 125; discusses Fourteen Points, 44–46, 48, 51, 52; discusses Armistice terms, 49; opposes Wilson's attendance at Peace Conference, 65, 66; in relations with Hungary, 135, 138–140; in blockade discussions, 165, 166, 168–170; attempted assassination of, 192; in Peace Conference negotiations, 192–194, 203, 211, 220, 222; on proposed treaty with Germany, 197–198; calls for dismemberment of Germany, 212–218; proposes military alliance, 218–220; in Treaty negotiations, 242, 248–249, 251, 269; attitude toward Wilson, 254–256, 259–260

ADDRESSES

on balance of power, 74; on Treaty, 237

LETTERS, MEMORANDA, ETC.

on Armenia, 145–146; to Brockdorff-Rantzau on Treaty, 251

Clémentel, Etienne, 165, 166

Coal Administration, 12n.

Coal supply, 104, 105, 108

Cobb, Frank I., 2, 44; opposes Wilson's attendance at Peace Conference, 61–63

Colby, Bainbridge, 276; statement of Wilson's views on Communism, 150n.

Colonialism, 72–73
Commission for Relief in Belgium and Northern France, 1–2, 4–8, 76, 156
Committee of Economic Advisers (*see* President's Committee of Economic Advisers)
Communists, 115–116; in Austria, 137, 140–141; in Baltic States, 123, 126–128, 130–134; in Germany, 152, 176–177, 235; in Hungary, 135, 139; in Russia, 115–118; Wilson's statement on, 150*n.*
Concert of Europe, 179*n.*, 184
Congress of Vienna, 179*n.*
Congressional election of 1918, 14–17, 77
Congressional relief appropriation, 101
Constantinople, 78, 79; mandate for, 226
Coolidge, Calvin, 295
Cotton, Joseph P., 12*n.*, 91, 92
Coudert, Frederic, 17
Council of Relief and Supply, 86
Cox, James M., 294
Crowell, Benedict, 15*n.*
Curzon, G. N., Lord, 255
Czechoslovakia, 108; declares independence, 43, 263*n.*; Germans transferred to, 213; invasion of, 137, 138

Dalmatia, 203
Daniels, Josephus, 10, 39*n.*
Davis, Norman, on President's Committee of Economic Advisers, 85; in Relief and Reconstruction of Europe, 93, 95, 105; on Supreme Economic Council, 87, 163, 165; letter to Wilson on Treaty, 243; in Treaty negotiations, 243, 244
Dawes, Gen. Charles G., 221*n.*
Dawes Plan, 221*n.*
Democratic Party, 14, 16; Convention of 1920, 294–295
Denikin, Gen. A. I., 116, 123, 142
Dercum, Dr. Francis X., 272–274
d'Espérey, Gen. Franchet, 29, 54
Dodge, Cleveland, 142
Dulles, John Foster, 229

Ebert, Friedrich, 58, 234, 235
Eliot, Charles W., 295
Erzberger, Matthias, 29
Estonia, declares independence, 43, 263*n.*; relief for, 130; revolution in, 123, 126–130

Finland, 123–126, 263*n.*; blockade of, 124; recognition of, 124–126; relief for, 124–125
Fiume, 203, 205
Foch, Marshal Ferdinand, 54, 55, 57, 58; plans attack on Russia, 116, 117; plans invasion of Hungary, 137; in blockade discussions, 165, 166, 169; suggests reimposing blockade, 229
Food Administration (*see* United States Food Administration)
Fourteen Points, 18, 19, 28; discussion of, 44–49; text of, 20–23
France, alliance with Britain and United States, 218–220; in blockade, 156, 157, 161–163, 166, 176; demands at Peace Conference, 192, 212–218; mandates, 226–228; relations with Russia, 116, 123; in Relief and Reconstruction of Europe, 91, 104, 107, 110; secret treaties, 78–79
Francqui, Emile, 171
Freedom of the seas, 44–48, 52–53, 56, 57
Fuller, Joseph V., letter to J. C. Grew, 240

Garfield, Harry A., 11, 15*n.*; opposes Wilson's attendance at Peace Conference, 61, 63–64
Georgia, republic of, 142, 263*n.*
Gerard, James W., 8*n.*
German army in typhus control, 110
German colonies, mandates for, 226–227
German railway equipment for relief purposes, 107
German ships for relief purposes, 102, 160, 163

Germany, Armistice requested by, 28–
30; Armistice signed by, 58; in
Baltic States, 126, 127, 129, 131,
133; blockade problems, 152, 154–
155, 157, 162, 163, 170–172; Delegation to Peace Conference, 233,
237, 238, 250–252; dismemberment
of, 213–218, 236; invasion of Belgium, 75–76; in peace negotiations,
28–41; Reichstag revolution, 29; relief for, 171–173, 235; reparations
payments, 220–221; republic established, 58, 263n.; submarine
warfare, 5; war crimes, 222
Gibson, Hugh, 93, 171; diary quoted,
94n., 95
Gilchrist, Col. Harry, 109, 110
Goltz, Gen. Kolmar von der, 127, 131,
133
Goodyear, Col. Anson C., 108
Grayson, Adm. Cary T., 198, 272
Great Britain (see Britain)
Green, Capt. Joseph, 142, 143
Gregory, Capt. T. C. C., 135, 137,
139, 140
Gregory, Thomas W., 16, 67
Grew, J. C., 106
Groome, Colonel, 133

Harbord, Gen. James G., 229
Harding, Warren G., 295–299; on in-
ternational relations, 296, 298
Harrington, Lieutenant, 131–133
Haskell, Col. William N., 142, 144–
146
Heath, Maj. Ferry, 126
Heinz, Howard, 142
Hertling, Count von, 23, 29
Hindenburg, Paul von, 41n.
Hitchcock, G. M., 275, 281, 289, 290;
letter to Wilson on League of Na-
tions, 188
Hitler, Adolf, 236n.
Holsti, Rudolf, 126
Holy Alliance, 179n.
Hoover, Herbert, as Chairman of Bel-
gian Relief, 1–2, 4–9; advises Col.
House, 2–3; study of European
economic conditions, 7–9; as Food

Administrator, 8–9, 12–13; supports Wilson's appeal for Democratic Congress, 17; in peace negotiations, 36, 37; opposes Wilson's
attendance at Peace Conference,
61; organizes postwar relief, 67;
criticism of, 75; and inter-Allied
agencies, 83; on President's Committee of Economic Advisers, 84,
146–150; on Supreme Economic
Council, 86, 87; in Relief and Reconstruction of Europe, 87–96, 99–
114; reports to Wilson on Russia,
117–119; and proposed relief for
Russia, 119–123; in relations with
Finland, 124–126; in relations with
Baltic States, 127–134; in relations
with Hungary, 135–140; in relations with Poland, 141; in Armenian relief, 142–146; in blockade
discussions, 151–156, 158–162, 164–
167, 170–173, 175–178; suggestions on League of Nations, 183–
184; in Peace Conference negotiations, 198, 201–202, 213, 214; proposes moratorium on war debts,
221n., on mandate for Armenia,
228–229; on reimposing blockade,
230–232; in Treaty negotiations,
233–235, 239, 244–246, 248, 265–
269, 270n.; in Treaty ratification,
290–292; in Presidential campaign
of 1920, 295–297; on World Court,
299n.

LETTERS, MEMORANDA, ETC.
to Big Four on Hungary, 137–
140; constitution of Supreme Economic Council, 86–87n.; to J. P.
Cotton on Relief and Reconstruction of Europe, 92; to Col. Groome
on Latvian revolution, 133; to Col.
House on entry into war, 5–6; to
R. Lansing on Armenia, 144–145;
statement on Treaty, 267–269;
Why We Are Feeding Germany,
172–173

to Wilson: on Armenia, 143, 144;
on Baltic States, 127–128; on Bavaria, 215; on blockade, 152–155,

158, 160–162, 177–178, 230–231; on commissions created by Treaty, 147; on Finland, 124–125; on Germany, 154–155, 177–178; on Hungary, 135–136; on inter-Allied agencies, 83–84; on Peace Conference, 202; on Relief and Reconstruction of Europe, 91, 103–106, 111–112; on Russia, 117–119; on Treaty, 245–248, 282–283

Hoover, Irving, 287n.

Hope, Adm. G. P. W., 129, 130

Hope, Walter, 12n.

House, Col. Edward M., Hoover as adviser to, 2–3, 5; suggests relief for Russia, 12n.; claims credit for Fourteen Points, 19n.; delegate to Peace Conference, 67, 82–83; on President's Committee of Economic Advisers, 84; character of, 84–85; in blockade discussions, 152, 165, 170; in establishment of League of Nations, 181, 183, 184, 188, 189; in Peace Conference negotiations, 192–193, 195–196, 210; in Treaty negotiations, 239, 242; Wilson's break with, 286–287n.

DIARY

Balfour quoted on secret treaties, 80; on break with Wilson, 287n.; criticism of Wilson, 13; on Italian demands, 211–212; on peace negotiations, 39n.; on renewal of blockade, 232; on reparations, 220; on Rhineland separation, 215–216; on Saar annexation, 217–218; on Treaty, 241; on Wilson at Peace Conference, 199–200; on Wilson's attitude toward entering war, 4n.; on Wilson's paralytic stroke, 271–272

LETTERS, MEMORANDA, ETC.

to Balfour on Relief and Reconstruction of Europe, 96–99

to Wilson: on acceptance of peace terms by Allies, 55–56; advising Wilson to attend Peace Conference, 65–66; on Armistice preparations, 54–55; on Belgian and Italian objections to peace terms, 51–52; on discussion of Fourteen Points, 44–49, 51–54; on Relief and Reconstruction of Europe, 95–96; on Treaty ratification, 284–286

Houston, David F., 11, 13, 16; opposes Wilson's attendance at Peace Conference, 61; on Senate criticism of League of Nations, 187; after Wilson's paralytic stroke, 275–277

Hughes, Charles Evans, 67, 211n., 221n., 295, 298, 299

Hungary, 108, 263n.; relief for, 135–137; revolutions in, 134–140; Rumanian invasion of, 138–140

Hurley, Edward N., 11, 36, 84, 102–104

Hymans, Paul, 52

Imperialism, 72–73

Independence, encouragement of, 73, 76, 263

Inter–Allied agencies, 71, 83–84, 86, 174, 178

Inter–Allied Blockade Council, 155

Italy, Austrian territory transferred to, 213, 228; in blockade, 156, 174; demands at Peace Conference, 192, 203, 206, 211–212; dispute with Yugoslavia, 105, 106; objections to Fourteen Points, 51; relations with Hungary, 137; in Relief and Reconstruction of Europe, 91, 104, 105, 107; secret treaties, 78, 79

Jadwin, Gen. Edgar, 141

James, Arthur Curtiss, 142

Japan, claims in China, 79, 81, 207–208, 228; compromise on, 207–211; relations with Russia, 116; secret treaties, 79, 81

Jews, persecution of, in Poland, 141

Johnson, Homer, 141

Joseph, Archduke, 138–140

Kellogg, Vernon, 110

Kerensky, A. F., 116

Keynes, J. M., 165, 234, 235, 238, 239
Klotz, Louis-Lucien, 160, 165, 166, 170
Kolchak, Gen. A. V., 116, 123
Kun, Béla, 135, 137, 138, 140

Lamb, Dr. Albert R., 198
Lamont, Thomas, 171
Lane, Franklin K., 7, 8, 11, 16
Lane, Gertrude B., 12n.
Lansing, Robert, 7, 16, 37, 39n., 86; opposes Wilson's attendance at Peace Conference, 61; delegate to Peace Conference, 67, 82; in blockade discussions, 165, 166; in establishment of League of Nations, 184n., 188–190; opposition to League of Nations, 184n., 191; in Peace Conference negotiations, 210–212, 214, 220; on French proposal for alliance, 218–219; in Treaty negotiations, 246; after Wilson's paralytic stroke, 271–272, 275–276
LETTERS, MEMORANDA, ETC.
  on compromise with Japan, 208, 209; to Germany on changes in peace terms, 56–57; peace terms submitted to Allies, 43; on Treaty, 239–240; on Turkish Armistice, 50–51
Latvia, 263n.; blockade of, 174, 175; revolution in, 123, 126–133
Lawrence, David, on Wilson's paralytic stroke, 272, 277
League to Enforce Peace, 180
League of Nations, constitution drafted by Wilson, 181; Covenant, 181, 183, 184, 187–190, 224, 266, 267; discussed by Allied leaders, 44–45; early ideas for, 179n.; establishment of, 179–190; mandates, 222–224; plans for, 67–68; proposed by Wilson, 22, 25, 26, 180
Legge, Alexander, 12n., 15n.
Lenin, V. I., 122
Libau, 131, 133
Lindley, Curtis H., 12n.
Lippman, Walter, 44

Lithuania, 263n.; blockade of, 174, 175; revolution in, 123, 126, 134
Lloyd George, David, 54, 56, 74, 116; discusses Fourteen Points, 44–46, 48, 52–53; discusses Armistice terms, 49; proposes financial plans, 148, 149; in blockade discussions, 164–165, 167–168, 170; in Peace Conference negotiations, 192, 193, 203, 211, 220, 222; memorandum on treaty with Germany, 197; in Treaty negotiations, 234, 238, 242, 248–251; attitude toward Wilson, 253–257
Lodge, Henry Cabot, 1–2; on League to Enforce Peace, 180n.; resolution against League of Nations, 187; opposition to Treaty, 279, 295
Logan, Col. James, 126, 131
Long, Walter, 255
Loudon, J., 8n.
Lovett, Robert S., 12n., 15n.
Lowden, Frank O., 295
Ludendorff, Erich F. W., 40–41n.

McAdoo, William G., 11, 294
McCall, Governor, 66, 67
McCormick, Vance M., 11, 36, 37; opposes Wilson's attendance at Peace Conference, 61, 64; on President's Committee of Economic Advisers, 84–87; on Supreme Economic Council and Superior Blockade Council, 87, 124; in blockade discussions, 159, 161, 165, 230; in Treaty negotiations, 239
DIARY, 84, 86, 146, 159n.
  on blockade discussions, 162–163, 174–175, 178, 230–232; on Council of Economic Advisers, 147–149; on Treaty, 244; on Wilson at Peace Conference, 199, 204–205, 260–261
McKnight, James, 229
Mandates, 222–229, 236
Mantoux, Paul, 208, 211, 214
March, Gen. Peyton C., 10
Marie, Queen of Rumania, 140

Max, Prince of Baden, 29, 30, 41n., 58
Merry del Val, Marquis de, 8n.
Mesopotamia, 78
Miller, David Hunter, 181, 183, 284
Morgenthau, Henry, Sr., 141
Murmansk, 116

Nansen, Fridtjof, in Russian relief proposals, 119–122
National Security and Defense Fund, 100
Nationalism, 73, 76
Near East, British spheres of influence in, 228; in secret treaties, 78, 79
Near East Committee, 142
Nitti, Francesco, 212, 260

Orlando, Vittorio Emanuele, 54; discusses Fourteen Points, 51, 52; in Peace Conference negotiations, 203, 206, 212; attitude toward Wilson, 260

Pact of London, 78, 192, 203, 210–211
Paderewski, Ignace, 141
Page, Walter Hines, 1, 4, 7, 8
Peace Conference, American delegates to, 66, 67, 77; Back Blocs, 115; committees of, 83; Council of Ten, 82–83, 106, 129, 192, 213; issues of, 70–81; nations represented at, 70–71; organization of, 82–84; preliminary plans for, 67–68; Superior Blockade Council, 87, 124, 174, 178, 229, 232; Supreme Allied Council of Supply and Relief, 159
    Supreme Council (Big Four), 82, 109, 266; financial plans, 149; letter to Nansen on Russian relief, 121–122; negotiations, 196, 203; in recognition of Finland, 125; in relations with Hungary, 135, 137–140
    Supreme Economic Council, 86–87, 101, 108, 124; blockade discussions, 163, 165–170, 174–176, 178, 229–232
    Supreme War Council, 94
Peace negotiations, 28–41
Peace terms, accepted by Allies, 55–56; changes in, 56–57; discussion of, 44–53; presented to Allies, 42–43
Pericles, oration of, 300
Pershing, John J., 10, 15n., 93; in relief work, 90, 107–110, 113n., 145
Persia, 78
Petrograd, 116
Pichon, S. J. M., 123, 165, 213, 220
Plumer, Gen. H. C., 164
Poland, William B., 229
Poland, 108; declares independence, 58, 263n.; German territory transferred to, 213; persecution of Jews in, 141; secret treaties on, 79
Polish Corridor, 213
Polk, Frank, 137, 138, 266
Polo de Bernabé, Luis, 8n.
Presidential campaign of 1920, 294–299
President's Committee of Economic Advisers, 83–86, 146–150; members of, 84–86
Prime Ministers, accept Fourteen Points with reservations, 47–49; discuss Fourteen Points, 44–48, 52–53; object to Wilson's attendance at Peace Conference, 65–66; oppose Wilson at Peace Conference, 192; in Peace Conference organization, 82, 87, 101; protest on peace negotiations, 31–32
Prinkipo, 116

Red Cross Societies, League of, 109
Relief and Reconstruction of Europe, 87–91; Allies wish to control, 91–95; Director-General of, 96–99, 101; organization of, 91–93; railway transportation for, 104–108; shipping for, 102–104; telegraphic communications, 113n.; typhus control by, 108–111; Wilson's message on, 96–99

Reparations payments, 220–221
Republican party, 14–17; Convention of 1920, 295–296
Republicans appointed by Wilson, 15n.
Requa, Mark L., 12n.
Rhineland, proposed republic of, 192, 215–217
Rickard, Edgar, 12n.
Riga, 128, 129, 131–133
Robinson, Henry M., on President's Committee of Economic Advisers, 84, 85; on Supreme Economic Council, 87, 165; in blockade discussions, 165, 171
Rolph, George, 12n.
Roosevelt, Franklin D., 294
Roosevelt, Theodore, 2
Root, Elihu, 66, 67, 180, 190, 295, 299
Rosenwald, Julius, 15n.
Round Robin, 187, 188
Rumania, 79; invades Hungary, 138–140
Russia, Allied efforts to confer with, 116; Allies propose attack on, 116–117; Hoover's report on, 117–119; relief for, 12n., 119–123; revolution, 7, 12n.; secret treaties, 78–80; White Armies, 116, 142; Wilson urges peace with, 60; Wilson's statement on, 150n.
Ryan, Col. T. R., 107

Saar given to France, 79, 217–218
Scheidemann, Philip, 29, 235, 252
Schwab, Charles M., 11, 15n.
Self-determination, 73, 76
Senate (see United States Senate)
Serbia, 100, 263n.
Seymour, Charles, 223
Shaw, Arch W., 12n.
Siberia, 116
Simmons, F. M., 21n.
Sims, Adm. William S., 10, 15n.
Smuts, Jan, 181, 183; proposals for mandates, 223–224; in Treaty negotiations, 234, 238, 239, 252; letter to Wilson on Treaty, 242–243; tribute to Wilson, 301

Sonnino, Sidney, Baron, 106, 165; discusses Fourteen Points, 44, 45, 48
Spartacists, 152, 176, 235
Stettinius, Edward, 15n.
Stoever, Maj. R., 142
Stone, Melville, 2
Strauss, Lewis, 93, 171
Sudeten Germans, 213
Swem, Charles L., 211; on reasons for Wilson's attendance at Peace Conference, 64–65; on Wilson's plans for Peace Conference, 193–195
    Papers of, 104, 116, 181, 225
Sykes-Picot Treaty, 78–80
Syria, 78, 192

Taft, Robert A., 12n., 93
Taft, William H., 15n., 67, 180, 189, 190, 295
Tardieu, André, 197, 213, 249
Taylor, Alonzo E., 12n.
Taylor, Henry, Sr., 12n.
Thirty-eight points in Wilson's peace plans, 19–27
Thors, Lieut. John, 130
Treaties, secret, 77–81; separate, 298
Treaty of London (see Pact of London)
Treaty of Versailles (see Versailles Treaty)
Trieste, 105, 107
Tumulty, Joseph P., 16, 67; on Wilson in campaign of 1920, 295, 297–298; on Wilson's paralytic stroke, 272, 275
    LETTERS, MEMORANDA, ETC.
    on compromise with Japan, 208; to Wilson on Peace Conference, 200–201
Turkey, 263n.; Armistice agreement, 50–51; persecution of Armenians, 142; in secret treaties, 79
Typhus, 90, 108–111

Ulmanis, Karlis, 131, 133, **134**
Underwood, Oscar W., 284

United Nations, 302

United States, alliance with France, 218–220; anti-imperialism, 72; armed forces, 13; attitude toward Peace Conference, 71–72, 75–77; declares war on Germany, 8; supports White Russians, 116

United States Army, Liquidation Commission, 107; Medical Corps, 109; in typhus control, 110

United States Food Administration, 12–13; aid to Europe, 88–89, 100, 102, 113, 156; Grain Corporation, 100, 156; heads of divisions, 12n.

United States government, organization for war, 10–11, 13; separation of powers, 77

United States Senate, League of Nations discussed by, 187–188; reservations on Treaty, 279–281; votes on Treaty, 284, 292–293

United States War Department, 100, 101

Versailles Conference (see Peace Conference)

Versailles Treaty, 179, 233–252; and Covenant of League of Nations, 188–190; discussion of, 235–237, 244–245, 265–269; Senate reservations on, 279–281; Senate votes on, 284, 292–293; signing of, 252

Villalobar, Marquis de, 8n.

War Industries Board, 11–12n.

War Trade Board, 12n.

Wemyss, Adm. Sir Rosslyn, 170, 171

White, Henry, 67, 212; letter to Wilson on Peace Conference, 202–203

White, John Beaver, 12n.

Whitlock, Brand, 8n.

Wilbur, Ray Lyman, 12n.

Willard, Daniel, 15n.

Wilson, Woodrow, and administration of Belgian Relief, 2, 4, 7–9; reluctant to enter war, 4, 7; recalls Ambassador from Germany, 5; suggests study of economic conditions in Europe, 7, 8; wartime powers, 11; appeals for election of Democratic Congress, 14–17; proposes League of Nations, 22, 25, 26, 180; in peace negotiations with Germany, 28, 30–31, 33–35, 37–41; presents peace terms to Allies, 42, 44, 47, 50; informs Congress of Armistice agreement, 58; proposes peace with Russia, 60; urged not to attend Peace Conference, 61–64; reasons for attending Peace Conference, 64–66; plans for Peace Conference, 67–68, 193–196; arrives in Paris, 68–69; and issues of Peace Conference, 71–77; suspicion of his motives, 75, 76; knowledge of secret treaties, 79–81; and Relief and Reconstruction of Europe, 87–88, 90–91, 93, 96–102, 109–110, 113; and Russian Communist government, 116–117, 150; in relations with Finland, 124–125; in relations with Baltic States, 127, 129–130, 132; in relations with Hungary, 135–138; in relations with Poland, 141; in Armenian relief, 144, 145; and Committee of Economic Advisers, 146–150; statement on Communism, 150n.; and blockade problems, 151, 152, 156, 158–161, 173, 176–178; establishes League of Nations, 179–186; presents League of Nations to Congress, 187–188; hears of "conspiracy" on Covenant, 188–190; at Peace Conference, 196–206; illness in Paris, 198–199; plans to return from Europe, 199–201; resumes Big Four conferences, 203; in compromise on Japan, 207–211; on Italian demands, 211–212; on dismemberment of Germany, 213–218; on German war crimes, 222; on mandates, 222–226, 229n.; on renewal of blockade, 231; in Treaty negotiations, 243–245, 248–250; attitude of European leaders toward, 253–261; achievement at Peace

Conference, 262–264; campaign for ratification of Treaty, 265–266, 269–270, 281, 282, 288–290, 293; paralytic stroke, 270–278; in campaign of 1920, 294–295, 297–298; death, 300

ADDRESSES

on Armistice, 58; on balance of power, 27; on Italian demands, 204; to League to Enforce Peace, 180; on League of Nations, 181–183, 185–186, 189; on mandates, 225–226

on peace terms: basis of peace, 18–19; five particulars, 25–27; four ends, 24–25; four principles, 23–24; Fourteen Points, 20–23; thirty-eight points, 19–27

on reasons for attending Peace Conference, 65; on Russia, 60

LETTERS, MEMORANDA, ETC.

to American Mission against proposed attack on Russia, 116–117; to Austria-Hungary on peace terms, 34–35; to Balfour on Relief and Reconstruction of Europe, 96–99; to Clemenceau on Rhineland, 216–217; to Germany on peace terms, 30–31, 33–34, 36–39; to G. M. Hitchcock on Treaty ratification, 282, 289–290

to Hoover: acknowledging advice to Col. House, 3n.; on blockade, 161, 178; on commissions created by Treaty, 148; on Congressional election of 1918, 17; on Food Ad-

ministration, 12–13; on Poland, 141; on Relief and Reconstruction of Europe, 105, 113

to Col. House: on Armistice terms, 40; on blockade, 152; on Fourteen Points, 44, 47; on freedom of the seas, 47, 50; on opposition of Prime Ministers, 66

to E. N. Hurley on shipping for relief, 102; to R. Lansing suggesting resignation, 275–276; to Gen. Pershing on typhus control, 109, 110; to H. Robinson on shipping for relief, 104; to F. M. Simmons on trade barriers, 21n.; statement on Congressional election of 1918, 14–15; statement on Treaty ratification, 288–289

Wilson, Mrs. Woodrow, 189, 191; after Wilson's paralytic stroke, 272–275, 277

My Memoir quoted, on Treaty ratification, 281; on Wilson at Peace Conference, 196, 199, 205–206; on Wilson's paralytic stroke, 272–275

Wood, Gen. Leonard E., 295

Wood, Gen. Robert E., 15n.

Woolley, Clarence M., 12n.

World Court, 299

Wrangel, Gen. P. N., 116

Young, Dr. Hugh, 273

Young, Owen D., 221n.

Yudenich, Gen. N. N., 116

Yugoslavia, 108; dispute with Italy, 105, 106; unification, 43